LOVE LESSONS

Since 1945 Joan Wyndham has led a rich and varied life including opening Oxford's first Espresso Bar, running a hippy restaurant in London's Portobello Road, cooking at major pop-festivals, and more recently catering for the actors at the Royal Court Theatre. She has also worked in Fleet Street on women's magazines, and as a food and wine critic in London and New York.

She is married with two daughters and lives in London.

D0033864

LOVE LESSONS

A Wartime Diary

Joan Wyndham

FLAMINGO

Published by Fontana Paperbacks

First published in Great Britain by William Heinemann 1985

This Flamingo edition first published in 1986
by Fontana Paperbacks, a division of the Collins Publishing Group,
8 Grafton Street, London W1X 3LA

Made and printed in Great Britain by
William Collins Sons & Co. Ltd, Glasgow

BOOK I

Tuesday, 22nd August 1939

ORCHARD CLOSE, RAMSBURY

It's very hot this August, the hottest summer I can remember for years. There's thunder in the air which gives me a headache. I wish the rain would come to cool everything down.

Spending the hols with Granny is really quite an experience. The service is incredible, with everything done for you. I wish I could have seen the head housemaid's face when she unpacked my case, and found a grubby suspender belt and my signed photo of John Gielgud in *Hamlet* – not to mention a paperback of Casanova's *Amours*.

At dinner there is a sort of changing of the guards ceremony between courses – and when I asked for some aspirin for my headache, the butler brought them on a silver salver!

Granny is a bit of a bore, always chasing me to wash my hands and wear a dress – but luckily she's in bed a lot of the time, wearing a chin-strap and a little circle of tin pressed into the middle of her forehead to keep the wrinkles at bay – it's hard work being an ageing beauty.

The nicest person here is Aunt Bunch – Mummy says she takes drugs and goes around with Negroes, but I don't care, I really like her. I am in love with Harold the butler, and Macrae who looks after the horses. He is like a brown monkey and smells of wet ferns. Granny says Macrae hasn't had a bath within living memory.

I'm writing this in the music room, feeling quite sick with excitement, waiting for Daddy Dick to arrive – I don't know why everybody calls

5

him that, as if I had a choice of other, more suitable daddies. Unfortunately all I have is DD, maddening, self-centred and never there. I suppose he'll be late as usual, although it's nearly a year since he last saw me.

Later

DD finally arrived in a very expensive-looking car called an Alvis, and we drove out for a cream tea in Marlborough. His face is tanned and he wears a blue shirt with a red tie. He looks much better now he has stopped drinking. The tea was supposed to be a kind of treat, to make up for neglecting me for so long. He seemed unusually friendly and interested, and asked me about Mummy and whether she was OK. I said yes, but we could do with a bit more money if he could spare it, which he jolly well ought to, considering what his paintings fetch nowadays.

'And how is the exotic Sidonie?' he went on, very sarcastic because he can't stand her. 'Still painting her face white and going to Mass every morning?' I don't know why he should be so down on her, Mummy's jolly lucky to have someone to look after her and love her – it can't be much fun being divorced at twenty-three.

The clotted cream and scones arrived and we laid into them. 'We're both rather greedy aren't we?' Daddy observed. 'It's strange how like me you are, in spite of our hardly ever seeing each other. I wonder how you'd have turned out if you'd been brought up by me instead of by two religious ladies.'

'Just like Aunt Bunch I expect,' I said, 'getting drunk and rushing around after drugs and Negroes.' Which he seemed to think was rather funny.

On the way back I could see the speedometer touch 82. I thought the wind would blow my head off. We listened to the wireless after dinner and heard Chamberlain say we would stand by Poland against Hitler, even if it meant war.

Wednesday, 23rd

A lovely day – Daddy rode at the local point-to-point and didn't come off. Mummy says he came off a lot while she was carrying me, and I was born with my hands over my eyes. Darling Macrae was jumping up and down and yelling, 'C'mon y'bugger!'

Afterwards we had tea in the tent and Granny asked Aunt Bunch, 'What was that word Macrae used?' 'Oh,' says Bunch, 'what they're supposed to – er – *do* – down at the Gazelle Inn. You know, sodomy!' Granny practically choked on her cucumber sandwich and muttered something about '*pas devant l'enfant*'. She needn't have worried – I wasn't any the wiser. I once asked Mother Aloysius what it was they did in Sodom and Gomorrah and she made me kneel in church right through recreation. Next time I get Aunt Bunch alone I must ask her exactly what it means.

After dinner, charades in the drawing-room. Granny was the Queen of Sheba, swathed in silver lamé, and Daddy did *L'Après-midi d'un Faune*, looking rather silly I thought. I noticed for the first time he's beginning to get a bald patch on the top of his head, like a priest's tonsure. Acting games are a bit of an embarrassment. They all expect me to be brilliant just because I'm at RADA. I did Rob Roy, and Daddy said, 'You know you're really quite pretty without your specs!' Then we played a game saying what each person reminded us of and I ended up as a cross between Burne Jones, Vivaldi, apricot soufflé and *Just William*. V. flattering, but not quite how I see myself, apart from William – I've always wished I was a boy.

Aunt Bunch got very drunk in a firm and rebellious way, refusing to act or take part in games that made her look silly. I like Bunch very much. She smokes all the time and is rude to people she thinks are boring. Once during the evening I heard her say that famous word again – the one beginning with b!

Thursday, 24th

A blazing hot day, just right for the treasure hunt. I was winning – I knew the last clue must mean the sundial in the rose garden. Suddenly I saw Granny almost running across the lawn, a letter in her hand, and while I was distracted Daddy pounced on the prize. He's such a cheat. The letter was from Mummy, saying I must go back to London right away – it looks as if war is inevitable.

I read it out and no one seemed to know what to say. Daddy opened his prize, a box of chocolates, and handed it round. I chewed a caramel slowly, feeling the sun on my face and smelling the roses. I thought, 'What a bore!' It was terrible saying goodbye to Daddy and Bunch, and lovely Harold and Macrae.

Friday, 25th

Home on the morning train, to the smell and roar of London, and the hot dusty Fulham Road. Nothing felt any different, only our house looked curiously shabby and small after the grandeur of Orchard Close, as if it had shrunk during the holidays.

There was Mummy, desperately worried, and Sid in that awful mauve smock that clashes with her red hair, her face even whiter than usual. Cook was in bed suffering from nerves so there was no lunch, only cold meat and pickles. After we'd eaten it Sid took us up to the little altar on the landing outside her room. She lit the candles, and we all prayed aloud to Our Lady for peace. All I could think about was getting back to RADA – we have our holiday play to rehearse, *Hedda Gabler* in German, produced by the lovely Dorothea Alexander on whom I have a slight crush.

Sid looked terribly shocked when I told her. 'A *German* play! You don't mean you're still going on with it now?' I lost my temper and said, 'What on earth does war have to do with art or the theatre?' I admire Sidonie but she does frighten me – her saintliness tends to give me guilt.

Tuesday, 29th

Straight to RADA. It seems I've got a good part, Thea Elfstead. Learning to speak German is going to be hard but Dorothea says she'll help me. She is my ideal woman of twenty-seven or any other age, thin and brown with bare legs and sandals, and soft shiny hair held back in a net.

Spent most of the day rehearsing Anton as Lovberg. He is a very sweet boy but thinks of nothing but sex. I blush easily so it is a kind of game for him to call me The Innocent and I play up accordingly. No one mentioned the news.

After rehearsals we went to Poggioni's for spaghetti and on the way D and I turned and saw Anton just behind us talking to a little man with a square grey beard, wearing a big dark hat. They stood together at the end of Charlotte Street. Dorothea said, 'That is Professor Freud.' Back to Chelsea in a tube like an oven.

Wednesday, 30th

Rehearsed all day in D's room in Swiss Cottage. Bare yellow walls and a piano – afterwards everyone was talking about arty subjects, Verlaine, Toulouse Lautrec, Baudelaire, and so on, except for Anton who was deeply preoccupied with the question of whether girls are nicer to kiss with or without lipstick. Nobody talks about Hitler. It is absolutely taboo. Dorothea's father was killed in Vienna a few weeks ago and anyway we want to forget about it if possible. It wasn't till someone put on the wireless at nine that she finally lost control of herself and went off into a kind of silent, stony, twitching hysteria. I am becoming more and more infatuated with her.

After dinner we went for a walk on Hampstead Heath thinking it might be the last time we would enjoy the full moon with untroubled minds. The moonlight made the grass a silvery grey and the dew was falling, wetting our feet. I became aware that I am passionately in love with her, in the rather unreal way I do fall for people. She is so sweet, so clever and so exciting, and ten years older than me. We climbed the hill that looks over Highgate and lay in deck chairs at the top, smoking in the moonlight.

Thursday, 31st

Today Dorothea was going to teach me to cry. I thought how wonderful to be able to let myself go with her but when I reached Belsize Road I saw her coming down to me. 'Well, darling,' she said, 'having read the news I'm not sure I shouldn't send you home.'

'But I thought you were going to teach me to cry,' I said in dismay.

'You won't need any teaching soon,' she replied sadly and took me to her bank where she drew out all her worldly possessions – £127. Then we bought some pimentos and went home and stuffed them for lunch. There was no more talk of the play – that is finished. RADA is closing down.

After lunch the rest of the actors came in to say goodbye. Because we didn't want to think of the war we talked of the really important things in life like Bach, Mozart and Beethoven. Anton loves music almost as much as girls.

He put the Brahms violin concerto on the gramophone and we listened like people drugged. On the top note of the cadenza, a note as ethereal as air, the newsboys began to shout. We heard their voices far away, raucous, impersonal and frightening. As they came nearer we could just hear two words, 'Hitler' and 'Poland'. There are going to be hardly any buses tomorrow, owing to the children being evacuated, so we thought we'd better say goodbye and get it over with. Also I knew my mother would be worrying about me if I stayed out late.

I said goodbye to Anton and Dorothea. She kissed me on the cheek. I went out before we both became too emotional for comfort.

Friday, 1st September

The posters say 'HITLER INVADES POLAND'. Everywhere children are waiting in expectant noisy herds, but the mothers are quiet, grey and some of them are crying. Passing a side street I saw a Punch and Judy show playing to an empty road. Everything tilted at a slightly grotesque angle, like a surrealist film. Mummy and Sid went to church so I sat in my room and got completely drunk for the first time in my life – on rum. It was a very nice experience indeed. I no longer cared a damn what happened to anybody.

I rang up Dorothea: 'I'm completely drunk.'

'That's right, so are we.'

'Goodbye and good luck.'

'Goodbye, darling.' Everything now is goodbye and good luck.

Later on Mummy and Sid came back from the Servite church with

Alfred and Bertie. Alfred is the one I like best of all Sidonie's friends. He's tall and lean and wears dark blue shirts, and has a gigantic appetite for treacle pudding. I love his calm, deep, drawling voice and the way he shakes with silent laughter, the sound coming through his nose and not his mouth. On the other hand his room-mate Bertie is pretty awful, sensuous-looking and plump, with a girlish face.

After dinner Alfred played Debussy, his long thin fingers trailing over the keys, while Bertie crouched on the window-seat listening.

'It's a drug of course,' Alfred said as he finished 'La Cathédrale Engloutie', and I heard Bertie's velvet murmur, 'How heavenly drugs are!'

Saturday, 2nd

Awful news: they are planning to close the theatres! I rushed straight off to the New to see John and Edith Evans for the last time doing *The Importance*. Sat in the gallery. People in the street seemed really quite cheerful, and all the people in the gallery queue were talking to each other, which is unusual for the English!

When I got home Mummy and Sid were absolutely furious with me for going to the theatre. They seemed to think it was a dreadfully frivolous thing to do at such a time.

Sunday, 3rd

This morning war was declared by the Prime Minister over the radio.

Five minutes after the National Anthem, while we were still sitting around feeling rather sick, the air-raid warning went. For a moment we didn't believe our ears – we hadn't had time even to realise we were at war – then we went down to our gas room and began damping the blankets with pails of water.

When the room was ready we went and sat on the front doorstep waiting for the first gun. The balloon barrage looked too lovely in the sun against the blue sky, like iridescent silver fish swimming in blue water. After a bit the all-clear sounded. We heard afterwards that it had all been a mistake.

Kathleen had a nervous breakdown and left London. So now we have the cooking and washing-up etc., to add to our troubles!

Last night I woke up at three out of a particularly horrible nightmare, having dreamed I had murdered someone with my hands and couldn't get the skin from under my nails. As I sat up in bed, I heard, very faintly in the distance, the air-raid sirens again rising and falling. I said to myself 'the far waterfall like doom', and went to wake the others.

I shall always associate the smell of wet blankets with air-raids. We went out into the garden – it was very dark and cold. I have not been frightened at all yet, not the slightest bit, though the others are. This is very strange but I have no doubt the first bomb will change all that.

No all-clear went till nine o'clock. I believe seventy planes were intercepted and beaten off at the coast.

Today we all joined up at our local first-aid post, St Mark's College, to learn how to cope with air-raid casualties. Sid, Mummy and I work three days a week, nine till nine, alternating with night duty.

Our commandant, Miss Wigram, is like a grey cobweb floating on the wind, with only one end attached to the wall. She has a dropped bosom and is addressed as 'Madam'. There is also 'Quartermaster', whose bosom is rampant and who suffers from halitosis. Then there is Mrs Harley, who is as strong as two oxes and can throw a casualty over her shoulder with one hand; Mrs Vaughan who paints ballet pictures and is very much the lady (intensely gloomy about the awful fate that awaits us, rape etc.); and a shop girl called Daisy whom the others consider 'common'.

Mummy and Sid look too frightful in their nurses' get-up, particularly Sid, with her red bobbed hair, dead-white face and horn-rimmed spectacles. She really looks most peculiar, and I think the other nurses think she is a bit barmy. I, of course, know how terrifyingly intelligent and penetrating she is, having been scared of her since the age of two. Still, I suppose Mummy really couldn't manage without her.

The worst thing is that there is nothing to do. We while away the time practising bandages on each other and send totally insignificant phone messages by 'runner' to the Commandant. Today I was actually 'recommended'. Miss Wigram was 'extremely pleased with the way Wyndham had taken down that message – clean and foolproof! Congratulations Wyndham, we shall get medals soon.'

I have found three newts in the hospital laboratory, and have 'evacuated' them to my own aquarium at home, alongside the sticklebacks I caught at Orchard Close. But the best news of all is that I have found a friend. I first saw her in the mess-room. We were drinking the inevitable hot strong tea which is made practically every hour during the day. A head by Epstein with long half-shut eyes, full lips and blonde hair. In fact, the very type that I have always found irresistible. She came up to me, and said, 'Is this your *Candide*? You left it by the telephone yesterday. It practically saved my life on night-shift.' Her name is Laura Cavendish.

Later we took some bandages to the rest-room under pretence of practising. If anyone came in I would shoot out my hand, and Laura would make a few pretend spirals up it. We found we had almost everything in common. It is amazing really that we should have landed in the same detachment and found each other. She is an oasis of pleasant depravity in a desert of white-starched uniforms. Like me, she also suffers from mother trouble – that awful preoccupation with one's clothes, with one's warmth or lack of it, one's food, motions and emotions, in fact everything that should rightly be left to one's own discretion. Surely we have the right to starve, or freeze ourselves to death in our own way, should we wish to, without the horrible blanket of mother love and possessiveness violating our freedom as individuals? I am myself, and no mother on earth should be allowed to possess me. Needless to say Laura is also a convent girl.

Later on we got hungry, so we stole some cheese and chocolate and had a quiet picnic talking about Plato. I told her about how my father had left my mother when I was two, abandoning me to the tender mercies of my mother and her religious companion, the enigmatic Sid. I also told her all about my father and his mistresses, and she said, 'How nice immoral and unconventional people are.'

At the moment, Laura and I are enjoying a gentle lesbianism of the mind, but I'm afraid it won't last and soon I shall be in love with her properly.

Sunday, 10th

Home is ghastly at the moment. Mummy and Sid have frightful rows, dissolving in floods of tears, hysteria in the bedroom etc. Sid's love for Mummy takes the form of furious fault-finding, and quarrels which she declares are essential in her present emotional state. Poor Mummy doesn't share these frenzied emotions, so life is a bit wearing for her.

Monday, 11th

Laura and I lay in the garden under the mulberry tree at the first-aid post, the sun being hot. We were on one of those mattresses you blow up. I tickled her arm gently with a pigeon's feather – she is like a sleepy blonde bird herself. We studied first-aid and anatomy and dropped unripe mulberries into each others' mouths.

'God,' Laura said, 'I wish I was still a student! How I used to love sitting in that canteen, hideously decorated by the Slade, talking about life over black coffee.'

Me: 'Funny how it was a kind of snobbery that you always had black coffee, however much you yearned for white.'

L: 'Mmm. And it wasn't done to have a healthy appetite – but you could always be dying for a cigarette.'

Me: 'Terribly remote all that student business seems now.'

L: 'There was nothing like it was there?'

Me: 'Nothing.'

We lay back quietly and looked up through the mulberry leaves at a tiny barrage balloon, miniature and shining in its frame of green branches.

Wednesday, 13th

I am getting quite good at bandaging and doing the fireman's lift. The workmen all call me 'nursie' which is very gratifying but quite untrue. I get parked on the telephone in the McAlpine room where the workmen have their den. This is a greatly coveted billet as it contains a fire, and a six-foot-something blond who is the men's boss. He told me he was expecting a mutiny at any moment among them. 'They're not gentlemen, of course,' he explained. He reads Freud's *Totem and Taboo*.

Home for tea which we had in Sid's studio at the bottom of the garden. Her painter friend Cally staggered in with some huge sunflowers, and put them in a Van Gogh pot in the hall. Later Sid found Cally on her knees, quietly worshipping them, her face all puckered up with emotion. Sid is very fond of Cally, but says she suffers from the sin of spiritual pride, whatever that is. Cally is a fine painter, much better than Sid, who only does religious stuff anyway. Sid is always very critical of her friends' shortcomings which is probably why she is currently writing a book called *Guilt*.

Freud died today.

This war really isn't at all bad. We make the best of things, putting our trust in God and Arthur Askey. This week's 'Bandwagon' was the best ever. Big sang the 'Bee' song and 'Run Adolf Run', and did the sketch where they blacked out the skylight with one of Nausea Bagwash's lumbago plasters. We all felt so cheered and reassured after it. We have the radio on all the time, news bulletins mostly – our expeditionary army is going to France – and we listen to a lot of music too. I shall never think of the war without thinking of Chopin's 'Tristesse' – they played it all through the crisis, and now they've turned it into a jazz song as well.

There's another sound too that's running through my brain – it comes from the studio skylight behind the wall at the end of the garden. A pipe, or some sort of flute, that never stops; clear and shrill even at night, playing 'Au Clair de la Lune' and nursery rhymes.

Old J. C. Squire the poet called today from number 9 with a very amusing and conceited boy from Oxford called Denzil Batchelor. Although Sid tells me that Jack Squire is one of the immortals, a great poet, satirist and the best literary critic in England, he just looks like a pleasant and debauched old teddy bear with a lock of scanty hair combed across his forehead and a face like a tired clown. Young Denzil held forth endlessly on the subject of bad poets. At the end Squire just said quietly, 'Oh well, they don't do any harm.'

Night duty is hell. Only three hours in bed in a grim dormitory like a doss-house ward, with grey smelly prison blankets. I wrap myself up in my black coat like Sir John Moore after Corunna. At about six in the morning Laura and I run out into the garden and tear around the lawn, and watch the sun rise. When it's cold I wear my cloak and it flaps out behind me like a great black wing.

This morning it was warm, so we sneaked out early, climbed out over the garden wall and ran down the empty grey Fulham Road, creeping back before we were missed. Then the sun came up and I jumped on to the swing in the mulberry tree and swung up into the green branches in my green dress and Laura said, 'You look like a dryad.'

Some results of this life – an awful preoccupation with food, a tendency to say 'bugger' when beaten at ping-pong, and a craving for French books of an immoral nature. At the moment Laura is reading Prévost's *Femme*, me *Fleurs du Mal* and *Candide*. The fact that the food is awful seems to make no difference to our preoccupation with it. The canteen is just like school. 'Well, if I give you my carrots, you'll have to give me some of your pudding.' Yesterday the canteen cat tore in with a live rat. L came over queer so I had to seize it by the tail and drown it in the fire bucket.

Saturday, 16th

Tea with Rowena who was looking extremely glamorous in a powder-blue coat and skirt, with cyclamen lipstick. She has cut her hair short with a fringe, and looks totally different to those good old Holy Sepulchre days when we were both in love with Marion Gilmore (apparently M is now a nun at Mayfield).

We went to Lyon's Corner House and ate buttered toast while the band played the 'Indian Love Lyrics' and Rowena told me she has got a sugar daddy whom she calls 'Uncle'. She says she is about to 'take the plunge' – which will make her the first of my convent friends to go over the edge. I'm longing to hear all the gory details.

After tea we went to my first wartime concert, Henry Wood conducting Beethoven's Ninth, and Moisevitch playing the 'Emperor'. What more could one ask?

Later, while I was saying the Our Father beside my bed, I heard the pipe again, playing 'The Wind and the Rain'. I couldn't go on praying, it made me mad for a lot of things. I'd give anything to know who plays it.

Wednesday morning, 20th

Three o'clock. What have I done that I should be sitting in a telephone box at three in the morning with a Negro? Oh well, coffee-coloured anyway. At this worst hour of all he wakes from sleep to talk to me in careful, precise English about the state of the theatre in this country. Now, thank God, he's asleep again, head on arms.

When I don't have him there's that terrible, deaf, lady fencing-champion with an eyeglass, but sometimes Laura comes in and we sleep together on the floor and scratch each other's backs. Laura thinks a lot about death because she used to have consumption. Yesterday, when it got light we went down to the morgue, grim and cold with rows of hooks for the name tags, and Laura said in Greek, 'The flowers come up again in the spring but our sleep is forever.'

Thursday, 12th October

Yesterday was my seventeenth birthday. I got Purcell's *Dido and Aeneas* and a beautiful pale-grey coat with a hood, which I think makes me look very appealing! Also a scrummy cream cake with seventeen candles from Deschuyter's pastry shop on the corner.

Theatre-going is still rather frowned upon, but I was allowed to go to an afternoon concert with Alfred's friend Karl, to hear the Delius violin concerto played by Albert Sammons. Karl is quite old, about thirty, and wears a heavy black overcoat and woollen gloves.

On the way home we stopped at Deschuyter's to pick up the cake, also enough rum babas, apricot slices, and apple strudels to feed the German army. Karl has a terribly sweet tooth. Today Old Ma D, who is the most inquisitive creature living, said to my mother, 'Is your daughter engaged? Such a nice young man in with her yesterday. A foreign accent he had – what nationality would he be?' I suppose the nasty old bitch must have guessed he was German!

Saturday, 14th

ARP concert at Hortensia Road first-aid station. All Chelsea at the concert and nearly all in uniform. My mother was down below with the nobs, I was in the gallery with Decontamination and Demolition – the most awful collection of toughs and villains.

There were lots of vulgar sketches with men dressed up as commandants with false bosoms, and awful jokes about what goes on in the blackout. Grand finale came when Lewis Casson – last seen playing Polonius to Gielgud's Hamlet – dashed out to a fanfare of trumpets in his blue boiler suit and hurled himself once more, dear friends, unto the breach, raising the roof.

Karl has started to call quite often now and Mummy and Sid seem to approve of him. Sometimes we go to concerts, sometimes he just brings round cakes and flowers and plays with my newts and tortoise. He is very upright, very Teutonic, with a wry sense of humour, but he has a funny rather doggy sort of way of looking at me which makes me uncomfortable.

Yesterday he took me to Hampton Court. The light was strange, very clear yet sombre, white shadows shimmering in long dark walks, and the yews making black shadows on the pale grass. We paddled in the river, collecting weeds for my newts which we put into an old milk bottle. Then it started to rain and we caught a bus. Karl took off his grey woolly gloves and warmed my hands in his, holding them against the leaping vein in his wrist, till I felt uncomfortable and pulled them away.

I brought him in for a drink when we got back, and there was old Squire in the drawing-room in red bedroom slippers and very tight. He had come to borrow mugs for his party tonight and was as excited as a child. He said it was going to be a marvellous party with every walk of life represented, policemen, air-raid wardens, dukes, chars, artists, sculptors and soldiers.

'I have a particularly filthy sculptor,' he went on, 'who is my co-host. Ooh, so filthy!' he chuckled, looking out of the corners of his eyes at me. 'It will be beer on the bottom floor and gin and whisky on the top floor. Sid and Iris simply must come in their nurses' uniforms. I have promised the policeman there will be nurses!'

Nine o'clock. Went along to number 9. Only a few people had arrived so went up to Squire's room where the gin was, and dug ourselves in to wait. It's the sort of room I love, scrubbed inky tables, antlers on the wall, photos of poets (mostly signed), cricket caps, piles of books, broken-down velveteen sofas and great casks and tubs of booze.

I sat on the floor and talked to a nice old intellectual lady in a house frock, and played with a plum-pudding dog, only a puppy, who tore around me rolling and biting.

Then someone said, 'There's his master' and I turned round and saw – well how can I describe him? If I was feeling romantic I should say I saw Pan, if realistic, then the most depraved long-haired Bohemian, in a blue shirt and corduroy pants, that ever drank cheap red wine in the Artists' Café.

'Is this dog yours?' I asked, and he answered me in a pleasant, drawling voice with a foreign accent – German perhaps? – and came and sat beside me on the floor. Such an intriguing, perpetually amused sort of voice, such a thoroughly lovely and animal face. Nothing good about him at all I should think. The old trout seemed to think so too. She bullied him in a cheerful motherly way. 'Oh, you're such a rebel! Such an untamed savage young animal, just like your dog.'

'We'll soon fix that,' this apparition replied. 'Here you are, Woffle, this'll quieten you down.' And he poured some of his gin down the poor creature's throat and some over me.

'What do you do, paint?' the old trout asked. 'No, I sculpt.' (Aha! The filthy sculptor.)

I pulled myself up on to the sofa, so that he could see me better, trying to look as glamorous as possible in spite of the fact that my black cocktail dress was, by now, reeking of gin and covered in dog hairs.

'What sort of sculpture?' I asked, trying to sound intelligent.

'Abstractions,' he replied, giving me a rather bored glance.

The old trout pressed on however, trying to make him explain the meaning of abstract sculpture, but he shut her up with, 'Do you want a lot of phrases? What my sculpture says to you is the real truth, and if you don't get anything from it then it doesn't matter whether you understand it or not! But I'll tell you one thing that's behind it – the crystallisation of evolution.'

'Oh well,' said the lady in the house frock, looking a bit put out. 'There's no answer to that, is there?'

Him: 'Oh yes there is, and the answer is flux.'

I listened, absolutely fascinated, and managed to get myself another double gin without my mother noticing. I was beginning to feel rather drunk and on top of the world. He leant forward and touched my nose gently. 'How old are you, my little Pussy-willow?'

'Just seventeen.'

'Not English?'

'Of course I'm English.'

'Not just a little bit Irish?'

'Well a bit. How about you?'

'German, Dutch, Javanese, Jewish . . .!'

Oh dear, another German. Out of the corner of my eye I could see my mother glaring at us, obviously wondering how soon she could manage to get me away from this dreadful person. I turned my back on her and lapped up more gin.

'I've seen you wandering around the Fulham Road several times,' he went on, looking at me mockingly out of his yellow goat-like eyes. 'Last time I saw you you were wearing a grey coat with a hood – I thought, Mmm that looks rather interesting. So tell me, what do you do? How do you pass your time?'

'Oh I don't know – play the piano, read, go to concerts – write a bit.'

'I'm writing something myself. The working title is *Ecce Ego*!'

'What's it about?'

'Myself, of course, stoopid! What do you write?'

'Oh, rot mostly.'

'I'm not interested in your self-criticisms. Do you write short stories, poetry?'

'I suppose you'd call them impressions. I see something and it sets a rhythm going inside me, that spins itself out in words.'

'So what do you admire?'

'Eliot and Pound,' I said, trying hard to impress him, although I don't really understand very much of either of them.

'Good old Ezra, I used to live with him. Well how does it feel, your new-found freedom – leaving school, reading T. S. Eliot and so on?'

'I feel as if I'm in an aquarium – looking out at the world through glass. I don't really feel free at all.'

'Well I suppose I'm going to have to do something about you, aren't I?'

I could see my mother getting to her feet, ready to drag me away. Jack Squire, who had managed to drink himself sober – an amazing feat – was singing dirty songs at the piano.

> 'Never never never no more
> Will I go round the 'ouses,
> Never never never no more
> With anything in trousis!'

I started to get to my feet rather unsteadily. Gerhardt, for that is his name, looked up at me, his satyr's eyes glowing under dark lashes.

'OK Pussy, come and have tea at my studio some day. I'll lend you *Ulysses*, Henry Miller, all the bad books you've never read. My studio's number 3 Cavaye Place, over a garage beside the Forum – how about next Saturday at five? I'm going to Cornwall tomorrow but I'll be back by then.'

'He took my purse and said goodnight nurse –'

Squire was now in full spate. I thought triumphantly, he's going to educate me, change me, break the aquarium! I was very drunk indeed.

As soon as they got me home there was a full-scale row. It dragged on and on, Mummy shocked, Sid slightly amused.

'Well dear, if you like that type there are plenty to be had – they swarm in art schools, prisons, doss-houses; they're laid out in rows in morgues –'

Mummy: 'But I can't understand you having such depraved taste – he was filthy! And I told you not to mix your drinks!'

Tired and exultant, I told her it happened to be the type of man I liked best. I also told her that he was very intelligent, but when I told Sid about the crystallisation of evolution she just chuckled and said, 'In other words, plain balls!'

I went to bed but couldn't sleep, my legs were tired and aching and I was shuddering and sweating. At half past two I was still awake and heard the pipe playing softly in the night. I woke again at five and read *The Waste Land* to send me off again – 'And indeed there will be time to wonder/ will I dare and do I dare/ time to turn back and descend the stairs.' But of course I'll go.

When I woke properly I wondered whether it had all been a very pleasant nightmare. I didn't seem to have a hangover. Then I saw the dog's hairs on my black dress and smelt the gin stains on the skirt and I knew it had happened.

Friday, 20th

I stayed in today, nursing a cold, worrying and planning how to evade my mother tomorrow. My original plan was to go to a concert at the

Queen's Hall and pretend to be having tea with Rowena afterwards, only it wouldn't have been R, it would have been Gerhardt. But Mummy, who is fanatical about colds, has said I must come straight home after the concert and go to bed.

Saturday, 21st

Slipped away before the Brahms symphony, hoping to find Gerhardt at home to explain why I couldn't come. Found the studio at last: brightly painted doors opening on to a long balcony with stone stairs leading up to it, a mysterious and private world, a setting for *La Bohème* and 'Che gelida manina'.

Number 3 had 'GERHARDT (G. C. Feldmann)' written on it. The tawny curtains were drawn. By squinting through them I could see into the empty room. Big blocks of stone (presumably in the process of being made abstract), dust, space, bottles, and an untidy bed covered with a black and yellow check coverlet. Yellow chrysanthemums on the table beside it. It was starting to rain and I knew that Mummy would be worrying. I thought I had better write a note and not wait, which I did, saying 'See you next Saturday, same time.'

My mother had given strict instructions to come home by taxi, so with purpose to deceive, I took a penny bus ride to South Ken and a taxi home from there! How am I going to live till next Saturday?

Wednesday, 25th

Back to the post. Charming lecture on anal feeds and body lice!

Poor old Daisy is very depressed because her boyfriend won't marry her. She has bought a guinea wedding dress and keeps it lying over a chair in her bedroom hoping it will give him ideas. She is wondering if she can manage to get drunk tonight on five shillings, which is all she has for her weekend off unless the boyfriend manages to steal something (he is a thief).

I am still very fond of Laura but somehow it is not quite the same now that I have met Gerhardt. I think I have grown up a lot lately. Gerhardt has brought something out in me. I think I feel more of a separate person, not just a minor and dependent limb of the family octopus.

When I got home tonight Karl was there waiting for me. It is really very strange: I liked Karl quite a lot a few days ago, now I simply can't stick him! I was in such a state of nervous irritability that I was really quite rude to him. He treats me as if I was fourteen, saying things like, '*The Kreutzer Sonata* is a very good book but of course you're too young to read it – when you have been married for a year or two perhaps!'

He keeps following me everywhere and never leaves me alone. He wears those awful black woollen gloves. I can't stand to look at him. Oh Gerhardt, if you fail me I don't know what I shall do!

Saturday, 28th

Today's the day! Mummy thinks I'm having tea with Rowena at Lyon's Corner House. I hate deceiving her, it makes me feel rather sick but it's her own fault for being so narrow-minded.

After lunch, while I was in the garden looking for my tortoise, I suddenly noticed this extraordinary thing – I don't know why it hadn't struck me before! The wall at the end of our garden is, in fact, the back wall of Gerhardt's studio! He's been living within a stone's throw of me all the time. I bet he's the one who plays the pipe at night.

Later

As I came into Cavaye Place, I heard the sound of rhythmic blows, and looking up at the balcony, saw that his door was open. He was standing just inside the door, striking sparks from a huge block of granite, chips flying out like shrapnel – I ran in, dodging a direct hit, and was greeted ecstatically by Woffle but very casually by G, who hardly turned around from his work. I quite like this in a way – or at least I tell myself I do. I felt that I wasn't a guest, just a friend and equal, something that had dropped in for company like a cat.

'Look at this if you like while I get on with my work,' he said, chucking a huge volume of photographs and cuttings at me. I sat on the bed and flicked through them. He seems to be pretty famous actually, lots of his stuff sold to galleries, princess this and the cardinal that – and all the time bits of granite, hot from the chisel, were simply whistling round my ears, cracking into saucepans and against window panes, as Gerhardt, legs astride, attacked the block as if it was his mortal enemy.

After about half an hour he turned to me like the perfect gentleman he is. 'Here's half a crown – if you want any tea you'd better go out and buy it!' The nearest he ever got to conventional politeness was to say he liked my dress! Well, I went and got some cakes from Deschuyter's – in the rain incidentally – and he made coffee and we sat on the bed to eat our apple tarts.

'Is it you who plays the pipe?' I asked, when we'd finished. 'I'm always hearing it.'

For answer he went to a table and came back with an old stained wooden pipe tied together with string and, sitting down on a box, began to play 'The Wind and the Rain'.

What an awful novelettish coincidence – me lying awake, hearing the music and thinking, 'I'm sure I've got some sort of affinity with that person, if only I could get to know him!' In the middle of saying my prayers, I'd be torn away to look out of the window – and suddenly there I was watching the worn dark wood between his lips.

After tea we talked about the days when he was a stevedore on the New York docks, and I kept wondering whether my mother was right and he was going to jump on me. He must have read my thoughts for he suddenly said, 'I suppose your mother's worried sick about your being here – you're at the dangerous age, aren't you? Well you needn't worry about me. I'm a tired old man and I'm terrified of virgins.'

He is quite old actually, well over thirty in fact, but still terribly attractive.

It was beginning to get dark. He didn't have any blackout, just a shaded light over the bed. If ever there was a time for funny business it was then, sitting on his bed in the dark, but I felt so safe, as if I was with God. I realised that if I ever did want Gerhardt to kiss me I would have to throw myself at his head, good and strong, and also that I was likely to fall very heavily in love with him in the near future! Watching him ladling cooked dog biscuit out of a saucepan, I saw all my future feelings mapped out before me like a chart. Days of sour boredom, melancholia and touchiness, followed by days of bliss and delirium (usually quite uncalled for), living from one milestone to another. No more aquarium life.

He lent me a lot of books, James Joyce, and Ezra's Pound's *Cantos*, and said, 'Thanks for the visit, I've got to go now to try and scrounge a meal off a girlfriend. You'll come and see me again won't you?'

I was left in the rain, clutching *Ulysses* and the *Cantos*.

Sunday, 29th

Mass at the Servite. Walking back down the Fulham Road with Mummy I sneaked a look through the grubby checked curtains of the Artists' Café, in case G should be there. No customers, but a thin unshaven man in a dark pullover, putting fresh candles in Chianti bottles.

My mother, who had been walking beside me, suddenly said, 'Why do you never hold my arm any more, the way you used to?' I took her arm right away, feeling very guilty and ashamed because the truth is she has become my enemy since I met Gerhardt. As soon as she said all that stuff about how awful and depraved he was, it was like a curtain coming down between us. What makes it worse for her I suppose is that we were so very close before. I used to confide in her and tell her everything about the people I was in love with, which I suppose was all right as long as it was only the head prefect or John Gielgud, but somehow now it's a real man everything's different.

Tea with Rowena. Met her 'uncle' who looks terrible. Everyone is waiting to see if Hitler will invade Holland to get his air base in order to bomb us.

Jack Squire is giving another party tomorrow – that means GERHARDT! Jack is a very sweet old man, apart from his poetry, which is pretty terrible.

I have bought a pipe. Last night at midnight I played 'Au Clair de la Lune', and after a pause another pipe answered me across the bare cold gardens, with every note dropping clear into the well of darkness like a stone.

Saturday, 4th November

I washed my hair, and kept it done up in pipe cleaners all day so it looked really nice and curly when I brushed it out. I also tried a new parting, sort of slanting across from the left and held back on one side with Kirbi-grips. I think it looks sexier than my snood.

I took a lot of trouble over my make-up, putting on Max Factor pancake with a sponge and two layers of the new cyclamen lipstick I'd got in Woolworth's – I also wore my best black dress (what am I talking about, my *only* black dress!) for the second time. It's the one Miss Mannery made for me with the V neck and ruched shoulders. I really looked pretty hot stuff, if I say so myself!

Jack's sitting-room was full of smart clever people whom I didn't know, talking about Wyndham Lewis and Ezra Pound. My mother immediately became embroiled on the sofa with an Antarctic whaler who was talking to her about seals. Jack Squire pinched my bottom and said, 'It's no damn good pinching girls nowadays: they're all so bloody bony!' I sat on the floor and hid behind the sofa, listening desperately for every new footstep. After what seemed an eternity, Gerhardt came. He did the rounds, made a few passes at other girls he knew, then, like a knife slipping into a sheath, came to rest by me for the rest of the evening. He had really surpassed himself that night, as regards his appearance. Mummy took one look at his fingernails and blanched away into a far-off corner with her seal man.

'I heard you playing again last night – it was you, wasn't it? Did you hear me answer?'

He took out his pipe like a conjurer and began to play for me. Squire hadn't been able to afford any gin, so I didn't get drunk, but I was light-headed with excitement.

'Did you read any of those books I lent you? The *Cantos*?'

'Well – I –'

'Don't bother to lie, you wouldn't understand a word of it anyway. I don't know why people talk so much about Ezra – he wasn't interested in Italian history, he was interested in Venetian whores. Christ,' he went on, looking around, 'everyone here's in bloody uniform!'

'Why don't *you* get yourself a uniform?'

'It's not my style – anyhow I'm a filthy German, or hadn't you noticed? I suppose I'll be interned soon and then you won't see me any more.'

He must have seen the look of despair on my face and suddenly lifted my chin with his fingers and said, mockingly, 'Oh, so you love me?'

Of course I love you, I thought, I love you because you're low and depraved and uninhibited and beautiful, and wear corduroy trousers and don't shave – that's what I *thought*. But I said, 'Of course not, I don't love anyone!'

'Except yourself?' he mocked.

'Least of all myself.'

'Oh yes you do, you're at the narcissistic age. I'm very cruel to you, aren't I?' he went on, taking hold of my hand. 'That's why you like me, I suppose, because I treat you cruelly. That really attracts you, doesn't it?'

Feeling stripped naked I laughed rather hysterically, but didn't deny it. He knew where he'd got me all right.

By now Jack Squire was at the piano, singing rude songs, like the one which begins:

> One night I lay tickling my grandfather's balls
> With oil on the end of a feather,
> But what seemed to please the old gentleman most
> Was knocking them softly together.

I caught Mummy's eye and saw it was time to go, so told G I'd see him next Friday at four.

Tuesday, 7th

Big upheavals on the domestic front: Mummy is moving a small electric stove into the dining-room, and we are going to cook on it, so that we don't have to go down two flights of steps to the deserted servants' quarters every time we want to make ourselves beans on toast.

Wednesday, 8th

Mummy keeps saying how much money we're going to be saving now Kathleen has gone, but it doesn't seem to be working out that way. After ten years of eating Kathleen's boiled puddings with hairpins in them, and never being allowed to cook, Mummy is really going to town and making the most amazing things. Yesterday we had croissants from

Deschuyter's for breakfast with hot chocolate instead of tea – she made it by melting down a whole big bar of Cadbury's, and adding cream.

Then in the evening we had baked oysters in cheese sauce! Alfred came to dinner and everybody was sick – somehow I don't think this is going to turn out to be such an economical idea after all. Maybe someone should give Mummy a pep talk about wartime austerity.

Thursday, 9th

Awful rows today. Sid won't eat Mummy's food. She never eats much anyway because she thinks it's sinful, and Mummy gets terribly worried about her health. I, on the other hand, have to hold myself back from it so as not to appear too greedy by asking for second helpings.

The other thing that makes Mummy mad is Sid's chain-smoking. Even when she's drawing or writing she always has a cig hanging out of the corner of her mouth so that lately she's got a kind of brown stain running down her chin, very unattractive, especially as she's taken to wearing all this very white make-up – a kind of paste, which she somehow thinks makes her invisible. Of course it has just the opposite effect, particularly with her bright red hair, and everyone turns to stare at her in the street.

Friday, 10th

Last night I lay on the floor beside the radio after everyone had gone to bed and listened to Flagstadt singing Isolde. After the last crystal-clear note of the 'Liebestod' had melted into silence, I opened the blackout curtains to look up at the stars. Heavy snow was falling. I felt shivery and excited because tomorrow was Friday. Snow is always my lucky weather.

About half past three, I put on my new tartan skirt with a green jumper, my best pair of nylons, and my grey coat with the hood, and started walking towards Cavaye Studios. I saw Woffle first – she was jumping around in the snow snuffing at it in amazement and scattering the drifts with her paws. Then Gerhardt came down the stairs to meet me, dark and rather shrunken-looking, wearing a beret and a black scarf. I noticed the end of his nose was quite pink – cold weather obviously doesn't suit him.

He said very casually, 'Hello Pussy, are you coming to see me?' as if he didn't know. 'Of course,' I said. 'You asked me to tea, don't you remember?' He looked a bit doubtful. Obviously he'd forgotten all about it. He said, 'OK, come back at six if you like. I need some mending done. I can't ask you in now I'm too busy working.'

'What do you want mended?' I asked, feeling rather put out.

'My trousers – I'm going out with Bianca and my only good ones have got a hole in them.'

'Who's Bianca?' I asked, hating her already.

'Oh, she's a very beautiful woman, a patron of the arts – I met her last year in Antibes. She's about fifteen years older than you and she's going to buy me dinner.'

The stove was glowing in Gerhardt's studio when I got back at six, and G was jumping around energetically in a towelling bathrobe. He tossed some trousers at me.

'Here Pussy, get these mended quickly, then I'll swill them out in some Lux and we'll put them in the oven to dry. I've got to look spruce for Bianca, she might be sponsoring my next exhibition – she's already bought the bird.' He pointed towards a rather beautiful little structure in red sandstone.

'Do you know Beethoven's Fifth?' he went on, when the trousers were safely in the oven.

I said I'd never heard it right through, just the 'V for Victory' bit, on the wireless.

'Oh well,' says Gerhardt, turning on his gramophone which has a huge horn, 'you've got a treat in store.'

He threw himself down on the divan bed and I perched nervously on a chair nearby. 'Come on little girl, the big wolf's not going to eat you.' He gestured towards the bed. Rather nervously I lay down on the edge as far away from him as I possibly could and pulled the black and white bedcover over my chilly legs, but not before Gerhardt had spotted them.

'Smart stockings Puss! Not like those awful brown lisle things I've seen you around in – are they for my benefit?'

'Of course not,' I lied crossly.

As the beautiful music began to pour out of the horn just beside my right ear, I felt myself slowly relaxing. I wasn't even frightened when, half way through the second movement, he took hold of my hand. His palms felt very rough and calloused – from chipping stone I suppose. I thought – this is it. He's going to kiss me! I couldn't imagine what it would be like. It had never happened to me before. He propped himself up on one arm and I saw the brown face and hypnotic yellow eyes come looming down over me. At first his lips felt dry and firm, then I felt a snake-like tongue trying to force mine apart. At the same time I was aware of his other hand creeping down to the edge of my skirt, and starting to push it up over my knees. I sat up stiff with terror, pushing him away as hard as I could.

'What's the matter?' he asked, looking rather surprised. 'Little Red Riding Hood frightened of the big bad wolf? Don't you like being kissed?'

'I don't know – I've never kissed anyone before,' I admitted.

'Jesus God!' Gerhardt exclaimed, sounding not so much surprised as downright frightened. He jumped off the bed and turned off the music. 'Well, little girl, you'd better run home to mummy, hadn't you, before Wolfie does anything else naughty!'

He broke off suddenly and sniffed the air. 'Christ, my bloody trousers are on fire!' I couldn't help laughing. He looked so funny dancing round the studio, stamping on the smouldering trousers and howling with rage. Luckily he thought it was funny too.

'Oh well, old Bianca will just have to take me as she finds me. She probably expects artists to be filthy anyway, and it's only the Café Royal.'

I was feeling so miserable by now, and so ashamed of myself for behaving in such a childish way that I longed to discuss it with him, but he seemed only too anxious to get rid of me. I don't suppose I'll ever get a second chance.

It was hell this evening. I kept thinking Mummy and Sid could notice something different about me, as if I had a brand on my face, saying 'I've been kissed!' I told them I thought I might be sickening for another cold, and went to bed early.

No sound of the flute tonight, and no light through the skylight window either, although I kept waking up in the night to look.

Saturday, 18th

I feel very strange these days. I've often thought of my brain as being like one of those ants' nests under glass you can buy at Harrods, with my thoughts scurrying along the brain's corridors. Now Gerhardt has poked his stick in, and the whole nest is in an uproar.

I go out all the time on pointless errands hoping to meet Gerhardt, haunting the shops opposite Cavaye Studios in case he should come out. Once I saw him emerge with a tall, slim elegant woman in trousers, who must be Bianca, so I hid in Dossi's drinking cups of tea I didn't want.

I can't enjoy anything or concentrate on anything; it's like hell. If only I could roll back time and be on his bed again, returning his kiss with all the love I now feel – but he obviously thinks I'm a prissy little idiot and not worth bothering about.

BOOK II

Sunday, 10th December

The skylight at the bottom of our garden has been black for nearly three weeks now Gerhardt is away, living in a cottage in Cornwall with Bianca. In a way it's almost a relief – I've behaved like a fool, and I don't suppose I'll ever see him again.

On Monday I had a lovely day with Rowena. Brought her up to date on G. Her advice: forget him! We'd gone to Soho to buy her some leg warmers from Gamba's, then wandered home slowly through back streets. We saw a most beautiful lesbian come out of a house, in trousers, with a coat over her shoulders. Her face was painted, and her red-brown hair cropped short.

Soho is a scream – although it was only eleven o'clock in the morning we saw the most gorgeous dames in full and frowsy evening dress with feathers! Also arty young men, a real dream, and swarms of dark foreigners. There is a bookshop next to the Royalty Chambers, where we saw little boys with goggling eyes, sucking their fingers in ecstasy as they looked at *The Pleasures of the Torture Chamber* or *The Sex Life of Ancient Rome*, and everywhere we looked we saw pansies and lezzies!

The streets had a faintly sour smell, like old garbage, and a barrel-organ jangling out the *Rhapsody in Blue*. Our feet were beating in time to the music and I began to feel happy for the first time in weeks. To hell with G, Christmas is coming! In the excitement of the moment I bought myself some eyelash curlers, and a second-hand book of Donne's poems which I'd had my eye on for ages. Then we had a bilious cheap lunch at Lyon's Corner House – lobster mayonnaise and ice-cream.

Everyone at home is in a frenzy of Christmas shopping – my shopping list for Mummy and Sid consists at the moment of:

1 Gogol's *Dead Souls*
2 *Inhibitions* by Sigmund Freud
3 A dirty-clothes basket
4 *Madame Bovary*
5 A nest of live ants
6 Indecent pink gauze nightdress, the kind you can see through.

We are also very much taken up with our Christmas panto, *Aladdin*, which we're going to perform for friends in our dining-room, to raise money for the Loaves and Fishes – our society for helping distressed gentlefolk who live alone – we're charging sixpence a ticket.

Christmas Day

Midnight Mass at the Oratory. Lovely prezzies – got my ants' nest and *Madame Bovary* and Freud.

Everyone over-ate. Alfred ate so much he got indigestion and couldn't go to the carol service.

On Boxing Day we did our panto – huge success! I played Aladdin, and had to run on, crying, 'I am that naughty boy Aladdin whose trousers always need some paddin'!' chased by Alfred as the Widow Twanky in a long curly wig, mob-cap and apron, waving a cane! His friend Bertie was divine as the Princess Zadubadour, in a transparent black evening dress, swooning on the floor and murmuring hoarsely, 'Leave me, leave me!' Alfred and Bertie had a great fight over a roll of cotton-wool for their busts. 'Give me my bust, you swine. You can't have it all, damn you!'

Everybody paid sixpence, and we raised 18/– for the Loaves and Fishes. Later we had a tea party for the Sea-horses [the old people], who are often lonely at Christmas. I made Viota cakes with pink icing, and we lit the candles on the tree and sang carols. Mummy and Sid have secret nicknames for the Sea-horses, like Hungry Harry, Dreary Alice, and Dopey Diana – if only they knew!

New Year's Eve

Alfred came over to see it in with us and Mummy made some hot punch, and we all got rather tiddly.

Alfred did his impersonation of one of Wagner's Rhine Maidens – he says it's much better with three people; he and Bertie and Sammy do it a lot at home. Then he and Mummy changed clothes, and he looked simply marvellous with ostrich feathers on his head, doing a hula dance.

I don't know what I'd do without Alfred; he's the only bright spot in my otherwise boring life. I love his calm familiarity with me and the way he holds both my hands when he greets me. He really treats me like an intelligent adult, his artistic and intellectual equal, not like a child.

Just before midnight Bobby Cartland arrived, looking divine. She really is the best-looking woman I know, with her short, sleek grey hair brushed back, curling slightly at the nape of the neck, and lovely chiselled features like a boy. She always wears a grey coat and skirt and her voice is low and husky. Alfred says she has been neutered!

He played the piano and she crooned 'Smoke gets in your eyes' and 'There ain't no good man worth the salt of my tears'. She has a deep throbbing voice like an organ, extraordinarily low for a woman's.

Then Alfred played 'Auld Lang Syne' and we all sang, and kissed each other. I just hope 1940 turns out to be a bit more exciting than 1939.

Sunday, 14th January 1940

Food is now being rationed, at least certain things are, like butter and sugar, not to mention bacon which Mummy has a passion for. I'm more upset about sugar, as I'm used to having four lumps!

Ballet club with Rowena – *Dark Elegies*, *Sleeping Beauty* and *Masques*, with darling Bobby Helpmann dancing.

I was eating liver sausage sandwiches in the bar, and listening to the ballet talk – 'But of course, darling, I always did think Margot's left point was rather weak!' – and admiring the boy next to me who had blacked his eyebrows and wore mascara, when Rowena dashed downstairs, saying she'd seen Bobby in his dressing-room! He had false eyelashes an inch long and pink nails, and he simply reeked of scent! She said he was wearing his *Masque* get-up, with an ostrich plume on one shoulder, and was standing in front of a long glass practising keeping his bottom in by stroking it down while tucking in his stomach. I caught a glimpse of him later, swanning downstairs with Soames and Edwards in tow, both most alluring in light sun-tan make-up. We think Bobby is absolutely gorgeous, even if he does look a bit like a goldfish.

Still no sign of Gerhardt coming back. The winter seems endless. The only bright spot is that now he's away I am getting on much better with Mummy and Sid. I can hear Sid's chisel and hammer tapping away down in her shed at the bottom of the garden. She is carving me a pregnant Madonna in limewood. Ears of corn grow up from the plinth and curve round the centre of gravity, her womb. Sid's latest eccentricity is to join a circle of lesbians, who meet every Thursday to discuss Plato and define things like vulgarity. She is thinking of bringing Bobby Cartland along next time, to get them excited – Bobby being so handsome – and then whisper, 'Keep off the grass, she's got a mistress in the peerage!' It's funny really, now I come to think of it, Sid not disapproving of Bobby when she disapproves so much of Bertie. But perhaps Bobby doesn't actually do it? And if not, what exactly is it that she doesn't do? I wish I knew.

Friday, 19th

My old schoolfriend Thetis came to dinner, and we talked about art and men till quite late and I told her about Gerhardt. I was pleased to find someone else who frequently wishes they were dead. Her trouble is that she says she can't co-ordinate religion, art, and life into a sane and purposed whole, and she worries herself sick because she can't put order into this chaos. Like me, she's still a virgin. Her family are very intellectual and give poetry readings in their drawing-room, which Thetis says are very embarrassing.

Saturday, 20th

To Alfred's for supper – sausages and cheese. Then on with Alfred and Sid to hear a debate between a white-cowled, hair-splitting Dominican,

Father Gilbey, and a psychiatrist called Eric Strauss, who wore a monocle, about the differences between Freud and Thomas Aquinas. I really didn't understand too much of it, and finally gave up trying when a man with side-whiskers swayed forward and demanded, 'Father Gilbey, as a Thomist, what is your opinion of the actuality of the absolute otherwise?'

Tuesday, 23rd

This war that isn't like a real war still drags on. Poor Laura has left the first-aid post – the conditions there have apparently brought back her TB and she may have to go to a sanatorium. I miss her terribly.

We still do part-time work at the post, but it's very boring. Even Mummy and Sid are getting fed up with endlessly bandaging healthy limbs!

Alfred to tea, and we sang *Tosca* and sat on the floor eating winkles off the pin of my brooch. He has had a quarrel with Basil and doesn't see him any more. I think he must have realised how much Sid disapproved of him. Sid got another letter from her lesbian circle today; they write, somewhat ambiguously, 'Enough of Platonics! Let us know when you're ready for Sin!' which apparently is the next subject they intend discussing.

Father Carato came to supper and we had it in Sid's shed in the garden. He looked so picturesque by the flickering candlelight with his black beard and dark eyes, eating liver sausage and throwing back large whiskies. He really likes his booze! I kept thinking about how I go to Confession to him every Friday, and all the things I tell him. I just hope he doesn't recognise my voice!

I have vivid memories of when I was two, being dragged to the font for my second baptism, this time as a Catholic, and how I screamed blue murder when I saw the water, and how he slapped salt on my tongue to shut me up.

As we were walking down the garden, saying goodbye, something made me turn and look back and, like a miracle, Gerhardt's skylight burst into glowing light. He was back! I said goodbye to Father Carato and ran upstairs to my bedroom and cried with excitement. During the night I heard the pipe playing again.

Thursday, 1st February

Went to a film show at Hortensia Road – Chaplin in *A Dog's Life*. What a lovely artist he is, so thin and small with the most perfect hands. Then had a cup of tea with Daisy in the canteen. She is thrilled because she finally got her boyfriend to the altar. She goes around saying, 'I'm the naughty, naughty nurse who never has the curse'!

On the way home I ran into Jack Squire and tried tactfully to probe him about G's return. He said, 'Oh yes – the old bastard's back.'

I gathered he'd spent Christmas with Bianca at her house in Cornwall – it must be nearly three months since I saw him last, but I haven't the courage to go round in case Bianca is there. If only Squire would give another party.

Friday, 2nd

Went to Confession at the Servite – Father Carato, *again*, three Hail Marys. While I was kneeling in front of the altar saying my penance, I suddenly thought of G kissing me and a kind of delicious stabbing pain ran through my stomach, so sharp and strong that I winced.

I was walking back past the dairy towards Milborne Grove, thinking about kissing and whether I would like it better next time, when the door of the Artists' Café burst open and a hand shot out, pulling me into the murky interior, which smelt of stale cooking fat and garlic. It was Gerhardt! I felt quite faint with the excitement of seeing him again so suddenly.

'Hey Jo, look what I've caught' he called to a dark unshaven man, who was boiling up a big pan of spaghetti in the kitchen. He was very attractive in a depraved sort of way, wild dark hair, black eyes, blue stubbly chin, navy-blue polo-necked sweater that looked as if it hadn't been washed for years. I gathered he was the café's owner.

'This is little Pussy-willow,' G said, pulling me on to his lap. 'She's a virgin. Joan, meet Jo Matutinovitch, the worst artist in Chelsea.'

'A virgin, eh?' Jo looked suitably impressed. 'Well Pussy, how are you? Enjoying life?'

'Well, I haven't been recently,' I said. 'In fact I've been terribly bored.'

'Nobody at seventeen has a right to be bored,' G said. 'You're only bored because you don't know anyone in Chelsea except your mother and me, and you haven't got a boyfriend.'

'How about me?' Jo strode out of the kitchen and tilted my chin with a filthy finger. 'Mmm, not bad, why don't you sit for me?'

'Are you any good?' I asked.

Jo looked offended. 'Of course I am, I'm a bloody genius actually. Aren't I Gerhardt?'

'You're a dreadful dauber, but at least you keep real artists like me in food – come on Jo, how about a couple of spag bols?'

Jo picked up a handful of spaghetti and hurled it at the wall to see if it would stick, but it slithered slowly down to join the rest of the garbage on the floor. 'There, you see, it's not ready yet – it reminds me a bit of the way old Jack Bilbo did his paintings, remember?'

'That's right,' Gerhardt said. 'He used to cover the canvas with glue and then stand back and chuck things at it. Old French letters, rusty razor blades, burnt sausages, fag ends – if they stuck it was a collage, if they fell off – oh well, it all helped to mess the paint around. God, if he could be an artist, anyone could! Why don't you be an artist, Pussy? You could get away from your mum and meet exciting people.'

'But I can't paint!' I exclaimed weakly.

'So what? Neither can Jo, or anyone else in this road for that matter. You could go to Chelsea Poly. Who's there now – Sutherland, Henry Moore? They'd soon teach you the ropes and it would only cost you about twelve bob a term. Then you could talk your ma into getting you a studio!'

Jo's eyes brightened. 'And then *I* could paint in it!'

I could see Gerhardt smirking at us both in a cynical way. I jumped to my feet. 'I must go now,' I said. 'My mother's holding a meeting of the Loaves and Fishes!' There was a stunned silence.

'What in hell's that?' Jo asked.

'Well, it's a society we've formed,' I said, 'for helping lonely gentlefolk who have fallen on hard times. The helpers are called Sprats and the old people are Sea-horses. I'm a Sprat.'

Jo and Gerhardt exchanged despairing glances. 'The sooner we fix this girl up with a new life the better! Which do you think would suit her best, painting or sculpture? Bearing in mind that she's not serious, just friggin' around.'

38

'Oh sculpture, I should think – clay's cheaper than paint, and she'd like old Moore. But there's nothing to stop her doing both.'

Oh, I'm so glad he's back! I didn't dare ask where Bianca was. As I was going out Gerhardt called after me, 'Oh, by the way, there are some decent studios to let down Redcliffe Road just round the corner from you – Prudey's place is swell. If you want to see it, drop by tomorrow night, she's having a party.'

'Will you be there?'

'Sure, I'm taking Bianca.' He glanced at me to see my reaction but I remained impassive.

Sunday, 4th

I spent most of yesterday wondering what on earth I should wear. My black dress seemed too grand for a studio, so finally settled for trousers and a soft white shirt with full sleeves, and my cameo ear-rings.

When I got to number 34 I found the door unlocked, so pushed it open. I could hear a distant roar of voices, that seemed to be coming from the first floor.

I was shaking with nervous expectancy – my first *real* party. Not just a literary gathering but people staggering up the stairs with bottles, music pounding, people dancing.

The studio was all white, with a gallery running round it, candles everywhere and pink scarves hanging over the lights. A short boyish figure with spiky hair and bare feet was taking the bottles and pouring them rather haphazardly into an old garbage bin – my hostess presumably. I sat myself on the edge of a divan and started smoking nervously, not inhaling but using the cigarettes to cover my embarrassment. I didn't know anybody there and nobody was speaking to me, so I smoked till my mouth was dry and my throat scratchy. When I was wondering if I could bear it a moment longer, Gerhardt came loping up the stairs, Bianca and Woffle in tow. He caught sight of me and grinned derisively.

'Hello Pussy, having a great time? Why aren't you drinking?'

He went over to the garbage pail and bowled me out a mugful of the murky mixture. I gulped it down greedily, but as I looked up to continue our conversation he had already moved away, talking to a large bald-headed man in a check shirt, one arm round Bianca's waist.

On the pretext of getting myself another drink, I wandered across the room and sat down beside a thin dark boy who was playing a guitar. He looked friendly, and rather lost, and not quite as frightening as the others. He told me his name was Luis and that if they called him up he was going to kill himself. Strumming a few minor chords he began to sing:

> ' tried to keep my secret
> From every shot and shell
> But one came along
> That made me tell –'

'What's that called?' I asked. 'It sounds terribly sad.'

'It's called "Ghost Soldier Blues".'

By now the drink was beginning to warm me, dissolving my fears. I could even bear to watch Gerhardt, who was lying on a nearby divan with Bianca and stroking her hair.

'What do you think of Leonard's new still life?' I heard her asking him, raising a languid hand to indicate a heap of melons and a blue jug that hung over the mantelpiece.

'La seule nature morte que j'aime c'est une femme nue sur un lit,' G intoned, slipping his hand under her shirt.

By now lots of people were dancing to the radiogram, which was playing 'St James Infirmary Blues'. I watched them with my face set in a stiff grimace of simulated happiness, as I tried to look as if I was participating. I didn't know which I dreaded most, to be asked to dance, or not asked to dance.

Just as I was giving up hope, a tall Negro crossed the room and held out a hand like a paddle towards me, pulling me up to my feet in one movement. His palm was hard and dry and he smelt of coconut oil. I clung to him like a drowning man, trying to follow his steps as he pulled me into the sea of dancers. Gosh, I thought, as he swung me round on the floor, I wonder should I tell him that the last time I danced was with Molly Maguire at the Holy Sepulchre, and even then I had to lead because I was so tall? Too late! Already I was being pulled in and thrown out like a yo-yo, then unexpectedly released, to spin away down the room and crash humiliatingly against the wall.

When I recovered, all I could see was a tall black back strutting away from me across the room with a muttered 'Didn't come here to teach chicks to jive!'

I was still standing rooted to the spot, hot with embarrassment, when I felt two sinewy arms slide around my waist from behind, and a prickly cheek was pressed against mine.

'Hi baby,' said a hoarse voice. It was Jo from the café, reeking of red wine and garlic. 'How ya doin'?'

'Oh, it's awful,' I said, 'I don't know how to dance!'

'Forget it,' Jo said, turning me around to face him, and pressing the lower part of his body against mine in a most peculiar way. 'Just relax and take a lesson from Uncle Jo!'

I leant against him, breathing through my mouth because of the garlic. I'd never really danced close with a man before, and I take back anything I've ever said about modern dancing! This was surely the most thrilling and satisfying thing I've ever experienced. Jo danced slowly and very well, like a doped panther, holding me so tightly I could feel the movement and interplay of his muscles against my body. We really seemed to be moving like one person. All my life I've suffered from self-consciousness, watching myself from the outside like a performing puppet, but now suddenly there I was, right inside my own skin, and moving beautifully without thinking about it, in a happy dream. It was rather like swimming or riding, only much nicer. As the record came to a stop he bent his head and kissed me on the neck – I started as if an electric shock had gone through me and tried to pull away. To my dismay I could see Gerhardt's sardonic eyes watching me from his horizontal position on the couch.

The next thing I knew, they were both plying me with drink and everything became a bit hazy. I remember Jo asking me whether I was going to get a studio and whether he could come and paint there – apparently there's one going at number 48 down the road, much smaller than Prudey's but only thirty bob a week. I also remember practically passing out on the sofa at one point, and hearing Luis playing 'Careless Love'.

When I opened my eyes I saw the big Negro and his girlfriend jiving alone in the middle of the floor, moving very slowly. The girl's mouth was open and her eyes were glazed. She seemed to be lost in the music, controlling its flow with the movements of her long hands and the whipping edges of her red skirt. As she slowly spun and twisted, I lay back on the sofa in a drunken daze watching her through the smoke and stroking Woffle's ears.

Just then a door opened on the staircase to the left of my head and I was aware of someone looking down at the party and making 'tut tut' and 'oh dear, oh dear' sort of noises. From the corner of my eye I could see that whoever it was was wearing a paisley dressing-gown and carrying a coal-scuttle. The caretaker, I thought, come to make a fuss about the noise. Then I turned round and saw that it was no caretaker but an absolutely beautiful young man with dark curly hair and beard. He looked rather like a very handsome seal.

'Hello,' the apparition said in a jokey kind of voice. 'What an absolutely dreadful crowd! I was going to ask Prudey for some coal, but on second thoughts' – he broke off and studied me more closely – 'I suppose you don't by any happy chance play chess?' I shook my head dumbly.

'Pity, I've just checkmated myself three times running and it's getting awfully boring. Ah well, off to beddy-byes, I suppose.' He gave a last disgusted look at the prostrate bodies and trailed away up the stairs. I suppose this must be the one they call Rupert who lives with Prudey and hates parties. He's certainly devastatingly attractive.

By now I was feeling surprisingly sober and the awful thought came to me that it must be after midnight. My mother would be going crazy! Gerhardt was still entwined with Bianca and Jo certainly couldn't be trusted in the blackout so I thought I'd better go home by myself and not say goodbye to anybody.

I sneaked out and went rather unsteadily down the stairs. I'm quite sure nobody even noticed I'd left.

Saturday, 10th

Sid's away on retreat at Eastcote this weekend, so I've been able to work on Mummy about taking up art lessons.

She seemed a bit surprised at first, because she'd got so used to my wanting to be an actress, but she said yes, provided I could get into the Chelsea Poly and provided I went on doing war work part-time. She has also agreed to let me rent a studio! I told her about the ones in Redcliffe

Road and we went to see Wheeler and Atkins, the agents, who said the top floor at number 48 is vacant. It's only 30/- a week, and we've got quite a bit of furniture in store. I am going to be allowed to work there in the daytime provided I come home if an air-raid siren goes off – not much chance of that! All our fears of bombing seem to have receded into the distance. Grass is sprouting on the roof of our air-raid shelter.

Monday, 26th

Today on my way home, I ran into Jo from the Artists' Café and he seemed very excited at seeing me again. He seemed particularly happy to hear about the studio. I have a feeling he may have designs on it himself! Anyway, he has asked if he can paint me and I am going to sit for him on Friday. Anything to keep my mind off Gerhardt. He paints in a room at the back of the café. I hope he doesn't think I am going to sit for him in the nude!

Friday, 1st March

I couldn't sleep for excitement – at last something new is going to happen to me!

Got to Jo's café soon after ten, and found he had been up early, scraping down an old canvas, and hadn't even had time to wash or shave. Luckily he didn't seem to expect me to pose in the nude, as he'd got a beautiful, off-the-shoulder pale-blue evening dress for me to wear, which he says will be the very devil to paint! His room at the back was small and rather dark – no wonder he wants to use my studio!

The pose was quite an easy one, seated in an armchair in front of the open stove, with Jo's two rather smelly dogs asleep at my feet. Jo, silhouetted against the window like a shadow-play, was the inspired artist incarnate, slashing away with his palette knife, with occasional cries of 'bugger' or 'Christ, that's good!' Soon my arms got cramped and I began to droop visibly, owing to lack of sleep. Before I knew what was happening, Jo had put down his palette and was bearing down upon me.

'You're tired my lovely, my precious petling! Wouldn't you like to take a rest?'

What happened after that was so quick and unexpected that I had no time to protest. My neck and shoulders were bare, and Jo was covering them with kisses. I could feel the unshaven bristles rasping against my skin. To my amazement, I felt a great shiver of pure delight run through me, rather like the way I felt in church when I was thinking about Gerhardt.

Well, I thought, I'm not going to be so stupid the second time round, so this time when I saw Jo's face looming over me, blue stubbly chin and rather thick sensuous lips pouting for a kiss, I decided to shut my eyes and bear it. Actually it wasn't as bad as I had expected. In fact I even found myself responding a little, kissing him back. A pity he smelt of garlic.

Just as things were beginning to get hectic the doorbell rang furiously. It was the dustman. Jo said, 'This pisshole is just one damn thing after another,' and went to the back door. By the time he had disposed of the dustman the atmosphere of passion had somewhat evaporated and so we resumed the sitting.

Tuesday, 12th

Every night at about six, Gerhardt turns on his light and the skylight glows like a rose. As long as I see the light I can feel the atmosphere of that studio and see where the furniture is standing. I know where the bed is, I can smell the dust and imagine the slouch of his shoulders and the way his hair falls forward over his ears when he is working.

Then the blackout is drawn across and Gerhardt ceases to be a reality, and I stop being aware of his life flowing and burning on the other side of the garden. I wish it could be like that all the time. I wish he would go out of my blood.

On the other hand, I have been thinking a great deal about Jo and with a certain tenderness. When I went back to the café this morning to arrange for another sitting, I found I was seeing him with a new kind of vision. I watched him with pleasure and curiosity, and almost with pos-sessiveness. He seemed physically attractive to me in a way he hadn't before and I found myself positively yearning over his bent head and the lines of his body. My casual interest and excitement at the last visit had suddenly become something strong and exciting inside me. Oh no, surely not – I can't be going to fall in love again! What's wrong with me? Why does this happen to me all the time? So when Jo asked if he could paint in my studio, of course I said yes.

'You mean you'll really let me paint there?' Jo looked at me as if I was giving him the earth. In no time at all we were discussing the exciting details of north lights and brown linen curtains and whitewashed walls and easels, and the different ways you can cheat your landlord out of the rent, and all the customers telling me what a lucky bastard I am.

Jo's going to teach me how to make canvases out of potato sacks, so altogether we'll be a self-supporting industry. I have always hated being alone or working alone. When I think of Jo painting at my place I wonder what I've done to deserve such happiness.

I spent the afternoon walking across the park making up songs and singing them to the empty air, then had tea at a milk bar and bought myself a new skirt for 5/– in Regent Street, feeling on top of the world.

When Jo saw me coming back in my new skirt, he said, 'Holy Mother you're dressed to kill. Are you going somewhere tonight or is it just that spring feeling?' He grabbed me to give me a kiss and I found to my amazement I was nearly crying. My arms tightened round him convulsively and I could hardly control myself. We stayed in each other's arms for a little, rocking to and fro, and I was terribly moved, taken unawares by my emotion. Only another ten days before I get the keys to the studio.

Easter Sunday, 24th

I thought of nothing except being happy. The cherry tree in front of the house has come into flower. For Easter my mother gave me paint brushes, a palette, Gertrude Stein's *Picasso*, and a grass snake.

After lunch I went down to Redcliffe Road and climbed the stairs to my studio, and stood under the skylight for the first time as an owner. I felt that here was something no amount of unhappiness would ever take from me. The windows were stiff from disuse and the sun made a yellow square on the wooden floor. The paper was peeling off the walls and the skylight was filthy. The room was very high, shut off and self-contained.

From the big front windows you could look down and see the whole of Redcliffe Road; life quietly going on on roofs, balconies and pavements.

From the little windows at the back you saw the never-ending houses of the poor, children playing in yards, trees, coloured strings of washing like flags at a carnival, and behind the church spire the smoking chimneys of the power station.

The room was so high up that the intense life all around didn't touch it, you felt alone there without being lonely. I measured up all the corners and windows and saw the furniture taking form in space. It isn't big like number 34, but cosier.

After dinner Jack Squire came in looking very ill, and talking about the new edition of his poems that he's bringing out. 'Of course it won't bring in any money,' he said, as he struggled into his huge overcoat, which had two bottles wrapped in brown paper protruding from each pocket. 'Still,' he went on, glaring at me over his glasses, his eyebrows bristling like antennae, 'the longer I live the less I worry about money.' He turned to lurch down the stairs. 'That's what old Belloc used to say,' came a parting growl, 'only with him it wasn't true.'

Tuesday, 26th

Got up early, made sandwiches, bought some apples and carted my paints and some old canvases round to the studio. Then I lit a cigarette and sat on the window seat, leaning out and watching the corner of the road. The curtains of the house opposite drew back and several women watched me. After about ten minutes I saw a small figure coming round the corner into the road, its hair standing on end and carrying an easel. The figure came nearer, saw me and waved.

The stairs are very dark until you come out on to my landing and then it's light and my door is painted bright red. I waited, full of anticipation, but when he finally reached the top, Jo was seen to have flu and a hacking cough. Romance was obviously out, so we got down to work right away. Jo had the easel and I painted on the mantelpiece. I did the view from my window, Jo embarked on a large pink nude lying on a green sea-shore – pretty frightful. Jo's method of teaching is to come up behind me and say, 'Christ that's lousy! Let me show you how to do it!' And before you know where you are he's finished the picture and is standing back and saying, 'Mmm – damn good! One of the best things I've done!'

By the end of the afternoon Jo's pink nude had red hair and purple armpits and he was using up my slate white with a glorious abandon that made me flinch. I do hope he'll bring his own paints next time. The rain pelted down on to the skylight as we rested and ate garlic sausage and apples. Jo felt much better as soon as he smelt the garlic.

Had to leave at six to go to Sadler's Wells with Rowena. During the interval we had cocoa and Welsh rarebit at the Angel Café, while Rowena told me about her 'uncle', and how nice sex is. She says it's the best indoor recreation she has yet discovered, particularly in the afternoon which is the only time he can get away from his wife. She says it's like an old French song which just goes on and on, and I really ought to try it. I asked her what she did to prevent herself from getting pregnant, and she said there are things called Volpar Gels which are quite effective, but the best thing is to go to the Marie Stopes clinic and get a Dutch cap.

I told her all about Gerhardt and Jo, and she said it sounded very boring and rather decadent. Of course I'm not decadent at all really, I only wish I was.

Just before the curtain was due to go up on *Dante Sonata*, I suddenly said, 'Christ there's my father', and tore down the aisle. He was in uniform, very bald and looking, as they say, 'distinguished'. As I caught up with him, he was just stopping to say hello to his friend William Walton in the stalls. I touched his arm and he looked very surprised and said, 'Hello my darling how sweet to see you again!' Just then the first chords of the ballet broke in, so I had to rush back to my seat. It wasn't a terribly good ballet but there were some nice solo writhings by Bobby Helpmann, stark naked save for a snake.

In the interval I went to have a drink with Daddy. He's amazing, just like a child, much less adult than I am. It seems he is now a brigade major on some anti-aircraft unit, and he kept on saying, 'You know, I'm very important' or, 'That man I was talking to just now is very famous, he's a great friend of mine! June Brae is a great friend of mine too. I'm taking her out after the show. We're dining with Connie Lambert!'

'Oh yes,' I said, getting a bit bored, 'he drinks doesn't he?'

'No more than I do,' said Dick. 'By the way, have you read my new book, it's bloody good.'

'No, I can't afford it.'

'I'll send you a copy tomorrow.' (Of course he didn't.)

It's like Wyndham Lewis says in *Apes of God*: Dick lives in a vacuum, a vacuum with glass walls and each wall reflects Dick.

The noise in the bar was deafening – we sparred for a bit, neither of us feeling any great affection. His eyes never look at you when he talks, they are moving the whole time, scanning the room over your shoulder for something better. I watched him steadily, thinking his teeth are bad but he's still handsome. He only mentioned my mother once. 'Well,' he said finally, 'next time I'm on leave I promise I'll ring you. Take you out to a nightclub or something.'

We fought our way out of the bar and he left me abruptly in the foyer with, 'Have to go to the lavatory – goodbye darling.' So that was that.

Monday, 1st April

My first day at art school – it is quite near, in Manresa Road. It takes up a whole floor and has beautiful big rooms.

I sat with the other new students on a bench outside the head's room, watching with fascination as the old students began to arrive: young men who slouched in with hair flopping over their foreheads, lots of well-developed healthy girls with flat feet, in dirndls and brightly checked blouses. They fell on each other's necks with cries of 'Nuschka darling!' or 'Bobo!', and so on.

I was interviewed by the head, who is long and thin, and after signing various forms and paying my thirty bob, I was escorted to the sculpture room and introduced to Henry Moore. The great man is small and brown with magnetic blazing blue eyes. I thought he looked about forty. He had rather flat brown hair, wore a navy sweater, and smoked. I checked a morbid desire to address him as 'Maître'. As I had done no modelling before I was put into a little cubby hole off the main studios and given a plastic head of an oriental lady to copy. Moore knocked me up an armature, flung a lump of clay and some calipers at me, and told me to enjoy myself.

In the next room the more advanced students were modelling from a very cold pink nude, with red hair and bad circulation. After a bit the head sloped in looking like Groucho Marx. 'Heavens!' he said. 'You've got on fast.' And he called old Moore in and they both seemed very pleased. So tomorrow I am to be allowed in the main studio.

Wednesday, 3rd

The furniture is in. My grandmother's divan, two basket chairs, a bookcase, a second-hand piano I got for £4, and a rather beautiful dining table of Mummy's with four chairs. The studio now looks lovely, my ideal of a room.

The old girl in the studio underneath used to be Aleister Crowley's mistress. She calls herself Madame Arcana. Her novel (*The Hieroglyph*) is still popular in libraries, and she contributes to the *Occult Review*. She is a huge lady draped in shawls, pinned at the neck by a gilt bird in flight. Her hair is in coils around her ears with a boudoir cap perched on the top of them and she has a dove called Cooee which sits on her shoulder. It is very fond of Bach, and does a dance if you play 'Jesu, Joy of Man's Desiring'. Jo says to avoid her like the plague.

Thursday, 4th

Today an awful thing happened. I saw Gerhardt and he saw me and crossed the road. I looked at him and saw that he was pale and very thin. He wasn't laughing any more, and there was no mocking glint in his eyes. They are more like the eyes of a sick dog than a goat. He was wearing a filthy old mackintosh.

As I watched him, I knew in an instant that I no longer loved or even liked Jo. I love Gerhardt. In a calm and unsmiling moment of pure love I went back to my old state of misery and fears, back to where I started. But I willed it to be so. I said in a rather flat dull voice, 'You look bloody ill,' and then I told him about the room and said that Jo painted there.

'Oh Jo,' Gerhardt said in calm contempt. 'That thing.'

It was terrible. With that one sentence Gerhardt destroyed Jo. I asked him if he had done any work and he said, 'No, none, all I can think of is

49

how long it will be before I'm interned. Or if I'm not interned and the Germans come, whether I will be able to shoot myself before they can get me. You know of course that I am Jewish?'

Betrayed by his pale thinness, by the quietness of his voice, I forgot about my past sufferings and asked him to come and see me – I said, 'Come this afternoon.' Everything about our meeting was lovely and comforting. To feel the way I did was in itself a good and healing thing. I would die for him tomorrow, but I wouldn't stir a finger for Jo. And that in spite of the fact that Gerhardt never came.

It was very cold and I sat at the window for four hours, hardly able to believe it. I was miserable in a way I had never known before, without any energy, either physical or mental, unable to move or cry. I bit my nails to the quick.

Leaving the studio at seven, I went straight to Cavaye Place. I could see the lights on behind the drawn curtains, but they were short and didn't quite reach the windowsill.

I bent down and peered into the dimly lit interior. A woman's legs passed across my vision, long and brown and naked. After a little while they passed me again, going in the direction of the bed this time. After that I didn't see them any more but I heard the slow movement of Beethoven's Fifth, and then the lights went out.

They say in novels 'something died in me', but that's not true. It's all you ask for to have the love die. The worst thing is that it goes on living and redoubling its love, and is wounded to the quick and cries aloud. I only wish a lot of things would die in me.

Friday, 5th

When I woke this morning it seemed strangely cold and dark.

'You'd better put on thicker shoes,' Mummy said. 'I think it's going to snow again.' Even the weather wants to push me back into gloomy winter, and I thought it was spring!

I went round to the café, and there was Jo, sitting at the kitchen table gutting rabbits and singing 'Mets ta main dans ma main'.

I didn't feel the slightest affection for him – even his face seemed different, hard and selfish, with deep lines from nose to mouth. When I thought of the things I had permitted him to do, thinking that I loved him, I nearly died with shame.

The studio is almost finished. It now has a rubber plant and an oil stove. The oil stove, apart from keeping it warm, is fine for cooking stews on.

Jo came round to paint after lunch. I can see he's going to be a permanent fixture in the studio. He knows when he's on to a good thing. Still, I don't mind him there when I'm working – it's like having an animal around. He must have sensed the difference in my feelings towards him, for he didn't attempt to touch me. Once he kissed me lightly – I didn't respond but stood quite still, and after a little while I put up my hand and rubbed my lip.

What an extraordinary thing this love is that comes and goes, making a completely different person of you while it lasts. And when you're young it's a kind of unreal fantasy, based on something that doesn't exist. The best fantasies are when you are not seeing the person, when they are inaccessible. They fall to bits as soon as you get the person. But Gerhardt isn't fantasy, he's something deeper. The Jo fantasy only lasted a week, just a substitute for Gerhardt, I suppose, and a most extraordinary delusion. Even your eyes can't be trusted. You think you see with a new vision, then suddenly your old eyes are given back to you – you see the reality and then where are you? Right in the process of making a bloody fool of yourself usually. You have to be terribly careful when you are young.

Monday, 8th

Went to the Chelsea Polytechnic for a life class. The model is a big tattooed man, rather like Charles the Wrestler. Coxon and Day taught. Mine wasn't bad but I really hate drawing muscles. You sit on small slipper-shaped bits of wood and your behind gets pretty sore after a few hours. Everyone was very nice to me.

Ran over to the café in the lunch hour. I was hardly through the door, when Jo hurled at me, 'Do you want to paint a Negress?'

'Yes,' I replied rather nervously, 'that would be lovely.'

'OK, that's fine, she's coming to your place at ten next Tuesday to sit in the nude. She's enormously fat, coffee-coloured, has bad legs and charges 2/6 an hour. We share costs and you supply the draperies.'

I was a bit dazed but tried to act as if nude Negresses with colossal thighs charging around my studio were quite a common experience.

'Of course,' he went on, 'we may not get the bitch. She's in great demand. We'll have to have a screen, and some yellow or red hangings. Olive-coloured flesh would look fascinating against yellow or red, don't you think? – and, of course, a fire.'

'OK,' I said, 'I'll see what I can do.'

'You know 2/6 an hour is monstrous but I must have the nude,' Jo went on. 'Here you are, Pussy, have some goulash.'

Just then a rather weak-chinned English-type intellectual called Huxley came in for some coffee and started teasing Jo, asking why he wasn't in uniform. Jo leapt wildly at the bait.

'Who betrayed Austria? Who sold Czechoslovakia? Who sold Spain? Who sold Finland? And now they wish to make me fight as a British subject and for what? Pah!' he spat on to the filthy floor – 'For a narrow-minded, self-satisfied, stinking little island run by that pharisaical Bible-punching bastard Chamberlain, the bloody capitalist who engineered this war! *Me*, in a monkey jacket! Look at this!' he dramatically produced his passport and waved it under Huxley's disgusted nose. 'My British passport! Pah! I spit on it.' (He did so.) 'Christ why didn't I go to Mexico four years ago? I've had nothing from this government, they take every penny I make and what do they give their unemployed? Nothing!'

'On the contrary,' Huxley replied. 'They gave me 8/6 this morning, probably filched from your earnings – I'm very grateful to you, Jo!'

'And what is this 8/6? It is to make them contented with their shameful condition when they should be rebelling.' Jo collapsed back against the stove. 'Ah well, drink your coffee, let's not fight. By the way, Joan, did Gerhardt come to see you on Saturday? He said he was going to.'

I got hot with excitement and said, casually, 'Oh I guess I must have been out. How is the bastard?'

'Oh very depressed one minute, wildly elated the next. He thinks he's going to be deported any minute now.'

I spent the rest of the life class in a dream, thinking about Gerhardt and eating peppermints to counteract the garlic.

Tuesday, 9th

Wore my trousers – still a little nervous of going out in them. Went to the studio and painted a still life of irises against the blue screen with a red silk shawl thrown over it.

Jo came round and said, 'Christ, I wish I'd painted that! It's so fresh, young and naïve – my work's so sensual and sentimental. I only wish I could get away from myself in my work.'

We cooked a couple of lamb chops on the oil stove. When we'd finished gnawing the bones in our fingers, Jo wiped his mouth with a turpsy rag and glanced back towards the divan. After that, I am ashamed to say, it was just the same old routine. Jo pretending to be tired, then taking my hand and pulling me down beside him. I don't love him any more, but why make a fuss? When you're tired it doesn't seem to matter, and after all, the touch of his body is familiar and companionable, and I feel sorry for him. Warmth, tired relaxation, peace in all my bones. If only Jo would lie quiet and not get so excited. 'Sweet soft thing – you're getting me all het up!'

'Oh go to sleep, Jo. Is this your idea of a rest? Listen to the rain on the skylight and go to sleep.'

After lunch Madame Arcana came up, on the pretext of telling us that Germany had invaded Norway and Denmark but really to show off her latest acquisition – a beautiful young pansy whom she calls 'Bambino', who pranced around my furniture saying 'Ooh how delicious!' (I didn't tell him that most of it came from jumble sales.)

After he had gone I cleared up the incredible mess: cigarette ends in the sink, piles of greasy plates from the day before, fruit cores on the floor etc., and was glad I wasn't married to Jo.

Wednesday, 10th

Still-life at the polytechnic – no one came near us, there was only me and an old woman painting stuffed birds. I bought a canvas and started on the inevitable guitar with a few broken vases. I painted to please myself, very bright colours and no perspective. If they don't like it they can go bugger themselves, as Jo would say. But seeing that it was meant to be my first attempt at painting, I do think they might have come and given me some help.

Afternoon class with darling H. Moore. My head's nearly finished. HM very pleased with me. I suppose this must have given me confidence, for I suddenly decided to force the issue as regards Gerhardt.

As soon as I had washed off the clay, I went over to Cavaye Place and knocked. He wasn't there so I tore the blotting paper out of my cheque book and wrote on it in charcoal 'GERHARDT – PLEASE COME AND SEE ME TOMORROW ABOUT FIVE – NUMBER 48 IN CASE YOU'VE FORGOTTEN – TOP BELL. JOAN'.

Thursday, 11th

Of course I knew he wouldn't come – all the same I filled the studio with flowers and bought some milk and some apple tarts. It was a long wait. Half past five came and went. I painted the still life with irises so as not to think, losing myself in the painting.

Then suddenly the bell rang – I had that sense of shock and awakening you get when an alarm clock goes off. After a frozen minute, I tore downstairs with my knees stiff and tense like some paralytic old man. There he was, new and strange, wonderful and terrifying. I turned to watch him at each turn of the stairs – he ran up behind me, quick and light as a wolf. He settled himself in the armchair by the bookcase and I put the kettle on. I started to make polite conversation but he stopped me dead. He seemed to know exactly the state of depression I was in, with a keen perception that was almost psychic. He just said, without preamble, 'You make yourself very unhappy over things that don't really matter. You worry over things that don't exist at all, except in your imagination – you shouldn't do it, you shouldn't make yourself so unhappy.'

'How do you know I do?'

'Oh I've watched you, I've observed you.'

'Well, I suppose I do – I think too much about myself, I suppose. Unselfish people aren't unhappy.'

'Oh, so you think you're selfish, do you? Well, I'll tell you one thing, you'll never be an artist if you're not. Do you really want to paint?'

'Yes, I think so. I'm feeling my way.'

Gerhardt looked around the studio and seemed to sniff the air. 'How about Jo?' he said, his face wrinkling with distaste. 'Doesn't he bother you at all?'

'Oh no, it's just like having a dog around the place.'

Gerhardt chuckled maliciously. 'If he heard that! You know at your age you should be in love with Jo, you should think him wonderful –'

'My God, in love with Jo! Why are you laughing like that?'

'At you – so young and so cynical.'

'On the contrary, my trouble is I think too many people are wonderful.' I sat at his feet and drank my tea, listening in amazement to the kindness in his voice.

'The trouble with you is that you have the wrong idea of yourself. You think that you do everything badly, that you're clumsy, awkward and gauche – when really you react and behave in a perfectly normal and rather a graceful way. Apart from that, you're really a very pretty girl, or could be if you took off those dreadful glasses.'

'But I can't,' I said. 'I wouldn't be able to see anything.'

'No, but people would see you.'

His voice was so kind and quiet – he'd never spoken like this to me before. I was amazed.

'You want a lot of things you haven't got, isn't that so? What is it you want most?'

'That's my business,' I said blushing, pulling a geranium leaf to pieces in my fingers.

'Well, I'll tell you. You want friends of your own age, you want to have a good time and most of all you want a boyfriend. You want to fall in love.'

'But when you do it's worse hell than anything else! And what's more it's never returned.'

'Why not? You're a very nice girl.'

I shivered and said nothing. Then I put on the Brandenburg and started darning my stockings while he sat opposite me on the other side of the fire, whittling at a piece of wood.

'And what does your poor mother think of all this? Doesn't she want you to get a job?'

'Not particularly, she thinks I'm too young. Besides I've got £2 a week of my own, I could easily live on that.'

'You're not thinking of running away from home, I hope?'

'Oh no, I would never do that.'

'Not even for a young man?'

'Oh well, that's different,' I said laughing. He was laughing a lot too, mocking and probing, his eyes so bright and devilish that I had to hide my face. G is the only person I know it's no good posing or pretending with. He talked to me for a long time, rather like a psychiatrist, trying to reassure me and paint a rosy future. I take back anything I may have said about him being cruel. After today I must believe that he is kind and good.

Suddenly he looked at his watch and got up.

'I must go now but I'll come again – on Sunday. I'll come a bit earlier to give you more of my time – will you be in?'

I was speechless, twisting the stockings in my hand. Then he was gone very quickly, whistling a Bach fugue, and the front door banged.

I covered my face with my hands, took a deep breath and then lay down on the couch and started to laugh and cry hysterically. When the fit passed I knelt down in the middle of the floor and said the 'Our Father' three times. While I was tidying up the studio I took the cigarette ends that he'd smoked out of the ashtray and hid them in a drawer. Then I went home.

Sunday, 14th

It would be an understatement to say that I was distracted during Mass. I am not even very good at it normally, thinking about breakfast, the brown peppery sausages and hot sweet tea, and how good they taste together. Today all I could think about was Gerhardt.

He came earlier than the day before, wearing a coarse blue cotton shirt cut straight across the neck, dark sunglasses and sandals. He sat and smoked yellow cigarettes out of a paper bag. He was in the devil of a mood, his eyes brown and piercing, never leaving my face.

Much to my embarrassment he started on the subject of boyfriends again.

'You've really got to have one, it's what you need more than anything else, you know.' Then, very seriously and transfixing me with his eyes, 'You know it's time you went to bed with someone.'

I was taken aback, even shocked.

'Or are you intent on preserving your virginity for your husband?' His voice had an edge of sarcasm. 'After all, having sex is the normal healthy thing to do, most girls about your age do it with anyone just to get it over with. But don't you do that, choose someone you really like, preferably between twenty-three and twenty-seven, and then you'll see how different everything will look. You'll get life in the right perspective, you'll feel on an equal footing with other people, and it will lift your inferiority complex. Just make sure that you don't fall in love with the wrong sort of person – someone too old, whose necessities are different from yours. Someone like me for instance.'

My face was hidden by the cupboard door, the saucepan in my hand clattered on to the shelf as I said, a shade too quickly, 'But I'm not in the least in love with you!' I could imagine his smile.

'I was merely giving myself as an example.'

I came and sat opposite him tense and wary. 'Why would you be so wrong for me?'

'My life's different, my necessities are different – you don't want a tough old cynic like me. You're young, idealistic – I'm finished with all that sort of thing. What you want,' he went on, settling back into his chair and lighting another yellow cigarette, 'is some nice young artist, full of enthusiasm, who will read poetry to you and take you out. At your age you ought to be having a good time, going to little Chelsea clubs and Soho cafés, going dancing – if I took you to those places I should be bored stiff. It's a phase you pass through. When I was twenty-three I used to dance the Charleston all night and love it. Now I should just feel an idiot. Find some young man who'll take you about, show you a bit of life. Don't be alone so much. Fall in love – you should find it quite easy.'

And that, I realised, was the death blow – very kindly and tactfully delivered. I stared at the signet ring on his hand, and said nothing – it was really very decent of him to bother to disillusion me. A ridiculous picture of Gerhardt dancing the Charleston came into my mind – I wish I had known him at twenty-three – thin and wild and enjoying life.

I picked up my sketch pad and began drawing him, adding horns and turning him into a satyr. He picked up my copy of T. S. Eliot and sketched me on the flyleaf, a rather shocked-looking virgin with a long neck wearing a snood.

It was getting late so I started to peel potatoes. 'Do you eat up here?' asked Gerhardt. 'Alone?'

When I said yes, sometimes, he seemed quite upset, and said it was terrible the way I was always alone. But what can I do? Of course I long for someone young and vital and idealistic – but do such creatures exist? I seem to have only known the old, tired and cynical. I suppose I'll meet someone suitable in the end, but I'm a natural pessimist and meantime I love Gerhardt and he just sits there, a yellow cigarette between his teeth, hypnotising me with his mocking eyes and telling me I mustn't love him. I wish I was dead.

Monday, 15th

Back to work. Took out my feelings on the model. Little Coxon came round and said, 'By jove, that's a savage piece of work. It's wild, uncivilised, I like it! The violent way that arm sticks out at you – it fairly knocks you backwards. Where have you drawn before?' I told him it was my first try, and he seemed quite impressed.

Tuesday, 16th

At ten o'clock I threw down the key to Jo and a motley procession filed up: Jo dirty and unshaven; Janet in red canvas pants carrying her easel; her friend Joanna; a young pansy called Clifford wearing a woman's grey silk shirt with little frilly sleeves that left his shoulders bare; and last but not least the model, Jo's enormous negress.

Four easels were manoeuvred into position, paints spread all over the floor, furniture and carpets dragged back, and the oil stove lighted.

'Oh bliss, Stravinsky!' Clifford exclaimed, pouncing on my pile of records. 'I simply must have the rape scene to inspire me.'

To the opening bars of *Le Sacre du Printemps* we all set to work in busy silence. Out of the corner of my eye I could see Clifford covering his canvas with olive-green swirls, vaguely suggestive of the human figure, while Jo scraped on a magenta background with his palette knife, smoking, swearing and quietly appropriating my turps. The model sighed and scratched herself. The heat was thunderous and oppressive. I felt it was all rather unreal and I had no business to be there masquerading as an artist, splashing on colour as if I had been at it for years instead of weeks, pretending to be a Bohemian like the others. Still it was fun, and I pretended quite well. During the first rest Janet and Joanna flung themselves on my books like locusts with loud cries of appreciation.

'Darling, will you lend me this?' Janet cried pulling out *Gaudier-Brzeska*, 'or do you mind lending?' She put it into her basket without waiting for an answer. Joanna filched my T. S. Eliot.

I made strong tea and handed it round, and Clifford was heard to remark that, 'This is the only place I've felt at home in for a long time – barring my own little room of course!'

The tea was so strong that we could have the same pot, watered down, for the second rest. My nude was beginning to look most peculiar, but then so was everybody else's. The floor by this time was inches deep in cigarette ends.

We went on painting until three and then I provided them with bread, sausage and mustard, for which they seemed profoundly grateful. It disappeared in about five minutes, together with my entire supply of fruit and all my cigarettes. Then Jo made coffee in the teapot, and it tasted very good except that we had to strain the grounds through one of Joanna's stockings.

After the model had gone, we sprawled on the floor and divan, becoming very intimate and talking intensely about art, ballet and music, etc. Joanna, still stuffing herself with the remains of the garlic sausage, was off on *Sweeney Agonistes*. Jo, having eaten three bananas with fierce concentration and thrown the skins out of the window, finally threw himself on the divan and went to sleep. Clifford played Chaliapin on the gramophone.

It was nearly five before I finally got rid of them, having arranged to share another model next week. I was left in the midst of indescribable chaos, dirty cups and plates piled everywhere, thoroughly exhausted by the heat and so much intellectual talk.

Thursday, 18th

Started my first figure from life with Henry Moore. The model smelt awful. She has red hair. Today the Germans captured Trondheim.

Painted with Jo in the afternoon. He has a new thing, which is covering everything all over with alizarine red, thinned out with turps – unfortunately it's my most expensive paint. He says provided the Germans give him six years he will be a genius. He believes that geniuses are made and not born.

I didn't paint as I hadn't a canvas, but darned my stockings instead. When I was tired I lay down on the divan and Jo came and lay beside me. We've got to the stage now when familiarity makes it almost innocent – no mystery or fear, just a hearty good-humoured sort of atmosphere like schoolboys scuffling.

'Christ,' he said, pinching my waist, 'you're wearing a roll-on or something – that's a new departure for you, isn't it?'

'Please Jo stop that and let me sleep, I'm tired.'

'But don't I make you feel naughty?'

'No – you never do,' I said unhappily, hating my stagnant condition and wishing I was in love. I hope I'm not frigid or something. If only I could find someone to love who is capable of responding to me.

Thursday, 25th

Modelling with Henry Moore. He theorised for hours about sculpture and it was very interesting. When he comes into a room it's like a spark being struck. Had lunch in the canteen for the first time, huge plates of steak and kidney pie. Sat next to my new friend Susan who wears emerald green corduroys and a cerise blouse, and hangs shells around her neck. She said, 'Hell, I'm so sick of being arty! I think I'm going to marry a stockbroker.' She is a jolly nice girl.

Saturday, 27th

Mummy's birthday party. Alfred came with his new friend Basil. Sid doesn't seem to like him any better than Bertie, calling him decadent and perverted. Alfred did his take-off of Madame Butterfly's entrance in Act I, in red silk shawl with a parasol and a flower behind his ear. Mummy and I did the *Swan Lake* adagio.

Alfred has a new word he uses rather a lot, which is 'camp'. He uses it mainly when he is talking about the opera. He says it's got nothing to do with Boy Scouts but just means anything outrageous, or over the top – camp in fact! He thinks Basil's new tie is camp.

Sid is still very disapproving of my activities but Mummy seems to be getting nicer. The other day she ran into Jo and me walking down the King's Road together, and when we got home she said that she thought he looked 'very interesting' and she wouldn't mind an afternoon in the studio with him herself! Sometimes Mummy comes out with some really quite extraordinary things.

Friday, 3rd May

Life class with Moreland Lewis, a Welshman with black curls sticking up like a halo. I did a charcoal drawing, smudging the shadows with my finger in that tricky cheating way the teachers are so against. He says my work is 'fearless' but otherwise pretty awful. He has hairy arms and whistles through his teeth when he is drawing. Felt very depressed.

Home for tea. Alfred came and did the first act of *Tristan and Isolde* in costume. White gown, very long feet in socks, Celtic bangles, and a wig with plaits. He was wearing an incredible make-up, lots of my cyclamen lipstick and talcum powder on his blue chin.

Mummy made some cup and I got rather tight, laughing myself sick at Alfred, who has had a row with Basil, which is why he came on his own.

Tuesday, 7th

The model fainted, so went back to the studio to paint. I think she had the curse poor girl. Had to borrow money from Jo for turps, bread and liver sausage, as I had no money. This is the first time I've really had to worry over every penny, now that I've got a place of my own. It makes life more interesting.

A big bearded artist in a floppy hat, called Jimmy, joined us for lunch with his wife Francine, quite attractive, with purple lips and eyebrows like gnats' antennae. They run a café in Hollywood Road. Jimmy is worried because his wife must go abroad for her TB, and wants to start a pub in Majorca after the war.

'Or failing that m'wife and I could work the old second sight – but it's a hell of a life for Francine with her lungs you know, shut up in a box, passing me messages while I do the old *blague* outside! By the way, that German fellow Gerhardt was over at my place the other night – amazing fellow – he seemed suicidal.'

'Luis committed suicide,' Jo said. 'You know, that boy who played the guitar at Pru's party? You were talking to him, weren't you Joan? He was called up so he put his head in the gas oven. I daresay I'll be doing the same thing soon. I looked up my passport yesterday and realised I'm only thirty-three, so the buggers will probably rope me in by the end of the year. Oh well, in a few weeks' time I daresay a bomb will drop through the skylight and nothing will matter anyway. Thank God I'm off to Cornwall tomorrow.'

Jo had packed up ready to go with the other three when the bell rang, and I knew immediately who it was. The muscles in my stomach contracted and a tingle of excitement ran through me.

Gerhardt, thin and brown like an Italian peasant, blue cotton pants in tatters with a large triangular tear on the seat. Strange, like someone off a high mountain where sheep lie in the shade of hot rocks.

He said, 'I've torn my pants – mend them for me.' His sarcastic eyes hurtled around the room, and everything went out of focus. The room seemed to take on some of his strangeness, becoming the uniquely weird vacuum in which Gerhardt walks and has his being.

I said, 'Would you like to take your trousers off?'

'No Pussy, you might not be able to control yourself,' he muttered with relish, lying face down on the divan and unbuttoning his pants.

I got some darning wool and tried to sew the tear without hurting him.

'Go on, put your hand inside, don't be afraid! It won't be the first time someone's done it – but no monkey tricks mind.'

I sewed it up very badly, my hands shaking, feeling the heat of his body. After I had finished mending it we sat by the open window and he played his pipe for me. He was playing 'Little Miss Muffet' very meaningfully when I suddenly saw that man from Pru's party, the one who'd asked me to play chess, loping along on the other side of the road. He was wearing a blue and white stripey shirt and looked very brown and glamorous. 'Hello Gerhardt!' he called up. 'At it again?'

I wish I could find some way of meeting him.

After a bit Gerhardt said, 'I must go and put on smarter clothes, I'm going out with one of my expensive girls.'

'Do they pay?'

'Sure they pay! You can come around and talk to me while I dress if you like.'

The first thing I noticed when I got to the studio was that all his frames were empty – he must have sold all his pictures. The whole studio smelt of lilac. I lay on the bed and read E. E. Cummings, while Gerhardt swept off into the lavatory to wash his hair in lemon juice which he says gives it golden lights. He came back rubbing his hair with a towel, and threw a sheaf of typewritten papers at me. 'Some of my poems – see what you think of them.'

The main idea was the elimination of all capital letters and punctuation, in order to make their meaning as obscure as possible – apart from that they seemed to be mainly about sex.

'I expect they'll be too difficult for you, too obscure and too bitter, but maybe you'll understand them in your subconscious,' Gerhardt said. I tried to read but found it difficult to concentrate because he had just taken off his trousers. He has a beautiful body.

When he had made himself comparatively respectable for his 'expensive girl' he said, 'I want you to do me a favour tonight – take the dog – I shan't be back till three and she gets lonely.' Of course I said I would.

I took Woffle home with me. When she had finished gnawing my shoes to pieces she attacked the furniture and finally, worn out, went to sleep with her head on my shoulder and her feet on my hot water bottle. I lay awake till two, and heard Gerhardt come in and play his pipe. It was lovely having Woffle with me, she is the only dog I've ever really liked.

I took her back next morning at twelve – Gerhardt was in bed, naked, with the filthy red coverlet pulled up under his armpits.

Wednesday, 8th

Mummy took me to a fortune teller, an awful old witch called Madame Guthrie, with white hair and long jade ear-rings. She gazed into the crystal and told me I was attractive to older men, but the one I was with at present was a 'bad hat' and I should give him up as soon as possible. Then she gave me a wish. Thinking of Gerhardt's advice, I wished for a young artist of about twenty-three, full of ideals and enthusiasm and preferably a conchie, but not a pansy.

She turned up the cards and said, 'You'll get your wish much sooner than you expect, my dear.'

Thursday, 9th

The poly. A thin wispy young man gave us a lecture on Goya – quite attractive really. Baby-fair hair brushed back from his peeling forehead, big clear eyes behind round glasses, red sunburnt patches on high cheek-bones. He wears a red tie and green pants and sandals. I thought he looked vaguely familiar, and sure enough, while I was eating baked beans in the canteen, he came up and said, 'Haven't I seen you around somewhere? Walking up and down Redcliffe Road perhaps?'

It turns out that he's a painter called Leonard Purvis and lives at number 34 – Prudey's place where the party was – and that he's had his eye on me for some time, and wanted to meet me! Most flattering and just as the gypsy told me: a nice young idealistic artist, completely lacking in cynicism and a conscientious objector to boot!

He has offered to teach me to paint – I can see he will be very useful if I can only keep him under control! Anyway, it makes a nice change to have someone tracking after me instead of the other way round, so I asked him back for tea after class.

At first I was very nervous, moving around clumsily and tidying things unnecessarily, but after a bit I found him very sympathetic and started to confide in him. Soon I was telling him all about Gerhardt and how badly he treated me. It seems he knew him quite well.

'Well, well, *well*, Joan,' he said in slow amazement, watching me with big eyes. 'So you're in love with Gerhardt. It never ceases to amaze me how women love to be imposed upon.' It sounded strange to be called a woman. I started to fidget around again, carrying dirty crockery to the sink, and wondering what had made me confide so unashamedly in a complete stranger.

To change the subject, I asked him what *his* problems were, and he told

me that his wife doesn't understand him, and he worries about their relationship. He also worries a lot about the war and the position of the artist
in society. I kept hoping he'd say more about his wife, but instead he held
forth for ages on the artist in society and how he is a social outcast and so
on, which was rather boring. Then he helped me clean my palettes and
told me that if I pay him 5/– a week he'll give me painting lessons.

Rowena, who came in just before he left, said, 'Who's that, dear?
He seems all set for a nice love affair with you, don't you think – I can
see it in his eye!' Then she went out and bought some cold liver sausage
and we ate it and played the gramophone, and Rowena pushed back the
carpets and we danced to Stravinsky. She also showed me some marvellous
photos she'd had taken of herself, all draped in newspaper, by a very clever
young man.

Friday, 10th

Went round to Leonard's studio at number 34. It is definitely the same
house where I went to the party! His studio is very arty, all white with a
red divan and a plaster statue of a Greek goddess, a guitar, and tapestries
designed by his wife Agnes. We drank china tea on the divan and looked
at copies of *Verve*. He has a very interesting bookcase, everything from
The Wind in the Willows to *Marital Hygiene*.

After tea we had a long talk about masturbation. Leonard approves of
it and gave me the reasons why. He says everybody masturbates, it's
perfectly normal and a pleasurable way of getting satisfaction when other
means are impossible. Just as it was getting interesting and I was going to
ask him how it was done, another artist conchie rushed in waving a
newspaper. 'They've invaded Holland and Belgium!' he panted.

So there it is. We looked at one another. The war had really started.
Things seemed to be moving so fast, I felt suddenly quite dizzy. Leonard
and the conchie looked pale and horrified. They will probably be forced
to fight now, for every man will be needed.

Leonard poured the conchie a cup of tea and he read us a statement he
had prepared for the tribunal, saying why he won't fight. It was very
intellectual and high flown, all about the physical and spiritual planes of
life, and Leonard didn't seem to think the judge would like it too much.

Later we went out to buy a paper and he took my arm and we walked slowly down the Fulham Road each holding one side of the paper. All around us others were doing much the same. It was hot and dusty and as we went down Redcliffe Road we saw people sitting reading the papers under the striped awnings of their balconies. There wasn't any noise, only a man with a piano on wheels who played 'It's a lovely day to-morrow'.

Leonard looked at the green trees at the end of the road and said, 'Isn't it unbelievable, seeing the sky and the leaves and smelling the air and thinking how good it is to walk on the earth, that anyone should ever want to make war?' He thinks we ought to try and get back to the simple life, just eating, sleeping and copulating.

Back at the studio as we leant out of the window, a bearded satyr-like face looked up from the cactuses on the sun roof below. 'Hello Leonard, still talking rot?' he asked, putting down his watering can. It was that handsome man from the party again. L didn't reply and the red patches on his cheekbones grew darker. 'I see you're reading all the lovely news,' he went on, spotting our newspaper. 'Wicked old Germans disguised as nuns and Red Cross nurses dropping from parachutes – my God, what a farcical war! By the way, I've just had my hair cut – don't you think I look distinguished?'

Leonard didn't answer but moved inside rather angrily.

'Who's that?' I asked, trying to sound casual.

'Oh that's Rupert Darrow. He lives with Prudey. Lives off her, I should probably think.'

The sun was beating down on the skylight. When we looked up we could see nothing but hot blue sky, the silver blimps becalmed over the trees. Leonard, who seems to be given to abstract philosophising, began, 'Isn't it amazing that we two should be sitting here shut up in a kind of ivory tower, with a piano in the street still playing on, while the greatest catastrophe that the world has ever known –' I was beginning to get rather tired of all this and found my mind wandering. 'But *we're* doing the right thing, aren't we?' he was saying when I surfaced again. 'Sitting here and smoking after a good cup of tea with good talk about art and things that are really lasting – maybe I'm wrong, maybe one day I'll wish I'd fought the Germans!' Meantime his hand which had been on my shoulder had now moved down to my waist where it was moving in a strong rhythmic caress.

I don't quite know what I am going to do about Leonard. He quite obviously wants a mild sort of love affair, but he isn't sufficiently attractive to justify the awful guilt feelings I would have about his wife. When his hand started feeling its way inside my blouse I got up and said I was sorry but I had to go.

As we stood on the steps he put his arms around me and said, 'I'll be seeing you when I come back from Bath next week.' I think he would have kissed me, but I gracefully freed myself and ran down the steps, because it's rather embarrassing to kiss a man smaller than yourself standing up. I think I'm becoming the most awful bitch. I seem to spend most of my time arousing but not satisfying male desire.

Saturday, 11th

Wonderful sun, everything green bursting out. As I stand by the window in a spring daze, thinking about bombs and buds, Gerhardt suddenly started to work again, his hammer strokes ringing across the garden. All the daffodils were out round the air-raid shelter.

Went to Confession at the Oratory, just for a change, and when I said I had let men kiss me when I wasn't in love with them the priest said, 'Is there anything wrong in that, my child?' I was absolutely amazed, said the 'Veni Creator' for my penance, and departed in high spirits. Bought some gentians from Harrods at great expense, the deepest blue this side of heaven, and took them round to Gerhardt's studio. He had knocked up an armature, and was starting a new work using a pot of reddish cement which he was modelling on to it like clay. This is something new that hasn't been done before – it hardens like stone, and can be filed to a lovely surface, rather like red sandstone. G says it's very quick and cheap. I watched the muscles in his bare arms as he filed away, and loved him passionately.

After lunch – bread and cheese – we lay on the bed, and Gerhardt fell asleep with his head on my shoulders. On the table beside the bed I could see a large bottle of brandy, my bowl of gentians, a gas mask, and two books – *Alice in Wonderland* and the Bible. I couldn't move because I didn't want to wake him.

Later he opened one eye and said, 'What would you say if I violated you? You'd like it wouldn't you! But don't worry I'm not going to, not with your mother just round the corner!' Then he got up and made us some tea. He says he doesn't think it will be long now before Germany wins the war, and then he'll be shot as a traitor.

After tea he went on working while I lay on the bed and read some typewritten pages of *Ecce Ego*, all about Gerhardt's life when he was starving in New York – drinking from public fountains to fill his belly, shooting crap with bums and Negroes behind the garbage cans, and all the time dreaming about sculpture. If Gerhardt wants to keep hidden behind his barriers of cynicism he really shouldn't write such revealing books.

When it was dark we stood on the balcony and leant back looking at the sky and the barrage balloons, and G said, 'I've never known it so warm in the evenings, not in three years. All the blimps are up tonight, they should paint them blue like the sky for camouflage. Somehow I don't think they'll ever raid London.'

It was a lovely day, with Gerhardt talking to me so normally and quietly, just like an ordinary person. I could hardly tear myself away to go on duty.

Monday, 13th

Return of Jo from Cornwall. I went round to the café at eleven, wearing my new hat that I got from Woolies – cyclamen with a veil – that really knocked Jo's eye out. He was looking pretty good too because he was brown, in a blue linen shirt open to the waist, wicked and amorous and laughing like hell all the time. He filled me with vitality and I found myself thinking he was really quite attractive.

We had a wonderful morning, all young and excited again like it was at the beginning, kissing and fighting and hurling insults, laughing till we had to stuff our fingers in our mouths. Jo bit me till my neck was marked, and said, 'Oh how good and soft you are to feel! How do I feel? Do you like it?' But I wouldn't let him undo my blouse.

'Christ, this is bad for me,' Jo said. 'I really shouldn't do it, it gets me all worked up and nowhere to go, because if there's one thing I don't do it's sleep with virgins.'

'Too much trouble I suppose.'

'My God yes, and no fun for the virgin either. I'll give you one word of advice – when it does happen go all out and give it everything you've got, don't hold back or have any inhibitions, because if you do it's the one thing that can turn a young girl into a lesbian. Didn't your mother ever talk about these things?'

'No, she never told me much – I don't think she knew much herself, in spite of being married. Oh, she sort of told me how it's done, driving around Hyde Park in her little Austin 7, with the engine revved up very loud to hide her embarrassment – actually, her own mother didn't tell her very much either, just to use lots of scent and not let her husband see her cleaning her teeth.'

Jo shook his head in amazement, then kissed me several times very gently, without putting his tongue between my lips. I felt completely happy and quite fond of Jo again, and told him he could come round and do some painting at my place if he liked.

The result was a very impressionistic landscape in brilliant green, purple and yellow, a real Matutinovitch masterpiece, and afterwards we lay down and kissed rapturously.

Poor darling Jo, I don't love him a *bit* but I am divinely happy playing the fool with him. I know I shouldn't, because he keeps saying, 'Oh what an absolute bugger, oh you little bitch!' We do sometimes reach the farthest point of passion after which coition should naturally occur – only it can't. Also he complains that I don't respond much or wiggle as he'd like me to. I really don't get much urge to wiggle.

I think for a girl without experience the most awakened parts of her body are her breasts – it must be something to do with the maternal instinct. I'm not really moved much by all that rhythmic panting but when Jo touches my breasts or lays his head on them, then I find it lovely and beautiful. He's really quite decent and considerate with it all – if you say you're tired of striptease he'll do up your buttons again and be sorry, and he always shares his cigarettes and lends you money when he's got any. Now that he's brown he's really very attractive and his breath is clean and sweet, and I like the feel of his bare arms now that it's summer.

After Jo had gone I looked at my flushed face in the glass and tidied my hair, thinking what an awful tart I am. There was a terrible love-bite on my cheek, so I got a pin and made a few scratches across it, and told Mummy a cat had scratched me, but I don't think she believed me. Later we listened to a very stirring speech by Churchill about 'blood, toil, sweat and tears'.

Wednesday, 15th

Holland surrendered today. Henry Moore said he was surprised and pleased at the way I'd got on with my first figure, so felt terribly exhilarated. I do hope I'm not going to get a crush on him. He really looks amazing at the moment, in a violet shirt with a lemon yellow tie, and his face all ruddy and shining. We played the fool a bit, flicking hard clay pellets at the model's twimmock, using our modelling tools as catapults.

After class I called on Leonard to ask him to share a nude on Friday, and he said, 'Come on up, Agnes is here.'

Agnes was combing her long hair. She is small and round and very pretty. She wears sandals and has a large behind and small breasts, and wears stays. We sat around talking war gloom till seven. L says he is definitely going to commit suicide if Agnes is killed in a raid, or if the Germans make his life at all uncomfortable. I think that's a weak, spineless sort of attitude.

He is coming on Tuesday with Gerald Wilde, yet another artist who can't pay the model, but I said that would be all right. I think I'll get Sallé, who according to an article in *Everybody's* is known as Soho's Trilby on account of her perfect feet. She also has varicose veins and heavy hanging breasts which are good to paint. She is a darling, so kind to everyone, and goes around wearing damask curtains and blown hens' eggs in her hair, but that's just a stunt to get engagements, she's quite simple really.

My mother has now relaxed her ban on theatre-going, so went to see *The Beggar's Opera* with Thetis. I really liked it when Macheath said 'Kiss me you slut!'

Friday, 17th

Sallé arrived late, complaining about her veins. I draped the divan with a red shawl and she lay on it looking lovely. Jo said, 'You'd better make the

70

pose a bit more uncomfortable; it's the only way to stop the silly bitch talking!'

Leonard came with Gerald, who has long red hair, a bit thin on top, blue eyes with a cast in one of them, a long upper lip and a turned up nose. He looked incredibly dirty, his clothes so worn they were positively gangrenous, and he wore boots without socks. He said he was sorry about not paying. That means that with 7/6 for the day, and four of us paying, it will be 1/10 each, which isn't bad.

Jo painted a nude of unsurpassed vulgarity, even for him, on a very big canvas. Leonard, on the other hand, produced a work of great sensitivity on a very small canvas. Jo is always saying things like 'You know my new thing is "Light"', or 'Pure Colour', or some such thing, and at the moment it's 'Monumental Form'. This came as a great relief to me, as when it's 'Colour' he uses up all my best paints.

Cooked kidney stew on the oil stove. While we were eating it, Jo began talking about religion, saying his ancestors were Catholics when mine were wearing skins, and I didn't really belong to Holy Mother Church at all.

'Now I'm a *real* Catholic, brought up by bloody Jesuits. I used to go to Confession and come out and rape the first girl I met! That's what it means to belong to Holy Mother Church! But you bloody English Catholics, you just don't know what it's all about.'

Leonard, who had been looking at me with some dismay, said, 'But Joan, you're not a *practising* Catholic are you?' When I said yes, they all seemed amazed but said I was young and would get over it.

The gas fire kept going out because we only had a few pennies for the meter. Leonard couldn't pay the model either – so I paid for him. It was a very jolly party.

Leonard stayed on after everybody else left, and sat on the divan talking about his wife, and almost against his will it all came out, how she didn't love him and was fascinated by another man, and how he would kill himself if she left him, and how he had discovered her making astrological plans to run away with her lover.

I asked him why he didn't leave her, and he said he couldn't even if he wanted to, because he lives on her money and he would starve, and in any case he falls in love with her all over again every day because she has such reserves of sexual excitement. And on and on, rather boringly I thought, talking about his wife, her talents, her temperament and the shape of her breasts, and all the time his hands were softly stroking my hair or caressing the nape of my neck. Suddenly he took off his glasses, leant over and kissed me. I thought I knew what kissing was, but this was like nothing I'd ever known, and made me forget myself completely. I wouldn't have expected such technique from a boy of twenty-three!

I had on a blue cotton dress that buttons up the front, and when he tried to undo them I put up my hand to stop him but he held up my wrist like a vice so that I couldn't move. When I felt his lips against my breast it was terrible, worse than anything that had happened before, because I was half-naked, terribly ashamed, and blushing like a schoolgirl and couldn't stop him.

He never spoke, except once to say, 'Joan, *please*, for Christ's sake, take this wretched dress off!' But I said, 'Certainly not, and don't rip it, it's new.' Then he made me put my hand under his shirt so that I could feel the smooth warm skin. I'd never touched a man's skin before. I liked the way the muscles moved. He bit my neck, which I like too, though I wish men wouldn't do it so hard – there are dark bruises on my neck already and I'll have to keep my hair over them for days, not to mention his four-days' growth of beard making my cheek red. I think girls call it 'stubble trouble'.

Later on when we were lying there tired out, he took my hand and tried to put it over his penis but I wouldn't put it there. Then after a bit he said, 'Joan, if you're really sweet you'll make me some tea.' So I got up cheerfully, buttoned up my dress and made tea.

While we were drinking it, he said, looking at me very intensely, 'Joan darling, do you mind if I ask you something rather personal?'

'No of course not Leonard,' I said, wondering what on earth was coming.

'When I was kissing you just now, did you notice my teeth moving at all?'

'Your *teeth*?'

'Well, yes. Actually I've got a sort of plate in the front and I'm a bit worried in case it moves when I'm kissing people.'

I said he didn't have to worry, I hadn't noticed anything at all. After he'd gone I found he'd pinched all my cigarettes – God damn all sponging bastards!

Monday, 20th

Coming back from college, I saw Leonard making for the cake shop, so followed his twinkling bare heels down the Fulham Road. He was wearing shorts and flapping sandals, and his ankles were long and thin. His brown and white checked shirt was open almost to the waist, showing a narrow chest with callow reddish-blonde hairs on it like a young bird.

He seemed very pleased to see me and we bought apple tarts to take back for tea at number 34. After we had munched our way through them, he sat facing me and set out, I think, to shock me. That cultured, rather charming voice, and those clear grey eyes made what he was saying even more intriguing. He started off by saying, 'Do you find yourself shocked by the things that are happening to you now? You know you really shouldn't, there's something fine and human and large about the person who's never shocked, a lovely robustness of outlook. I'm going to ask you something now that would have shocked me at your age – you'll think me terrible – maybe I'd better not!'

'Oh no, go on, please ask me,' I said, expecting something terrific.

'Well,' Leonard went on in bell-like tones, 'I was going to ask you if you'd mind if I peed in your sink.'

I laughed so much that I choked and became red in the face. When my voice came back I wiped my eyes and said weakly, 'No, no, please do, only make sure that you move the tea things first!' and went off into further spasms.

'You see,' he went on, ignoring my hilarity, 'I always pee in the sink at home, it's so much easier than going down to the lavatory which is two floors down, and Agnes doesn't mind. I really thought you'd be shocked,' he went on, seeming rather annoyed. 'I didn't know you'd find it funny.' Really men are amazing.

After he had finished peeing he sat down again and started teaching me words like bugger, fuck, cunt, cock etc., which he thinks should not be thought of as vulgar but should become part of the English language.

After he had gone on about this for quite a long time with the air of an Oxford don, he moved his chair nearer to me and said, 'I'm being terribly curious, and I suppose your friends would think me either silly or a cad to speak to a young girl like this, but have you ever thought that you would like to indulge in certain erotic practices other than mere face-to-face copulation?'

I told him that quite honestly I didn't know there were any, which is probably why I had never thought about it. Leonard looked rather taken aback, but went on to describe, with scholarly enthusiasm, how a woman could lie on top of a man or sit astride him, or how she could kneel upright with a man coming in behind, or how they could do it standing up, or the woman could lean back over a table.

'But of course,' he went on, 'it's more difficult for a woman to come in those attitudes than when you're face to face – do you follow? I'll demonstrate if you like?'

'Oh no – thank you very much, I'd really rather you didn't – what does come mean?'

Leonard stared at me in amazement. 'An orgasm of course. My goodness, I keep forgetting how young you are.'

'So what else can a woman do?' I went on, beginning to get interested.

'Well, she can hold the man's penis in her mouth – the only objection to that is that it's rather difficult to know what to do with the semen when it comes. I know some women like swallowing it – it acts like a tonic and makes them feel marvellous.'

I said I couldn't really see myself enjoying that very much, so he steered the conversation back on to masturbation, which we had just been starting on the day Holland and Belgium were invaded. When I said I had never done it, he seemed very startled and said, 'Good heavens, not even at your convent? I thought all convent girls did it? Well you really ought to, you've missed a lot! Goodness,' he went on, looking for some more cake, 'I'm being extraordinarily perverse this afternoon.'

Leonard believes that any normally attractive man can get any woman in the end if he is patient and soft with her. I looked at Leonard's skinny legs and decided it wasn't true.

After he had gone I sat thinking for a long time and my face was terribly flushed because I have never really discussed these things before. Funnily enough, he reminded me of Mother Mary Damian giving a sex talk at school.

Wednesday, 22nd

Very hot today. Leonard came at five and said he was very tired. It's strange how my studio seems to make men feel tired. He lay down on the divan and said, 'I should like to take all my clothes off, wouldn't you? It's so hot and peaceful here, it would be lovely to be naked.'

Peaceful, I thought, if my experiences with Jo were anything to go by, was the last thing it was likely to be, so I told him that although it might be nice, I wasn't going to do it.

Then he asked me to sit for him on Friday and I said I would, before I realised he meant in the nude, but I didn't take it back because I really must get used to these things. Then I made some tea and lay down beside him on the bed and he interlocked his knees with mine, so I was very glad I'd got my trousers on.

Friday, 24th

Sitting in the nude for the first time is rather like learning to dive. When you take your dress off it's the first plunge and after that you don't really mind. Leonard thought my figure was very good, but I had to keep remembering to hold my tummy in. I tried to seem very self-possessed, doing and saying all the things professional models do.

After lunch L felt less and less like work and lay around uttering moans of depression, thinking about his wife's infidelity, so I said firmly that he mustn't force himself and we went to the cinema instead.

When we got to the Classic we found it was a dreadful musical called *Sweethearts* with Jeanette MacDonald, but Leonard said, 'Let's go anyway, it's only sixpence and I must distract my mind.' So we went in, and it was even worse than we had thought. Leonard was so taken up with saying 'Oh my God isn't this awful,' that he quite forgot about his depression.

Walking back down the King's Road we ran into his wife, who looked terribly sour and said things like 'I'm in the way, aren't I', so I left them as quickly as I could, feeling awful and riddled with guilt.

Dropped into Jo's café to see if he could cheer me up and found Gerhardt sitting with him, eating rabbit stew. I was flooded with joy at seeing him again, and gave him my last cigarette.

The café was very dark and smelly. Jo lit the candles, although it wasn't night. G pulled me on to his knee.

'What a nice tense young stomach you've got,' he said, adding something rude in Italian which I wasn't supposed to understand.

'Oh don't bother,' Jo said, 'you can't shock Joan. She's tough as nails these days and really hard. Do you remember how dumb she used to be that day she first came round to the café, how shy and self-conscious she was? She's certainly learnt fast.'

'Well she fell into your hands didn't she, the unhappy girl! Why don't you take her, Jo, a fine strapping girl, and pretty too! A bit pale perhaps but that's just her intensity. Do you know who she's like? Svengali's girlfriend, what's her name – Trilby. You rape her Jo, and I'll have her afterwards.'

'No bloody fear, not with her mother living just round the corner! You're a raper of virgins Gerhardt, why don't you take her?'

'Oh I'm too old, I can't take up with a seventeen-year-old, besides, I'd teach her a lot of tricks she oughtn't to know for another five years. What she needs is a nice young boy.'

'Pah!' Jo said. 'He'd be clumsy and turn her into a lesbian for the rest of her days.' He suddenly remembered. 'And by the way, what the hell do you think you're doing going to the cinema with a married man?'

'Well, I was going to sit for him but he felt bloody so we went to the flicks.'

'Sit for him!' bellowed Gerhardt. 'Holy Virgin, here I am with no money, about to be deported – why don't you sit for me? What are your breasts like?'

I told him they weren't bad at all and I'd sit for him any time. In my present mood I'd sit in the nude for every bloody artist in Chelsea and Fulham. I don't care what I do now or what happens to me. I never felt this way before.

I told Jo that Leonard had been trying to teach me about sex, and Jo said, 'To hell with sex, I'd rather have a good shit or a good sneeze any day. I'm fed up with bloody women. All that romance stuff, "darling I love you" and "look how bright the moon is", it just makes my arsehole itch.'

'Jo, you're filthy,' G said, tightening his arms around me. He seemed sad. I could feel there was something on his mind. Jo chuckled. 'Gerhardt's girl chucked him today – tonight in fact. No girl's ever chucked him before. So what are you going to do now, maestro?'

'God knows – you don't know where I can find a nice Circassian, do you? I used to live with one called Nadjia in Rome, she called me Effendi and bowed to me, and sang to me in Arabic. Her eyes were long and lovely but her taste in jewellery was appalling. I used to beat her.'

I watched the two men, loving them both, seeing how Jo was coarse and to be pitied, and Gerhardt, finer and more sensitive, but also more dangerous because he was so beautiful.

G lifted me off his lap and walked out into the darkening garden, saying, 'L'ombre s'en fuit. Adieu mon rêve', thinking about his girl who'd bitched on him and the Germans who were coming to get him. I really love him, I would slave for him all my life and never ask for anything. This is not just words or silliness, it's true. How funny life is, always wanting someone you can't have but never wanting those who want you.

As I was going out of the café, a new girl came in, younger than me, looking rather nervous, and I heard Jo saying something to Gerhardt about her being 'so refreshing'. I felt funny, being more assured than her, and remembering how I was like that six months ago.

Thetis to dinner, got very happy on rum and listened to the Poulenc trio. I could hear my mother crying in the next room. She is having a *crise des nerfs* because she is afraid of air-raids.

Monday, 27th

The Germans are in Calais. I don't seem to be able to react or to feel anything. I don't know what's real any more. I don't think I'm real or that this life is real. Before this last winter everything seemed real, but since then I seem to have been dreaming. I wanted to mix with artists so I rented a studio, and because of the studio I'm pretending to be an artist, when I don't even know what painting means. Ever since then I've been listening to people talking a new language, filth and blasphemy, and heard myself talking it too. I see myself acting like a tart, and men hurting me and sponging on me and trying to make love, and asking if they can pee in my sink, and telling me to take my clothes off and I really don't know whether I'm awake or asleep.

The bombs, which I know must come, hardly enter my fringe of consciousness. Bombs and death are real, and I and all the other artists around here are only concerned with unreality. We live in a dream, and it may be desperate but it's not dull.

Tuesday, 28th

Belgium has surrendered. Had a drink with Squire at the local pub, and he read me a rather bad poem called 'The Renegade' about King Leopold.

Went to a lecture at St Martin's on primitive art, then to a musical party at Alfred's, where an Irish Jew sang Debussy.

Thursday, 30th

I haven't been near the studio for several days – we spend most of our time sitting by the radio waiting to hear the news about Dunkirk. No one talks of anything else and there are special prayers every day at the Servite. Squire's sons have taken their boat over to help with the rescue, so Jack is round here a lot, drunker than ever.

Saturday, 1st June

Mummy and I went to a matinée of Leslie Henson's *Up and Doing*. The theatre was full of returned men from the British Expeditionary Force who had fought their way back through the German lines, and been taken off the beaches. It seems like a miracle that so many of them got out. Leslie Henson and everybody sang 'They are jolly good fellows' after the show and we both cried.

Laura's mother has rung up to say her consumption is worse and would I write to her at the sanatorium.

Monday, 3rd

My feelings of unreality still persist. Sometimes I think I'm going mad. Today at the post I stared in the glass and talked to myself in whispers and then got scared because I heard the reflection speak. I kept saying 'I'm not real' over and over again. The reflection proved me wrong by hissing back at me. As soon as I turned away from the mirror I lost my sense of identity again so that I almost suspected that there would be no reflection. I got mad and wanted to hurt myself and dug a pin into the back of my hand, but when it bled I stopped, feeling a damn fool.

Tuesday, 4th

Two hundredth anniversary of the Marquis de Sade. Sallé and her boyfriend, who is a surrealist, staged a weird performance in Hyde Park, reading bits out of *Alice in Wonderland* and the telephone directory, but the police thought it was some sort of code and took it all down.

Wednesday, 5th

Leonard came round today on a sponging expedition and said, 'How fresh and clean and beautiful you look!', borrowed some Bach records, my *Le Sacre du Printemps*, and my portable radio, filled his pockets with my cigarettes and said, 'I'm afraid I haven't a penny so you'll have to wait for that half crown I owe you.' Then, after he had eaten all the fruit that I was going to paint for my still life, he staggered downstairs with his booty murmuring, 'What a generous creature you are!'

I'm really getting quite fond of Leonard.

After he left, had a strange visitation from a young man in a blue shirt. Even without my glasses on he looked familiar. He said, 'Gerhardt said it would be a good idea if I called on you – my name is Rupert Darrow and I live down the road at number 34.' Of course I knew him then, the face who had peered up at Leonard and me through the cactuses, the one who asked me if I played chess at Pru's party.

I said, 'Do come in, Janet and Gerald and I have got a model upstairs.' He blanched, and said he didn't fit in very well with that lot, but came up just the same and sat there all morning without speaking, playing chess with himself. I offered him lunch but he wouldn't stay.

'I loathe the Bohemian existence,' he said, picking disdainfully at a burnt sausage. 'Give me a butler and a good cellar any day.'

I wonder whether dear Gerhardt sent him round in the hope that I would fall for him, so as to get me off his back! He is certainly very ravishing but looks rather a cad. He has a brown skin, black hair and embarrassing eyes.

Thursday, 6th

The poly. Model was strong woman Josie, who tears up telephone directories. Growth of strong immoral passion for Henry Moore. Today he hammered his thumb doing something to my armature and said 'Bugger'. There was blood all over the clay. During the rest I sat on the wood pile outside Trafalgar Studios and ate apples, and watched the bronze beetles running in and out of holes in the bark.

Saw Gielgud's *Tempest* in the afternoon, sixpence in the gallery.

Monday, 10th

Nearly got raped today. Jo gave up at last, panting and exhausted and groaning for a cigarette. Had to restore him with tea. He is now convinced that I am undersexed or something, he says I am like someone fast asleep. God help me if I should ever wake up! After tea Jo painted yellow and alizarin crimson pears on a green table. Leonard arrived at five, pallid and glassy-eyed, saying, 'Italy has come into the war, my wife and I have $2/11\frac{3}{4}$ between us, and I can't get a job! It's suicide or the army.' I was very distressed and gave him some peppermints in a paper bag, which was all I had, and lent him Zola's *Germinal*, a tale of such incredible gloom and privation that no fate can but seem cheerful by comparison.

Jo then sneaked off, and Leonard, after a short dissertation on Freud's dream symbolism, expressed a wish to lie down. It is a curious thing how the one idea of every man who comes to see me is to assume a prostrate position as speedily as possible – also to get me to do the same thing!

Anyway I lay down beside him and we put our arms around each other and talked about our future after the war, and the artist's place in society.

He told me he saw Rupert Darrow ringing my bell on Saturday night – I must have been out. Pity, I should really like to know him better.

Friday, 14th

When I got home from the poly my mother told me that Paris had fallen, and she wants to evacuate me to Granny's place until they see if there are going to be air-raids. I couldn't bear it, I just *couldn't* leave London at the moment; there's far too much happening.

Alfred came round, and we all got tiddly on rum, and decided that if the Germans come we will die a martyr's death outside the Brompton Oratory!

Sunday, 16th

It rained all day. Alfred and I played Bach fugues together. I feel very strange, as if the world were about to end.

Monday, 17th

After an hilarious lunch at the café, with Jo doing imitations of Mussolini, I came home to find my mother as white as a sheet and telephoning wildly. She said, 'France has surrendered – you'd better leave London tonight! Granny isn't well, so you can't go there, but your Aunt Lalla says she'll have you. I'll take you down tomorrow.'

I fought tooth and nail but it wasn't any good – a lot of balls about being young and having your life before you – if London's going to be destroyed I'd rather stay with it as long as possible and go on working and being with my friends until we're all blown up. But my mother, who has no stamina, and is terrified of staying in London herself – *she* is staying on and sending *me* away, so that she won't have to worry about me! I think it's the bloodiest thing I ever heard of, being shuffled out of the way like this.

Tuesday, 18th

I leave tonight. Went round to number 34 to say goodbye to Leonard – also hoping I might meet Rupert – but no one was in, only Pru, the nice sculptress who doesn't wear a brassière. She peered at me, because she is very blind and doesn't want to wear glasses, and asked me up for a coffee.

Her studio is big, white and modernistic, with piles of dirty washing-up, and copies of *Verve*. There was also a big ginger cat called Henry, after Henry Miller – he once had an affair with Pru in the South of France.

Still peering at me she said, 'What a brown skin you've got. You don't look a bit English. More Italian I should say. Are you the girl who has the studio near here and has to sleep at home with her mother? Rupert Darrow's been talking about you.'

I didn't tell her my Italian complexion came out of a Max Factor bottle, but I was thrilled to hear about Rupert.

'How did he come to move in with you?' I asked.

'The poor devil came to me one night when he had an abscess, and begged me to look after him, and I've been feeding him ever since. He has this awful baby talk he lapses into when he's ill or frightened - his special language, he calls it – and I just couldn't resist him. Besides, he's so handsome, isn't he? Every morning I say 'never again!' But somehow – you know how it is!'

I told her I was being evacuated and she said 'Poor you!' Pru is not young, about thirty, but dresses and behaves like a debauched young girl. I like her very much.

Went round to Gerhardt's studio but he was out. A very smart girl in a grey costume was also peering through the window and cooing through the letter box. I glared at her and went away.

Goodbye to Jo, and told him to keep the studio on and paint as much as he liked. 'Don't let the place go dead in my absence and don't let people borrow my books,' I said. I was hectic and miserable and my head ached. Jo tried to cheer me up, saying I was a hysterical bitch. He seemed to think it would have been nice to rape me as a farewell gesture, but he says I'm sure to be had by a soldier as soon as I'm evacuated to the country. I made tea for the last time and gave Jo the key.

People were standing crowded in the streets, listening to Churchill broadcasting from a loudspeaker in the radio shop.

Everyone very excited. Invasion imminent. Churchill says it will be our finest hour – small consolation for me, shuffled off to the country!

Everything in chaos at home. Packed my suitcase. Terrible headache. Dashed out to try and find G but he still wasn't in, so left him a note.

Taxi to the station, train to Tunbridge Wells, car to Lightlands, Lalla's house in Kent.

Wednesday, 19th

LIGHTLANDS, TUNBRIDGE WELLS

Last night the country seemed extraordinarily beautiful, and *right* after London – I mean the way the trees and grass grew, their proportions and colour, the innocence of a sheep scratching its ear with its foot, the whiteness and solidity of the moon which I saw through the train window for the first time as a separate world sustained in space.

What didn't look right were my feet on Lalla's neat gravel path, the scuffed leather sandals and the red I had put on my toenails so as to look good when sitting for Leonard. I tried to visualise all my Chelsea friends in the garden of Lightlands, but they wouldn't materialise. It is a big, low-built house set in woods, not very old but very clean and neat, with beautiful furniture and bowls of hot-house flowers everywhere.

I couldn't sleep because my legs ached. They always do when I'm in a state over anything. I kept waking up and thinking I could hear Gerhardt's pipe, so I went in search of a book from the landing and read myself to sleep with *The Freak of St Frieda's*.

This morning was zero hour – the place, the country, seemed unbearably remote, cut off from the warm stream of life.

I found Mummy and Aunt Lalla on the terrace drinking Ovaltine and felt myself beginning to cry, so I ran blindly out of the garden in case she would notice, and looked for somewhere to hide. Cried terribly in the orchard.

Thursday, 20th

We had an air-raid warning last night but I slept through it.

Only bright spot here is two arty land girls living in Lalla's cottage in the orchard – one is ravishing, like a Greek boy, large eyes and short dark hair, she is called Vera Charles. They wear filthy trousers and sandals and the cottage is painted white and red.

Mummy went back to London today and is getting in touch with Granny to see if she'll be well enough to have me in a week or two.

Rowena came down for the day with another old convent friend, Angela, whom I hadn't seen since she was expelled and who told me the scandalous story about her and Father Anderson. Poor Angela – she'd never even been kissed, and then to be initiated by a bald Irish priest of fifty-two who took her for a drive into the beechwoods and turned off the engine. It really is a bit too steep. She said she used to have to play the organ in church while he was preaching on temptation below!

Rowena looking wonderful as usual, all in dark red corduroy like the inside of a dark tulip. She has finished with her 'uncle' and is having an affair with a boxer.

I live in a Gerhardt fantasy, dreaming about him every night and thinking about him all day – him and all the other people that interest me. Jo, Pru, Rupert and Leonard.

Friday, 21st

There isn't anything to do here except listen to the news or drive into Tunbridge Wells to change library books. The house is hung with pictures of the Boer War and smells of orange blossom, but I keep thinking I can smell stone-dust, acrid, pungent and bittersweet – the smell of G's studio. Today I fell to the floor and pounded the carpet, then got up feeling very foolish with dust all over my face. I hate solitude. I find myself thinking gloatingly of crowds and roads full of traffic, familiar faces, life going on. The country has lovely compensations, but wild strawberries and white horses and glow-worms can't compensate me for crowds of loving living people.

Saturday, 22nd

Wonderful news – I'm going home on Monday, thank God! Granny is still ill and can't have me, and Lalla's grandchildren are arriving next week.

Sunday, 23rd

Angela lives quite near, in Uckfield in fact, so I am going over to have lunch with her today. My father's house, Tickerage Mill, is just down the road from her, so we'll be able to nip over and look for him. He hasn't paid Mummy any alimony for ages, and she's been hearing strange rumours that he's in jail!

Got into Angela's beat-up old car, me in a man's cap, Angela in a bare-back sun-top with a Russian fur hat, and shot singing through scandalised Uckfield, making air-raid siren noises.

Afterwards we found Tickerage and slunk up the lane. There was the mill house and the pool with dragon-flies, and Daddy's studio at the end of the lawn. No one seemed to be around so we crept into the house, and tore upstairs before the petrified housekeeper could stop us, and came to the conclusion from the amount of unmade beds that quite a few people were in residence. The question was who? We were soon to find out, for down the path were now charging three people: two very elegant pansies and a middle-aged girl in a candy striped Schiaparelli play-frock, with a white celluloid bow in her dyed blonde hair.

The first pansy, huge and red-haired with open shirt and blue silk scarf flying, bore down on us. Angela cowered in my rear.

'What do you think you're doing here?' he demanded, pink in the face with rage and alarm.

'Looking for my father,' I replied in tones of bell-like innocence, 'Dick Wyndham.'

'You're not *Dick's daughter*?'

'Yes I am,' I replied, with a certain satisfaction. The amazement of the pansies was a joy to watch. Red Hair shot out his hand and seized mine and we were overwhelmed with apologies. Apparently they had thought we were parachutists.

Their names were Roger Babington-Smith and Aylwyn Saville, and the blonde was some sort of a countess. We were asked to tea and ate toast and honey while Aylwyn played the latest jazz on the radiogram – 'Begin the Beguine', 'The Lady is a Tramp', 'Tuxedo Junction', and so on. 'Rather a good number that, don't you think?' Roger kept saying. I liked them both very much, but was rather scared of the Countess who is an expensive society tart and not my kind at all. I think she is possibly a relative of Daddy's new mistress. Anyway, there she was, bunged full of Benzedrine and bitchery. It seems that they all take Benzedrine 'to clear their brains for writing', but there are obviously some casualties. 'But darling, do you remember that shattering night at the Boogie Woogie when Vladimir took six and faced madness for days?'

I asked if my father was in prison, as I had heard rumours to that effect, and they said, 'Certainly not. He's having a nervous breakdown in the London Clinic.' I also asked about dear Aunt Bunch and it seems she has run away to Harlem with a lesbian. After tea they settled down to talk snobbery for a bit – nobody mentioned the war at all.

After a bit Roger drove us back to Lightlands in his super, open-topped Rolls-Royce, before going on to fetch my father's new mistress from the station.

'You'd love her,' he said. 'She looks like a beautiful little boy!' I'm quite sure I'd hate her.

Back at Aunt Lalla's we all got ourselves up like tarts and went into the woods to look for soldiers, carrying a picnic of cakes and bottled lemonade.

We tried to get off with a lovely blond sentry by a lake, but the sergeant found us first and ordered the sentry off so that he could chat us up himself. Lovely picnic beside the lake – found glow-worms. Heard soldiers' voices singing, across the water from their camp – 'Get 'old o' this, get 'old o' that!'

Tore my skirt on the barbed wire getting home. Thank God, back to London tomorrow!

Monday, 24th

MILBORNE GROVE

Home to the familiar streets and smells.

At nine I was saying, I'm definitely going to break with Gerhardt. By

86

eleven I was looking at his skylight thinking, how soon can I see him? – do I dare? By one I was sitting on his bed sewing buttons on his pants.

The room was terribly bare and trunks were ready, packed in case of internment, but it still smelt the same. It seems the police had interviewed him at the station last week, and he didn't think it would be long before they hauled him off. He was lighting one cigarette after another and his hands were shaking.

'Hurry up with those trousers,' he barked. 'I'm going out with a new, rich girlfriend; the real thing, Turkish cigarettes, scent on her underclothes, a French maid! The bitch stood me up last week,' he went on furiously. 'I'd had my first bath for a week, ironed my trousers and even borrowed ten shillings! Then she sends her French maid round to say she can't see me! She'd better turn up this time!'

'Where's the gramophone?'

'Still pawned at Tuson's.'

'So what would you like me to do now?' I asked when I had finished the trousers.

'Everything,' Gerhardt said, sitting on the edge of his bed, and cleaning his toenails with a wood carving tool.

I made his bed, noting that the brandy bottle was empty, then did the washing-up, but the coffee grounds on the bottom of the cups were so hard that I couldn't get them off. I asked for a drying-up towel but he didn't possess one, so I dried frying-pans with a filthy old bath towel. All the time I was working he was kind and considerate and talked to me, so that I was quite in heaven.

When I finished, I turned round to him and said, 'Is there anything more I can do for you?'

'What would you like to do for me?' he chuckled evilly, fixing me with his hypnotic stare.

I didn't say anything, just put my arms round his neck and hugged him, and he kissed me, saying, 'This is the best kiss of all, to kiss standing up with your whole body touching.'

I thought he might want to go further, but he didn't, he seemed too sad and tired, so we sat on the balcony with our legs up and the sun on our faces. I felt completely at peace, like being drowned and under water. I said I'd come round tomorrow and lend him my gramophone.

Went round to collect my gramophone from the studio, which was filthy and littered in cigarette-butts. It wasn't too heavy so I wrapped it in newspaper and I found I could carry it down the Fulham Road quite easily. Even before I got past the garages I had a funny feeling. In a few moments, I thought, I shall know. I hardly dared to look. The curtains were drawn except in one place. I looked through and saw the bed was bare, the bookcases empty, and stripped of their ornaments.

I didn't feel or realise anything until the garage man came up, raising his hands expressively.

'No good. 'E's gone. They came at nine this morning. 'E had till eleven to get 'is things together. Some lady's got 'is dog till 'e can find it an 'ome. Poor devil – well at least he won't 'ave to look after 'imself any longer! Proper furious 'e was too!'

He said he had no idea where they're taking him, but if he heard any news he'd let me know.

When he had gone I went up to the landing among the rubbish bins and sat down on the stone floor. The bottom had fallen out of everything. I was faced with the unthinkable prospect of never seeing him again. There were some sketch books stuffed in with the rubbish and I concealed them inside the gramophone and took them back to the studio. Then I lay on the couch and cried till I was sick.

Leonard came round at five and gave me some sherry and I drank it like medicine. I felt as if all the clocks in the world had run down – how was I going to get through the rest of my life?

BOOK III

Tuesday, 9th July

That was a fortnight ago. Since then I have gradually become happier in a negative sort of way.

Squire is very caustic about the whole thing. 'Poor lad. Such an inoffensive creature,' he murmurs. 'Still, I'm sure if the governor of the camp has a wife she'll see things are made easy for him. Probably give him her drawing-room as a studio, don't you think?'

So life goes on.

Saw Bette Davis in *Dark Rapture*, saw a rainbow, drew a Negro, bought a rabbit and carried it home in a paper bag – it died within a week. Madame Arcana says someone called Darrow called round at my studio several times while I was away.

Went over to Jo's café. He was sitting at the kitchen table shelling peas. When he saw me he started to sing at the top of his voice:

'Rose of Castile, I adore you!
Take down your pants, I'll explore you!'

I took no notice, and started to help him with the peas. He wanted to put the wormy ones in but I wouldn't let him. He was cooking meatballs in a brown garlicky sauce.

'They're called Tchebabchiky,' he said. Funny how most of the exotic dishes on Jo's menu, Kloski, Kotletky or whatever, always turn out to be meatballs. Don't really fancy Jo touching me any more. He kept putting his arms round me and saying, 'You're excited aren't you, I can tell by the way your nipples stand up. I'm not thirty-three for nothing.' Told him I had to work with Belgian refugees, and made my escape.

Leonard rang up at six, to say he'd been round to the studio and the rain was pouring in through the skylight. He had put a waste paper basket under the drips, and he had borrowed my *Apes of God* and did I mind?

Went over to assess the damage and spent the evening on my own, playing the gramophone.

I've discovered a curious thing. Since Gerhardt went away I'm not frightened of being alone any more. On the contrary, it's good to be alone. I think about him and feel self-sufficient.

Sunday, 14th

Jo joined up yesterday as a rear gunner. The average life of an RG is supposed to be five flights.

'So what?' Jo says. 'Feed, fight, fornicate and die dramatically!' I told him he'd better be careful his wounds were dramatic ones, as he'd be sitting in the back of the plane. I still won't let Jo kiss me. 'Jesus,' he says, 'and this is the generation I'm going out to die for?' Meantime he intends to paint his last masterpiece, and is using up most of my paints in the process. The atmosphere when Leonard is around as well, giving me painting lessons, is quite electric. They absolutely loathe each other. Leonard is looking particularly unattractive at the moment because he is growing a beard – a gingery one. For some reason this makes his nose and ears look even pinker than before. He watches with horror as Jo squeezes out my alizarin crimson and smears it on like butter with a palette knife.

'This is my new method – very modern, very Matutinovitch! Romantic because I am a romantic, cynical because I am a cynic, but not intellectual because all that stuff makes me puke.'

'Absolutely fascinating, Jo,' I said, 'but for Christ's sake lay off my alizarin, it costs a fortune.'

I could see Leonard's lips tighten and his embryonic beard bristle with disapproval. Then Jo, who despises Leonard as a pansy and a conchie, began taunting him for doing nothing for the war and just sitting around on his arse. Leonard replied that he thought he was doing just as much to save civilisation by sitting on his bottom thinking the right thoughts, as by rushing round with a gun thinking the wrong ones.

I am still paying him 5/- a week for painting lessons – he swears he will get a good picture out of me yet.

Saturday, 20th

For several days I had been thinking up plans for getting in touch with Rupert Darrow. There is something terribly fascinating about him that makes Jo seem like a boor, and Leonard just a non-man. And what's more he was Gerhardt's friend, and has the same alert cynical eyes.

Today I went out just on chance and he passed the door as I opened it. He seemed pleased to see me and said, 'I called on you several times but you were always out. Where do you go all day?'

'Oh,' I said, non-committally, 'I just track around.'

'What do you mean track?' Darrow chuckled, but I could tell that he knew very well what I meant. 'Come up and see me sometime,' he said, 'I'm always making tea and I'm always gloomy.'

Tuesday, 23rd

Spent the morning in an awful state of indecision – should I go round to Rupert for tea? I hate it when it's left to me to make the first move, in case the person didn't really mean it.

In the end I compromised and called on Leonard, who was cooking one of his awful vegetarian meals – fried millet and chick peas. No sign of Rupert, though I could hear movement and voices upstairs. We quarrelled because L wants me to go full-time to Chelsea and take my exams and not waste my time on war work. The miserable little cheese-worm!

At four o'clock he got all dressed up to apply for some new teaching job: yellow boots, grey, pin-striped trousers, pink tie and green jacket. He even carried a cane. I roared with laughter and he stormed out in a huff, so I went downstairs hoping to find Rupert.

Prudey was standing on the landing looking flushed and rather pleased with herself. 'I've thrown Rupert out,' she said. 'My new boyfriend, the Baron, is moving in tonight.'

'Out of the house?'

'Oh no, just my room. He's got a perfectly good place of his own up-stairs. He just shacked up with me because it was cosy and I cooked for him, and also he hates being alone. If you want him I think he's gone over to Jo's place, it's the last day of the café.'

Filled with excitement I put on some make-up in the landing lavatory, took my glasses off and went round to Jo's. Peering around myopically, I spotted R sitting alone, looking gloomy.

'Talk of the devil,' Jo said, 'here she is.'

I saw R's face brighten as he spotted me. 'You've taken them off,' he said. '*Much* better! – you really were a gruesome sight before, you know.'

I sat down opposite him. 'So, Prudey's kicked you out has she?'

'Mmm, I've been all morning carting my things out of her room, I think I've strained my stomach doing it. I feel very peculiar.'

'Who's her new boyfriend?'

'Oh, some degenerate from the Studio Club called Cosmo, says he a Baron.'

'Well,' said Jo, 'you know what you can do now. Have Joan for your girlfriend. Get *her* to keep you.'

'I haven't any money,' I said.

Jo shook his head sadly. 'Bloody useless – bloody virgin too.' Rupert seemed a little shocked, but I was too used to this kind of thing to care. 'Of course if you broke her in I could have her afterwards,' Jo went on, in his usual charming way.

I was beginning to get tired of this game, it had been gone through so often. Rupert was just watching me with a tired, rather sympathetic smile on his face.

'Well,' Jo announced, 'this is the last day of the café – I'm definitely closing it tonight, in case my call-up comes.'

I felt sad - it's the end of an era - but already my feelers sensed a new beginning. All the old regulars began to trickle in, and Jo distributed his goods and chattels. I got a green enamel coffee pot with a dead bug inside, very useful but a bit unhygienic and redolent of 'Chez Jo'. Rupert still stayed on.

Jo, not wanting to waste anything, had made a huge farewell stew with weeks of accumulated left-overs in it. It was free, but even the poorest regulars couldn't face it, they kept finding souvenirs of last week's meals in it, old sausages, bits of spaghetti, rabbit bones etc., nostalgic perhaps but not very appetising. A few people produced bottles of wine. Everybody sat around talking about art, and Jo announced he'd got yet another new method of painting.

'The fourth dimension – the relationship between time and the thing painted!'

'What's that mean Jo?'

'Well, supposing I'm painting a flower-piece in the fourth dimension – it would take you a fucking long time before you realised it was a flower-piece – see what I mean?'

Rupert got up. 'I'm bored with this place. Why don't you all come over for coffee?'

Coffee in Rupert's studio. He played us some Spanish flamenco stuff on his guitar, beating with his hand on the wood between phrases – it's called 'zapateado'. After all the others had left I stayed on. The studio is high and whitewashed. Nothing much in it, just large cactuses, and guitars, a chess board and some big abstract paintings by Gerhardt. Downstairs we could hear Prudey singing lustily on account of her new boy.

When she came up R said, 'Oh hello Prudey, this is Joan. She's going to be my new girlfriend – don't you think it's a good idea?'

'What will Squirrel say?'

'Oh Squirrel lives in Knightsbridge, she won't know.' I was dumb enough to think this was all a joke.

Then Rupert, who had been eyeing me in a speculative way, got to his feet and said, 'I'm bored. Shall we have dinner at Jimmy's?'

Jimmy's café down Hollywood Road is even smaller and smellier than Jo's and Jimmy is an even worse cook. Rupert says each meal is like a fight to the death between J and his ingredients. 'Let's hope the ingredients have the upper hand tonight,' I said, as we ordered liver and bacon. Francine, Jimmy's wife, came over and lit the candles, she was wearing a Spanish shawl with a rose behind her ear, and white paste on her eyelids. After quite a long wait, Jimmy emerged with our dinner: two small pieces of ox liver, scummy underneath and baked hard on top with a slight greenish tinge around the edges. They tasted faintly of bile, and were flanked by drowned cubes of swede and turnip.

Rupert looked at his plate bleakly and said, 'Looks like Jimmy won.'

I don't know how I feel about Rupert – he's very handsome, but I suppose I really think of him as my last link with Gerhardt, because they were such friends. I kept asking him to tell me more Gerhardt stories thinking it would bring Gerhardt back to me, but everything he said made me think I'd never really known him.

When I said how jealous I'd been of all Gerhardt's women, Rupert just roared with laughter, and said that the main trouble with Gerhardt was that he was convinced he was a sex maniac, whereas in fact he wasn't sexy at all, just afraid he might be missing something.

' "Women!" he used to say, "I've had thousands of them, they've ruined my life and my work – if it hadn't been for women I'd have been a genius, see?" The truth was, when he got them he didn't really know what to do with them – most of them had to seduce him.'

'Why do you think he wanted me then?'

'He wanted you as a friend. He wasn't really interested in seduction. He was just a terribly, terribly, lonely man. He had no real friends, you see, they didn't get on with him or he didn't like them, but he certainly wasn't sexy. You know, the tragedy of Gerhardt was that sometimes in the middle of the night he'd wake up, and realise he was no good. All day he'd be telling himself what a fine sculptor he was and what a Casanova with women, and suddenly in the middle of the night, a small thought would come to him – maybe I'm no good after all – and he'd break out into a cold sweat.'

'But he had some beautiful girlfriends,' I protested. 'I met some of them.'

'Well maybe a few, Bianca was all right – but what about Sheila Hurst? She looked like an embryo! And Honorine – a sort of squashed viper!'

'Did he ever have Prudey?' I asked, jealously.

'He certainly tried – you know, Beethoven's Fifth Symphony, the one he always seduces his girls with? Well he started stroking Pru's foot in the middle of the third movement and she, being a strong lady, picked him up and threw him bodily across the room. If he ever did get a very sexy girl, like Honorine for instance, he just couldn't cope with it. After a week he'd come to me exhausted and say, "Can't keep up with her any longer" – so I told him to go to Hepples in Charing Cross Road and ask for some Blue Moon. That kept him going for another few weeks but at the end of it she left him for Dylan Thomas.'

'Well,' I said, 'at least he was a brilliant sculptor!'

Rupert smiled pityingly. 'What do you mean a good sculptor, he was the most imitative sculptor I've ever met in my life! I shall never forget going to a Henry Moore exhibition with him. Gerhardt slinks around – 'Lotta junk,' he says. After that I know exactly what's going to happen, and sure enough, three weeks later he's got a bit of stone and is furiously knocking a hole through the middle of it.'

'But he did have exhibitions, didn't he?' I asked.

'Oh yes, Gerhardt's exhibitions! One night I called round to the studio and found Bilbo and three other penniless sculptors from Redcliffe Road all sweating like demons, knocking up pieces of stone, and Gerhardt striding up and down in his orange shirt yelling, 'Hit harder, you bums, hit harder! I've got an exhibition in thirty days!'

I was beginning to feel a bit disorientated with all this new information. 'But you were good friends weren't you? I mean you lived with him for quite a long time, didn't you?'

'Oh sure,' Rupert chuckled. 'We lived in Wentworth Studios, where Gerhardt was kept by an old Irishwoman whose bosoms were so long she had to support them in wicker baskets. In fact we'd be there now if I hadn't played this wicked jape on him! You see, he was always saying how he was a titanic kind of man and these little bits of stone were cramping his style, so I ordered a block of porphyry from the quarry, six foot by six, and harder than granite. It was carted off to Gerhardt's studio where it took up the entire room. A bronze plate was put up – 'Presented to the sculptor Gerhardt by Rupert Darrow' – and parties were given for it with people drinking their wine on top of it because there was nowhere else to sit. A couple of months later he took out his chisel and cut a small groove two inches deep down one side. After that he never touched it again, and we had to move from Wentworth Studios to escape from it.'

R pushed aside his uneaten liver and poured himself some more red wine. 'Oh yes, Gerhardt was a nice chap, a very nice chap indeed. I was *very* fond of him.'

'So was I,' I said, but nevertheless I was beginning to see Gerhardt in a slightly less romantic light.

When we got back to number 34, Prudey was there and called us into her room. She was naked except for a wisp of orange chiffon which she was fastening on one shoulder like a Greek tunic. Neither she nor Rupert seemed embarrassed by this. I thought her breasts were lovely and I liked her straight classical toes.

I sat and watched them a little bewildered, thinking what funny people they were; the way they yelled at each other and made extraordinary okes and sang, and Prudey leaping about in the nude.

Her story is peculiar. She married a Greek don who seduced her in every field in Cambridge. He used to make noises like a wolf and get very annoyed if she wouldn't bleat. When she was unfaithful to him he was so amazed he had her put into a lunatic asylum, but she ran away to Greece and got herself three lovers.

Now she is divorced, with crowds of men wanting to sleep with her but she won't have any man that isn't six foot tall with pointed ears, which is why she liked Rupert. She is about thirty, and looks like an attractively ugly boy with straight shiny hair, a wrestler's shoulders and narrow hips.

While we were drinking coffee, Rupert's mother rang up. She told Rupert she hadn't any money and her husband wouldn't give her any, and she and Rupert's brother Christopher were living in tents in the drawing-room, sitting on rubber mattresses and reading Leslie Charteris. R says she is a bit potty.

As I was going, he said, 'What about my eating with you, now that Prudey's chucked me out? I'll pay my share.'

I said OK.

Wednesday, 24th

Rupert to lunch at my place. Liver sausage, salad and tea. It was terribly hot so we went to the Serpentine to swim.

Blue water, green grass, brown shoulders. I think this is heaven. I turned over to tan my front and saw Rupert, who had just come out of the changing hut, looking like a Greek god, bronzed all over in the scantiest of trunks; and not a hair on his chest! I would have fallen over backwards, if I hadn't been on my back already. He was certainly the best-looking man there, his dark beard and hair giving him the air of a young Hebrew king. He has an aquiline nose that curves slightly down at the tip, but I don't think he is Jewish. I like the way his neck sockets into his chest, and the curving line of his collarbone. Oh boy, oh boy!

We swam together in the filthy water, then lay in the sun talking about

Elizabethan drama, with our shoulders touching, smoking his pipe because we hadn't any cigarettes.

'Gerhardt used to bathe here,' Rupert said. ' "I've won medals!" he'd yell, holding his nose, screwing himself up into a ball and jumping in with a mighty splash, coming out with his hair sleeked back and a slight bump on the top of his head like a dachshund.'

Rupert is making it increasingly difficult for me to feel romantic about Gerhardt.

'By the way,' asked Rupert, as we sat in the cafeteria and ate a Lyon's fresh cream sandwich for tea, 'why are you a virgin?'

'I don't really know,' I said. 'It's never occurred to me to be anything else.'

He picked up my hand and studied my palm. 'I think it's because you sit aloof in an ivory tower, like me. We watch the saturnalia milling and beetling around below and wish we could join in – sometimes we venture down, but only for a moment. It does make life very boring, this aloof attitude. I expect if you had been more of the milling and beetling kind Gerhardt would have seduced you, in spite of everything. You're like me, you look as if you're always expecting something to happen, but it doesn't unless you make it. I'm the same, I bore myself to tears, but I'm far too lazy to try and make contact with life.'

When I got up to go home at six he said, 'How would you like it if I robbed you of your virginity?'

I thought for a minute.

'I don't *think* I should mind very much, but then I hardly know you well enough to say.'

Monday, 29th

Fried sausages and tomatoes. Rupert wore a white shirt and smelt clean and fresh like a spring morning. He lay on the divan and said, 'Come and lie down while we think what to do this afternoon.' A cinema organ was playing tremolo on the wireless. He put his arms around me and said, 'Shall I make love to you? Or would you knock me out?'

'I shan't knock you out.'

At the beginning his kisses were very gentle, then he suddenly became ferocious, bruising and crushing me, crying out like an animal in pain. He bit my lips and tore at my flesh, and I tried to respond to his passion but it was agony and ecstasy together. I snapped my teeth at him and we laughed aloud between kisses. It was so wonderful I really felt ashamed to think that Leonard and Jo had ever kissed me. For two hours we created our own world and lived in it, then the bell rang and Jo arrived for tea, with a hunchback called Bunny.

'Broken the ice yet, Darrow?' he demanded, giving us searching glances and throwing himself regally on the divan. 'Let me know when you've cleared the road and I'll be right over.'

Gosh, I thought, how *old* Jo is! And he's really quite ugly – if he touched me I should be sick.

Went to *The Marriage of Figaro* at Sadler's Wells with Mummy.

Saturday, 3rd August

Rupert and I sat on his roof in the sun. It was perfect – he was wearing a blue and white striped shirt and sackcloth trousers and playing Spanish music on his guitar, with one bare foot resting on a brick. The little gardens were laid out beneath us and flowers were growing in pots all around. I had brought him an apricot tart from Deschuyter's.

Through the open window above we could hear Leonard whistling nervously, and every now and then I could see his disapproving face peering down at me. The only drawback was the powerful odour from Henry Miller's earthbox, whenever the wind changed. The guitar strings hummed in the hot air, allegros, tientos, seguidillas.

When it got too hot for the roof we went inside and lay on his bed in the cool studio. He lay apart from me but held my hand.

'When are you going to go to bed with me properly?'

'I can't say.'

'Why not – are you tongue-tied?'

I didn't answer.

'Would you rather I raped you in the proper he-man fashion, or will you tell me when you're ready?'

'I'll let you know.'

'That's right, Joanie, you let me know.'

He said this so kindly and gently, I felt completely reassured. After a long silence he said, 'When I reached the age of twenty I thought the world had come to an end. When I realised in church one day that I'd never see my teens again, my ears buzzed and I fell down in a faint. Do you feel like that about your virginity? Are you fond of it?'

Inside me I could feel every moral code I had ever believed in since childhood begin to crumble away. 'Yes and no,' I said, 'I don't think I shall regret it, although being a virgin in Chelsea gives you a certain *cachet*.'

'More a stigma I should have thought! I didn't realise quite how much until that day you walked into the café and Jo called you a 'bloody virgin'. I must say I thought you carried it off very well.'

'But why does everyone go on about it so?'

'Well,' R said, 'you're in a peculiar position, you have a home but you really live here in this studio, and you have a mother but she's only a sort of myth. This is your home and you live in these surroundings, in this atmosphere, and yet you're a virgin, and the thing is there *aren't* any virgins in Redcliffe Road, so you automatically become an *objet d'art* – and people are inclined to look at *objets d'art* and criticise them.'

We lit the fire and sat on the floor in the circle of light and warmth, leaning against each other with my coat over our knees. 'Tell me the truth,' said R, 'do you want to be seduced or not? I can't help feeling it's rather nice for you to be a virgin.'

'I hate it,' I said, 'I hate my virginity! It's so unnecessary.'

'Oh well,' says my brave Casanova, knocking out his pipe, 'I suppose I shall have to make the effort one of these days. I should have done it ages ago, I think it's the London air – in the country I'm always full of beans.'

'How many virgins have you actually seduced in your time?' I asked curiously.

'None,' Rupert replied rather gloomily.

'What?' I said laughing. He squeezed my hand.

'None, you're the first. I haven't the faintest idea how to do it, but it'll be rather exciting finding out. You see,' he went on, 'I was seduced by a woman of twenty-seven when I was fourteen and since then I've only known experienced women. Now I suppose I shall have to get one of those French letters – dreadful things! It's years since I wore one. You know this business is going to half kill me!'

I looked at his rueful face, feeling very alone and very much older than him, and loving him very much. Then I shivered in sudden terror. I wish I wasn't growing up so fast. Every time I come under the influence of a new man I grow a bit older.

I went home seeing 'SEDUCTION', written in letters of fire on every wall, my head humming with thoughts of lost virginity. I felt my mother must be able to read my thoughts, and I felt afraid to pray.

Sunday, 4th

Rupert came to dinner at the studio. He was late and I nearly went out of my mind. After eating, he sat by the gas fire in the fading light and played the Grenadinos.

When the light was completely gone we blacked out and lit a candle, then lay down together. Rupert removed my ear-rings, my brooch, and the Kirbigrips out of my hair. 'Can't have all this anti-Darrow apparatus,' he said, laughing.

It was wonderful. I felt even happier than the last time and couldn't bear the thought of leaving him to go home. I'd like to live here forever, isolated, in this paradise of intimate joys which I'd never known existed. I suppose I had guessed at it, longed for it, and then been taken in by substitutes. Surely something as nice as this can't be sin?

My grandmother would *certainly* have approved of what I'm doing on this divan, the same one that she used to lie on when she was a *grande amoureuse*, with Lord French in the last war. No wonder my poor mother is so sour and irritable, living with Sid and never having a man for sixteen years! On one of the rare occasions when she talked to me about sex she said, 'I believe a woman is supposed to have "her moment", the same as a man does – some of my friends say they actually experienced it but I never did!' Poor Mummy, I feel so sorry for her. I can't wait to go to bed with Rupert properly and find out what it's all about.

When it was time for me to go he pulled me back on to his lap and said, 'First I'm going to tell you a bedtime story. It's a special Redcliffe Road story which goes, Once upon a time there were three princes, and each one was uglier and more cowardly than the last, and they were all pansies because this is a special Redcliffe Road fairy story, and when the dragon finally rushed out to attack them they just locked themselves up in their anti-dragon shelters, and played chess.'

Monday, 5th

Called on Leonard and told him he needn't come and teach me any more, and would he please return my wireless and my *Apes of God*. He looked a bit sour and was quite rude, but Agnes seemed delighted.

Coming down the stairs, I heard the guitar being strummed in Rupert's room, and found him practising rolls and trills with his foot resting on two volumes of Byron.

He seemed pleased to see me, so I fried him some sausages for lunch, then he put his head in my lap and asked me to sing to him while we went to sleep. I sang 'Youth's the season made for joy' and he said, 'Wake me up if the rent collector comes. This is fun, isn't it, like starving in a garret!' Then he fell asleep.

While he was asleep Pru came back from the hospital where she's been having a miscarriage. She is awfully thrilled with her new boyfriend, Cosmo the Baron, because he stands her on her head and does it upside down. 'Not like you damned unimaginative Englishmen,' she snorted at Rupert who had just opened one eye. 'By the way, have you seen our air-raid shelter?' she went on. 'They've finally finished it. It's got a red light outside.'

'Open for business, eh? Well, I think this calls for a celebration.' Rupert jumped up and we went out and bought custard tarts for tea, and danced round the shelter singing R's new bad-taste, anti-war song, which goes:

> Lots of our brave soldier boys
> Are fighting like the deuce,
> But all we care in Redcliffe Road
> Is whom we shall seduce!

> Lots of lovely sailor boys
> Are drowning in the sea,
> But all we care in Redcliffe Road
> Is what we'll have for tea!

Lots of British fighter planes
Are crashing down in flames,
But all we like in Redcliffe Road
Is having fun and games.

We danced round the shelter three times, waving our custard tarts, and then went home to put the kettle on. After tea Prudey said she must go upstairs to get ready for the Baron. Rupert pranced round her, cackling with glee and making up a new verse:

'Prudey is a funny girl, as funny as can be –
She goes to bed upon her head
And not like you and me!'

Prudey was not amused.

Friday, 9th

Got some scrag-end half price, and took it home to make a stew for Rupert's lunch. Several cats came through the skylight to visit me.

About noon I heard Rupert pounding up; he always takes my stairs at a run because otherwise he can't face the smell. It is mainly the cats and the caretakers but Madame Arcana and her stuffed animals don't help either.

After lunch I noticed R looking at me strangely.

'What are you thinking about?' I asked, nervously.

'You know I can't make you out at all,' he said. 'Sometimes I think you're just longing for me to tear off your clothes and hurl you to the floor in the traditional manner, other times I don't think you want to be seduced at all. The trouble is you're not like a proper virgin, all coy and embarrassed and ignorant. You may *look* innocent enough but every now and then you talk like an old French whore! So what is one to think?'

I knew he was right and felt rather ashamed of it. I think it's something I've caught off Jo.

'Not,' he went on gloomily, 'that tearing off your clothes would be too easy a task – never in my life have I seen anyone who wears so many unnecessary and unattractive undergarments. It's like some God-damned

obstacle race! Why don't you wear glamorous underwear like Squirrel?'
It is the second time that dreaded name has been mentioned.

'Is Squirrel glamorous?' I asked, trying to sound casual.

'You bet she is, except when she wears yellow. You see, she's got this
sallow skin because of her Polynesian blood, and yellow makes her look
like a colossal bilious attack.'

I couldn't help hoping that Squirrel often wore yellow.

We polished off the scrag-end which was bony but nice. After lunch
Rupert started talking about religion, insulting the Pope and saying that
priests extorted money for confession, and that everyone knew Jesus was a
homosexual in love with John, so I pulled his hair and beat him up. 'I
never knew a girl set so much store by Jesus,' R said. 'It's quite amazing.'
Madame Arcana came upstairs and said I should be careful as she thought
the ceiling was coming down again.

Rupert seems fascinated by the thought of Confession. 'What do you
tell them?' he asks avidly. 'Do you confess to having kissed a beautiful
young man with dark curly hair? Am I your Great Sin?'

When I said yes, he said the whole thing was making him more and
more nervous and he wasn't at all sure he was going to be able to go
through with it. Nevertheless, he's actually asked me *out* to dinner on
Monday! We're going to Soho – I just can't wait! I only hope and pray
Mummy doesn't make a fuss and stop me going. Tonight she's taking me
to see Arthur Askey in *Charlie's Aunt*.

Tuesday, 13th

Yesterday was my first night out in Soho, my first real dinner date, my
first visit to the Café Royal and the second time I ever got drunk – quite a
night to remember!

Rupert and I set out about seven and sat on top of the number 14 bus to
Piccadilly. I was wearing my blue cotton dress with orange sash, and was
determined to get good and tight.

'The vast metropolis unrolls before us!' Rupert cried.

So there we were at Bertorelli's, a lovely old-fashioned Italian place
with oak panelling. We'd got a corner table and it was minestrone first,
and then veal with spaghetti.

Rupert doesn't know one wine from another but I was very impressed by the *au fait* manner with which he ordered the Médoc. He even poured a little out and sniffed it when the fat woman in black brought it over.

'I don't know what it is,' he said to me afterwards, 'but it's the cheapest.'

'You sounded as if you knew all about it!'

'Oh I can always carry it off when cornered.'

We finished the bottle and I felt fine, but when I got up to go to the ladies I was mildly surprised to see the door of the cloakroom retreating from my outstretched hand at a fast rate. 'This won't do,' I muttered, and, clamping my cigarette between my teeth I attacked it with both hands, captured it and managed to get it open. 'Gee,' I remarked to the lavatory seat, 'I'm really good and plastered!'

My return journey was more successful, I threaded the tables with swan-like undulations, and only clutched at the woodwork once.

'Nice work,' Rupert said, as I sank gratefully into my chair. We counted up our joint resources and decided we could just manage the Café Royal. Rupert was pretty tight too, and on the way there we had one or two unfortunate encounters with sandbags.

'You can take it from me Rooples,' I crooned happily, 'my head will be resting on your shoulder before this evening's out.'

'I don't doubt it,' said R suavely. 'Look out here comes a kerb.'

We reached the Café Royal and went in through a back entrance with heavy velvet curtains. It was like making a stage entry. You pushed open the curtains in the darkness and there you were in the dazzling light and the red plush. It was a lovely place, crystal chandeliers and Napoleon's arms, and plush and gilt and yellow glaring lights, and lots of very dull people who had come to see everyone else, only there wasn't anyone much to see. Everyone thought Rupert was a celebrity because he had a beard. We sat in the middle at a marble table and ordered lager, thinking of Oscar Wilde and Shaw and all the great geniuses who had sat there before us.

'Everyone's looking at us,' I said happily. 'Do you think they think we're artists and drug fiends?'

'Of course they do! Have you noticed those two queens, a pawn's move from us? They've been watching me all the time – I expect they're thinking, that's a nice little number – pity he's got that dreadful girl! I wonder if he's camp my dear!'

'Oh,' I said, 'that's Alfred's word, I didn't know anybody else used it.'

'And who might Alfred be?'

'He's a friend of Sid's – that's my mother's companion – and he dresses up in women's clothes and does opera imitations.'

'Good grief,' Rupert said looking at me rather oddly, 'you must tell me more about your fascinating home life some time.'

I looked at my lager and it seemed very long indeed. When I had drunk half of it it didn't seem nearly so long but I was feeling most peculiar. Our table was covered in butt-ends and bottles, just like a real French café. 'Isn't this a nice place,' I said. 'I'd like to stay here all night. Aren't you happy, Rupert?'

'Yes, moderately.'

'Aren't you tight?'

'No. Unfortunately not.'

'Well I am and I'm *terribly* happy! Isn't this a lovely place?'

'Oh, do shut up.'

I looked up anxiously to see if he was cross, but he was smiling quite benignly. He looked like a nice, kind, whiskery seal with big eyes. The lights of the Café Royal were spinning round and round like a Catherine wheel, the people in the balcony revolving slowly round my head. looked at my empty glass and smiled foolishly. 'Who would have thought it,' I said. 'Half a bottle of Médoc and two lagers and I'm tight as a tick!'

'Are you going to be sick?' Rupert asked me rather apprehensively.

'Oh no – nothing like that.'

'Well you will be,' he said gloomily, getting to his feet. 'Here, hold on to my hand. We might just make it home!'

I gripped his hand tight and we managed to reach the door without causing a disturbance, but once outside I collapsed completely. Heaven only knows how we got across Piccadilly to the bus stop. Anyway, there I was, roaring tight, singing Handel's 'Largo' on the pavement outside Simpson's to the great delight of the bus queue. Luckily a number 14 arrived and R hauled me up on top because there were fewer people. He says I was a great trial – that I sang and recited the Lord's Prayer and tried to knock out the conductor, but I think he's exaggerating.

When I got home I tried to creep upstairs without my shoes on but Mummy was sitting up waiting for me, and called me into her room. I tried hard to stand upright, one hand gripping the wardrobe. She was sitting up in bed with cold cream on her face and her hair up in pipe cleaners, looking very stern. I kept my face as much out of the lamplight as possible while I answered her questions, but I don't think I fooled her. This morning at breakfast she was off again, asking how much I'd drunk and who'd given it to me and so on. When she heard it was Rupert, her eyes grew sharp with suspicion and she wanted to know whether he'd made any 'improper suggestions' to me while I was under the influence.

'Now you be careful,' she warned me. 'He'll probably tell you he'll use a French letter, and nothing will happen, but don't you believe him! French letters are very untrustworthy!' I told Rupert about this at lunch and he roared with laughter. 'If your mother knew more about the men in Redcliffe Road she wouldn't be nearly so frightened, in fact we could write a good book about a virgin who leaves school thinking she's going to be pursued by hundreds of virile men all desiring her body, and how when it comes to the point they all think up some excuse and back out.'

'So what's your excuse?'

'You know perfectly well what mine is. Why, oh why can't I seduce you without some filthy apparatus!' He looked at me slyly. 'I suppose I can't?'

'No, you can't,' I said firmly.

'I can't bear the thought of one of those French thingummies.'

'What do they look like? I've never seen one.'

'Oh, like a sort of rubber glove – ghastly things.'

'Perhaps there's something else. We could ask Prudey. I'm sure she'd know.'

'Prudey's never used contraceptives! She thought she was sterile till that last miscarriage.'

'How about Squirrel?'

'She'll think it funny my asking her.'

'Well spy on her then!'

Sunday, 18th

Sunbathed on Rupert's roof in brassière and trousers, reclining like an odalisque on a rose-pink pillow, with Henry Miller purring on my stomach. I could hear Leonard and Agnes quarrelling through the window overhead. We read aloud from back numbers of *The Booster*, *épatant* monthly, run by Gerhardt and his Paris friends, which has poems like 'Out of the gorse came a homosexual horse'.

Air-raid siren while we were cooking lunch, and lots of planes came over. I went on frying baked beans and Rupert went on reading *Madame Bovray*. No one took much notice except for Leonard and Agnes who rushed into the shelter carrying chairs. Next day we read in the papers that it had been the biggest day-time air battle since the war started, with 185 German planes destroyed over England.

Saturday, 24th

Sirens at two in the morning. We rushed to the first-aid post to man the switchboard. I hadn't worked there for ages. A very tiring day, lots of yellow warnings and telephoning, bombs on Cripplegate, some churches hit – the first time we'd been bombed by day. We heard that Mrs Harley's husband had been killed at Dunkirk, Mrs Vaughan had lost two sons, and Daisy is pregnant. Miss Wigram has been sacked and the new commandant, Miss Patterson, is beautiful as an angel. Every time I go into her office my knees turn to water.

In the afternoon taught refugees to make rag dolls and stuffed animals. Back at the studio at six to cook spaghetti and onions for Rupert, who used to hold the record for spaghetti-eating at Poggioni's.

Monday, 26th

Tonight we went into our garden shelter for the first time. There were loud explosions extremely near, Heinkels thudded overhead for hours, and the whole shelter shook and vibrated – I realised for the first time that the war had really started but, because it never occurred to me for one moment that a bomb might land on me, I didn't feel at all frightened. On the other hand, they might have landed on Rupert. So next morning I rushed straight round to Redcliffe Road to see if everybody was all right, with a fruit tart in a paper bag for my lunch. As I turned the corner I saw someone tall in a dark blue shirt coming towards me, and when I realised it was Rupert my heart seemed to thaw with relief in the warmth of his presence. He acted as if the previous night had been quite normal, standing over me like a radiant beneficent young god, smiling and tweaking my nose.

'I was going to the Serpentine with Squirrel,' he said, 'but maybe I won't now – shall we have lunch together?'

I said yes, and he could have half my tart if he liked. I was so relieved that he wasn't dead, and thought I'd never seen anything half so handsome in my life. After lunch Prudey came round and lectured him for hours on what a crashing bore he is, especially when he is talking about his guitar, and how utterly incapable of real feelings. 'Ow,' he said gloomily, taking refuge in his special protective baby talk, 'poor Rooples, is Rooples a borskles then? – how much is he, sixpence?'

He had to leave early because he is sleeping with Squirrel tonight and has to get dinner for her. 'Why don't you come over tomorrow and meet her?' he asked. 'You'd probably like her.'

'Oh no, I couldn't, I'd be scared stiff!'

'Nonsense, don't be so silly. We'll all go to the Serp together.'

Tuesday, 27th

As soon as I came into Rupert's studio I saw the bed. I didn't see anything else and I felt sick. Then I saw Squirrel sitting in an armchair with her legs crossed, bare to the thigh, wearing a fur coat over her nightgown and mending Rupert's pillowcase, and I felt even sicker.

Rupert introduced us. Squirrel looks like a *Vogue* cover with black hair tied back in a snood. She is very small and fragile, with a beautiful short nose like a Pekinese, and eyes like small black cherries. She has a pale yellow skin like chamois leather, because of her native blood, and brown smudges under her eyes. She must be all of twenty-eight. I hated her at sight, I hated the unmade bed and her bare legs, the smug look she had, like the cat that's eaten the canary.

Prudey came up and while Rupert made tea Squirrel was quite charming to me which made me hate her even more. We talked about the war and how disgusting it was the way we lay around all day doing nothing, and Prudey kept saying how she really ought to start going to concerts again, and Squirrel wishing she could pick up a man with a car. Then Prudey read us bits of her diary, which consisted entirely of dinners and seductions, punctuated with oaths: 'Dinner Peter Kimber – roast duck, crème caramel. Let him seduce me. Damn!' The rest is mainly about number 34 and everybody going to bed with everybody else. What a funny house, everybody knowing everyone else's affairs!

Squirrel disappeared into the kitchen with Rupert, and Prudey decided to de-flea Henry Miller; I watched her charging myopically around her beautiful off-white studio in her indecent sun-suit which showed her breasts, with her brown, prize-fighter's shoulders hunched forward, and straight hair sticking up in a crest on the crown of her head, while she peered around fiercely for the Keating's powder. She looked all her age, but even so I found her more attractive than Squirrel.

'Tell me,' I said, 'how often does R sleep with S?'

'Oh, about twice a week – she bores him a bit, but he's fond of her and she's terrifically sexy. By the way I hope you're not going to fall in love with him, he's quite mad really, and totally incapable of normal feelings.'

I said I knew how awful and egocentric he was, but I loved him in spite of everything, and couldn't be happy away from him. 'You see,' I told her, 'apart from anything else, he makes me laugh. I never stop when I'm with him, I laugh till my guts ache – that is when I'm not sulking or having hysterics.'

When Rupert and Squirrel came back he said suspiciously, 'You two seem to have formed a mutual admiration society. I suppose the bond is that you both think I'm boring.'

'What you need is a great sorrow,' Prudey snarled. 'It's the only thing that might make a man of you.'

Good old Prudey. I like her. I hate Squirrel. What a pity she dominates Rupert so. But what the hell can I do against a twenty-eight-year-old glamour girl who may be dumb but knows her onions?

After they'd gone to the Serp I went up and made my peace with Leonard and helped him wash down the sun roof, which smelt of cat's pee.

I scrubbed it with a lavatory brush, while Prudey sprayed it with her new scent which is called 'Amour Amour'. Afterwards she gave me coffee in the kitchen and I asked her if R had ever actually done anything – any work that is – and she said he used to be quite good at public re-lations and advertising but he gave it up because office work made him feel ill. She still thinks he's the nicest man in Chelsea even if he is mad.

Didn't see Rupert for a few days, as I was busy at the post – kept thinking about Squirrel and hating her.

Tonight when I went round to the studio just for a check-up, I was surprised to hear the door-bell ring. It was Rupert, who seemed to have something on his mind. After some casual conversation he suddenly said, 'Oh by the way, I was looking through my pockets for some money this morning and I found half a crown in my dressing-gown, so determined to prove my manly powers, I leapt on to my bicycle and went to the chemist down the road and bought *three* contraceptive apparatuses! "Three French letters! The cheapest you've got and be quick before I change my mind!" I cried. "You'll feel more through the three and sixpenny kind, sir," said the chemist. "I don't care about the feeling, this is a job of work," I replied sternly.' There was a pause. 'So what do you think about that, eh Joanie?'

I thought it was very funny and rolled on the floor laughing. 'Oh dear, dear,' I thought to myself. 'What a funny life.'

He went on to tell me that when he was at Marlborough all the boys had catalogues of French letters and the cheapest was sixpence. It would last a year if carefully washed, rubbed with French chalk and put away in the box after use. This 'low-priced sheath' was known as the Workman's Friend. At least Rupert had spent 2/6.

'I once asked Jo what seducing a virgin was like,' R continued. ' "Buggerin' awful," he said in tones of awe. "Your cock's sore for weeks – and buggerin' awful for the virgin too!" '

I said I had never seen a cock, at which R let out a whoop of surprise and proceeded to describe in detail the cocks of half the men in Fulham and Chelsea. His, he said, was bright purple, denoting royal blood.

Taking advantage of this opportunity, I asked R a few more questions. 'Well,' he said humouring me, 'you – er – stick it in – and wiggle it around, up and down, in and out and so on – then you get thoroughly excited, and – well – you have an orgasm! Only' – his face took on an expression of intense gloom – 'with a virgin, you *can't* stick it in, that is, not without an awful lot of hard work. And as for the virgin, you can only hope she gets sufficiently excited not to think it's like being at the dentist, which it probably is.'

He then told me that some women can't have orgasms, but I said, 'I bet

I could have one', and R seemed to think that was funny for some reason. He told me he had once seduced Squirrel four times in one night but he could only manage once now because he was getting old. The most he had ever managed was seven. Then he told me about something called soixante-neuf, v. interesting, lying head to tail so to speak.

'And what about lesbians?' I asked. 'I've often wondered what they do.'

Rupert said, 'Goodness, you are innocent', and went on to tell me in a fatherly way diverse horrid details of lesbians 'sucking each other's pussies' and the huge rubber things they strap on to themselves in Paris brothels, and how pansies sleep with each other, and how men get girls to suck their cocks – Jo, he said, was especially keen on that. I screamed with horror but R said, 'Methinks the lady doth protest too much!'

All this talk had got Rupert quite excited so we lay on the sofa, and got into some rather peculiar positions with R howling 'I wanna seduce you, I wanna seduce you!' At that interesting moment the sirens blew off. I jumped up to check the blackout, pulling my blouse on and looking for my shoes. 'Gosh,' I said, 'I must go, Mummy thought I'd be back by ten.'

Rupert didn't answer, he was lying on the bed face downwards, making strange groaning noises. As I was walking home, heard bombs in the distance and saw flares.

Wednesday, 4th September

My mother came to lunch and met Rupert. She thought he was very handsome and had nice teeth. He said she reminded him of a girl he used to know called Mabel, who was a sex maniac. 'These tall flat women are always sexy,' he observed.

After she had gone we went to the Serp and lay in the sun and bathed. Met Pru's new lover, the Baron, the one who stands her on her head. Didn't look too good in his bathing-pants. Rupert put on my new green bathing-cap and looked like a Babylonian archer. Prudey now calls him 'that handsome half-wit'.

The Baron looked me over and said, 'Who is this lovely creature?'

Prudey said, 'She's the only nice girl in Redcliffe Road, and the only one in living history who ever resisted Gerhardt playing the second movement of Beethoven's Fifth.' I think Prudey is a bit gone on me. She kept declaring that I looked like a sleeping madonna and how pretty my hair was, to which Rupert replied, 'Oh I was just thinking how repulsive it was. Isn't it extraordinary how everyone thinks Joan is attractive, apart from me that is! Of course, in the reflected sunshine of my presence even toads have halos, but it's a pity about the Kirbigrips and glasses.'

Thursday, 5th

Met Thetis for lunch at Quality Inn – believe it or not, Thetis has beaten me to it! As soon as I saw her I thought she looked different. She was wearing an orange angora sweater with no brassière underneath, which must have been awfully tickly, and poppy lipstick. She was also smoking a lot, inhaling deeply and blowing it out through her nose in a very intense way, like Bette Davis does in the flicks.

'My dear,' she said, 'I've lost my virginity! It was marvellous, so simple and easy and natural. He's a married neurologist of thirty-seven, and I don't love him but it's changed my whole outlook on life. I'm a warmer, more tolerant person, I feel like someone with a great secret that I want to share with the whole world – God, Joan, you don't know what you're missing!'

We had wienerschnitzel and apple pie and cream, then went back to Thetis's attic (decorated with pictures of Markova's feet). She was just showing me her Volpar Gels, which were hidden in her underwear drawer, when an air-raid began and hundreds of planes whizzed by like minnows overhead. Two planes came down with parachutes. The guns were firing on Primrose Hill, and the Italian family on the floor below were screaming on the balcony. Their dog leapt the garden wall and got at the neighbour's rabbits, the spaghetti burnt and everything was thrilling, just like on the cinema.

'What a life,' I said, 'never knowing if you're going to be bombed or seduced from one moment to the next!'

BOOK IV

Saturday night, 7th

The tempo's speeding up, tonight the blitz started.

About nine, Sid and I were looking through the top-floor window when we saw four bombs fall on Kensington High Street – flash, boom! – and sparks and debris shot into the air four times in quick succession. The sky over by the docks was red as if it were an enormous sunset.

Midnight

Well here I sit in the air-raid shelter with screaming bombs falling right and left, and Sir John Squire, roaring tight, sitting opposite me next to his Scotch Presbyterian cook. Squire's breath fills the shelter and the cook looks as if she's going to be sick. Sid is reading Maxim Gorky and I'm trying to write this diary, though I can't see very well as there is only a storm lantern. Squire keeps on saying he wants to read Wodehouse's *Uncle Fred in Springtime* once more before he dies.

The bombs are lovely, I think it is all thrilling. Nevertheless, as the opposite of death is life, I think I shall get seduced by Rupert tomorrow. Rowena has promised to go to a chemist's with me and ask for Volpar Gels, just in case the French thingummy isn't foolproof.

Another bomb, quite near this time. Squire's leapt to his feet and is making for the exit. 'I want some cigarettes. I'm going to the pub –'

'Oh no you're not,' says Sid, clutching his arm. 'You're not leaving this shelter until the all-clear goes!'

'Maam,' says Squire, evading her with dignity, 'I am!' He climbs over her, remarking indistinctly that he has never stepped over a lady before, and disappears into the shell-scarred night, walking with difficulty.

Monday, 9th

None of us slept Saturday night. The all-clear went at five a.m. All clear for my lovely Rupert, I thought. I'm really in a very nice state of mind over him. I went up and lay on my bed for a bit but didn't sleep.

At nine I got up, put on my new black and white trousers that make me look like a cross between Oscar Wilde and a Christy Minstrel, and a pale green jersey. I looked and felt as if I'd slept for hours. The papers said – 500 planes over London, 400 dead, 1,400 injured, the docks ablaze.

As it was Sunday, we all went to church – funny how devout people look after an air-raid, but all I noticed was that the priests stood in a line of decreasing height – you could have walked upstairs on their heads. I felt most undevout, and my stomach rumbled.

The studio – one o'clock. Rupert rang the bell. Went to De Cock's and bought beef rissoles and Campbell's tomato soup for lunch. The rissoles are very nice if you dunk them in the soup and eat it all together.

After lunch we lay down and tried to sleep, but there was another air-raid. Then Rupert finally put his hand under my jersey, took hold of my right breast and said, 'Do you still want to be seduced?'

'Yes,' I said.

'Shall we go over to number 34 and go to bed properly?'

I knew then that my hour was upon me, and said in a panic, 'Oh, must we go right now – today?'

'Yes I think so – don't you? Unfortunately, we'll have to do it right under Prudey's nose – she's hopping mad to know whether I've done the deed or not. You realise she's the village gossip and it'll be all over Fulham and Chelsea once she finds out?'

'Can't be helped, provided my mother doesn't hear about it! You go on and I'll follow. Leave the door on the latch.'

Rupert went.

'Well, well, well,' I said, looking at myself in the glass. 'Farewell, a long farewell to my virginity.' I lit a cigarette and powdered my nose. Then I slunk over to number 34, where I found Rupert playing Spanish records to keep his courage up. He had moved the bed into the back room and drawn the curtains, but it was still pretty light.

'Come on,' he said, 'let's get on with it before I change my mind!'

I stood on one side of the vast bed and felt like a block of ice.

Rupert slipped off his clothes, and I suddenly realised he looked terribly funny in the nude and began laughing helplessly.

'What's the matter, don't you like my cock?' he asked, rather taken aback.

'It's all right,' I said, 'just a bit lop-sided!'

'Most people's are – never mind, take your clothes off.'

'You turn over and go to sleep, then I will.'

'Shy and virginal Joanie!' Rupert chuckled, turning his back on me.

I took the opportunity to slip out of my things and was under the bed-clothes in a jiffy.

'I'm not really shy,' I lied. 'It's just that this sort of thing doesn't happen to me every day and I feel a bit peculiar.'

'What, never been in bed with a naked man before?'

'No of course I haven't.' Well I was now, and very queer it felt too, as if I was about to undergo an operation.

We made love for a bit and he kissed my breasts, then put his hand down to break the hymen. I waited for the pain, but nothing seemed to happen. After moving his cock to and fro for a bit he finally got it in and for a few moments it was bloody painful and I clutched on to him and groaned, and just as I was thinking I can't stand this any more, it stopped. I thought, 'Funny, it didn't feel as if anything happened – Christ, I wish this was over!'

'I suppose I'd better get that French letter now,' Rupert said grimly. I watched him put it on with interest, a sort of long white transparent sheath. After that, for a short time we were lying together like one person, panting and sobbing in unison and Rupert was in me without any more pain and my eyes were tight shut. When I came to again and opened my eyes I could see his face pressed against mine, covered in beads of sweat, and heard him making pleased exhausted sorts of noises and saying, 'Hello Joanie! Did you have an orgasm?'

Gosh, I thought, is it all over? Is that all it is? I didn't even know it had happened yet.

'No,' I said, rather puzzled, 'and what's more I think I'm still a virgin.

I mean, what about all the blood and everything that you read about in books?'

'Well,' Rupert said, 'it's most peculiar. There doesn't seem to be anything there – it felt exactly like sleeping with a non-virgin. There I was, expecting terrific mountains and obstacles and there wasn't anything at all!'

We examined the sheets for signs of gore but there weren't any.

'Of *course*, I've got it. Perhaps I did it to myself with a Tampax!'

He looked at me in amazement. 'My dear girl, didn't you know virgins can't use Tampax?'

'But I've used them for years!'

'Oh my God!' Rupert said. 'All the fuss and the drama and the toing and froing, and half the men in Chelsea and Fulham turning pale at the thought of seducing you, and what were you? A fraud! Not a virgin at all!'

'Swear you won't tell anybody,' I begged, 'particularly Jo. I could never hold my head up again.'

After we had stopped laughing, Rupert turned his back to me and dozed off. I leant on one elbow and lay looking at his bare brown shoulders. I looked at the pink sheets and the afternoon light filtering through the thin brown curtains, and the engravings over the mantelpiece, *Minerva visiting the Muses*, and *The Birth of Bacchus*, all brown and fly-specked, and I thought, 'Well that's done, and I'm glad it's over! If that's really all there is to it I'd rather have a good smoke or go to the pictures.'

'What are you meditating on so lugubriously?' Rupert asked, waking up and turning towards me.

'Whether shrimps make good mothers,' I replied coldly.

'Disappointed, eh? Well most girls don't like it the first time – cheer up Joanie, let's have some tea.'

I got up and walked across the room naked, without any embarrassment now that I'd got it over with. After I'd made the tea, we took it out on to the roof, and Rupert lay beside me on the striped mattress. He could see that I was still looking depressed, so he explained to me that people like us with a certain amount of intelligence find it difficult to lose our identities in orgies of sex – there's always a barrier, a kind of brain-barrage that holds us back – we watch ourselves making love instead of losing ourselves in it. What we need is a kind of yoga in reverse, to give matter control over mind.

'Jo doesn't seem to have any problems,' I said.

'Christ no, Jo would poke an exhaust pipe if all else failed. I, on the other hand, need some frightfully sexy girl to work me up artificially – like Squirrel.'

'Then why do you want to go to bed with girls like me who aren't very sexy?'

'That's a very difficult question,' R began, but just as he was going to think of an answer the sirens went again. I believe it was a very heavy night, but I slept right through it, although I was still pretty sore, and the bombs were close. In spite of it all being rather disappointing, I still love Rupert more than I can bear and would do anything for him.

The gas main's been hit so we couldn't cook today. I carted cold food over to number 34 and found the whole menagerie in the kitchen. Prudey and her lover the Baron, Leonard, Agnes and Rupert. There was a slight pause in the conversation when I came in and I wondered if they knew. Then I saw R wink at me and knew he'd kept our secret. 'Hello Joanie,' he said with a big grin, 'I was just telling Leonard that if he snored in the shelter again I'd knock him unconscious.'

The Baron was in a state of wild excitement. He is a short, square-headed fellow with tight blond curls who always wears dark polo-necked sweaters turned up to his ears. He was putting in trunk calls and sounding very important and continental. Prudey is still a bit pale after her miscarriage but otherwise bearing up. Rupert loves it all – he says it cheers him up no end and why go to the cinema? Sausage pie and corn on the cob for lunch.

After lunch R said, 'I feel queer – I have for three days actually. I've an awful feeling something is going to happen. My head buzzes and I've got glands and I feel in a fever.'

The guns came nearer. We were in the back room when we heard a loud crash followed by an explosion that shook the room. Rupert, Agnes and I dived for the floor like three ninepins going down simultaneously. The doors rattled and I began to laugh hysterically. Rupert was behind the bed with three pillows on his head and Agnes was saying the only prayer she could remember which was 'Gentle Jesus meek and mild, look upon a little child'. I felt quite thrilled and stimulated, but Agnes was petrified.

As soon as the all-clear went we strode off to find the crater. It was in

Bramerton Street, a whole house destroyed, the air full of smoke and dust, and all the inhabitants of that part of Chelsea beetling around the barricades like insects disturbed, pansies and lesbians and all.

Tuesday, 10th

Jo, Peggy and I drew Sallé. Jo asked me if I was still a virgin and I couldn't resist saying no, and old Jo said, 'Aah now you're a woman. Did you enjoy it?' and the model said in a bored sort of voice, 'No, of course she didn't.' I was dead tired and felt sick, and couldn't draw, and Jo wasn't too well either from getting drunk in air-raids. There was only a flicker of gas, so Sallé had to take up crouching poses, and in the middle of a pose the sirens went, and we had a machine-gun duel overhead, very exciting, so we all sat on the stairs with Madame Arcana and her dove, in case shrapnel came through the skylight.

Wednesday, 11th

About eleven o'clock we were all in the shelter drinking rum out of tea-cups. It had been quite a noisy night and we thought the rum might make us go to sleep.

Suddenly there was a flash of light and a sound like the crack of doom. The concrete shelter shook in the earth like a ship at sea and the storm lantern swung out. I didn't know it then, but that was *the* bomb – our bomb! And if I could have seen Rupert at that moment I certainly wouldn't have slept another wink. As it was, I didn't know anything about it till old Squire came round before breakfast and said they'd hit Redcliffe Road. I hurtled into my clothes and together we set off to see what they'd hit. I could see that my house was standing, but it looked as if the last houses in the row had gone. I said, 'My boyfriend lives at 34.'

'Thirty-four?' Squire asked. 'Number 28, 29, 30, 31, 32, 33 – oh dear, it looks as if it's 34 they've hit!'

I hope I may never live through such a moment again. I turned faint and sick and my head buzzed. There was the green door with the three bells, and after that two flights of stairs leading up to doors that opened on to nowhere. Below the stairs I could make out the splintered remnants of broken-down floors, Prudey's gum tree wedged upside down with its leaves moving in the breeze, and the bed I was seduced on hanging out over the street with three foot of solid mortar where Rupert's head should have been. Leonard's studio was completely gone.

I rushed up to a warden and said, 'Where are all the people from that house?'

'Couldn't say miss, no bodies though, at least none that I've seen.'

Old Squire was properly sympathetic and reassuring but I was shaking all over and couldn't get my words out. Choking back my sobs I ran down the street to my studio to see if Rupert might have gone there after the bomb. When I arrived I found I'd locked the door and hadn't got the key, but outside on the landing was deposited one guitar in a dented and dusty case, one un-neutered male ginger cat in a basket, very cross, and one gas mask inscribed 'RUPERT CHARLES AUSTIN DARROW, STILL LIVING BY THE GRACE OF HIS OWN INGENUITY'.

Arcana came out in her nightdress and said, 'Your friend came round with these in the middle of the night. He'd just been blown up, it was most extraordinary, he seemed to treat the whole thing as a joke. I couldn't believe him at first, he looked so cheerful.'

Thank you God, I thought, thank you for saving Rupert.

I carried Henry Miller home in his basket and was upstairs doing my hair when I heard someone talking to my mother in the hall. Coming to the top of the stairs I saw Rupert, covered in dust, his shoes broken at the toes and his hair smoothed down with a wet brush, smiling at my mother with suave green eyes and talking very calmly. I let out a yell, ran downstairs and put my arms around him.

'I thought you were dead!' I cried, overcome with relief at seeing him again. 'How were you saved?'

'By the skin of my teeth actually! I happened to go down to the shelter to borrow sixpence off Leonard for the meter when the bomb went off. Prudey was saved because she spent the night at the Players Theatre, sleeping on the floor.'

Mummy made Rupert a cup of tea, and I could see her giving him the once-over, then we went back to Redcliffe Road to see what we could salvage. Everyone there was wildly excited and talking to everyone else, the way they do when there's a crisis. An Irish policeman tried to stop us, saying, 'Don't you go near there miss, there's a one thousand pound unexploded bomb in Cathcart Road, and when it goes off Gawd help this street!' God help it, and us too! I thought, striding into the ruins. While we were scrabbling around some bombers flew over, and R stood in the middle of the road with a striped cushion on top of his head, screaming 'Go away, naughty bombskles' and pointing his gun-stick at them. After we'd rescued his bicycle we made up four bundles and carried them back to my studio, clothes, bedding and two suitcases of Prudey's things, including her precious novel and her Helena Rubinstein Apple Blossom Skin Fragrance. There was also a tin of pilchards hanging from the roof of Prudey's studio so we knocked it down with a broom and took it home for lunch.

Rupert's first thought was for his damned guitar. 'A little out of tune but otherwise uninjured,' he murmured and sat down on the piled-up bedding to play the Grenadinos as if nothing had happened. 'See how steady my hands are,' he boasted. 'I feel like a Spanish refugee playing amid the ruins of Barcelona!'

He was still strumming away when the bell rang, and there on my doorstep was Squirrel, looking very small and worried in yellow corduroy dungarees and a camel-hair coat, asking if Rupert was there. (He's quite right – she does look dreadful in yellow!) My hackles rose at the sight of her, but very politely I asked her to come up, in the calm icy voice of the female in possession. R had to go off to the Labour Exchange to try and get compensation, so I moved some dirty shirts so as to give her a place to sit.

'I guess Rupert had better sleep at my place tonight,' says Squirrel.

'Oh no, he can quite easily make up a bed here,' I reply sweetly. I mean *really*, she may be his mistress, but there's no need to buzz around as if she owned him!

Finally Rupert returned and settled the whole thing by saying he'd sleep at Jo's, and meanwhile he'd leave all his stuff in my studio and diddle the Government by telling them he'd taken an unfurnished room! Triumph! My eyes darted flames at Squirrel. He'd even given the Post Office *my* number as his official address and all. 'What exciting times we live in,' said R, and went off to diddle the Labour Exchange for some more money. Still no sign of Prudey.

I wandered home through the shattered streets. It's getting cold now, the autumn leaves starting to fall and a sharp wind blowing round the fallen houses. Six shops in the Fulham Road have been gutted.

Thursday, 12th

Mummy had made cold meat fritters with the bits left over from the joint, but I felt sick and couldn't eat them – surely I can't be pregnant already. I was beginning to think nervously about taking quinine, which is what the girls in Redcliffe Road drink when they get pregnant, but my mother told me it is something nervous called 'Siren Stomach', very prevalent at the moment!

On my way to the studio there was an air-raid. I ran into the brick shelter in the middle of the road. There were poor little Leonard and Agnes sitting on their suitcases, having lost their all. Luckily Leonard had been wearing his best trousers at the time. Madame Arcana was there too wearing a gold brocade toque and a blanket. It was bloody cold and I wanted to pee badly, but couldn't. Leonard wouldn't give me his seat as he believes in the equality of the sexes, so I sat on the floor.

We all laughed and joked and smoked each other's cigarettes and talked about bathing in the Serp, which now seems unbelievably remote, and I was quite happy except for wanting to pee. Madame A said, didn't I look just like that beautiful little picture, *Bubbles*, sitting there on the floor, only I must be careful, because apart from piles I might get lumbago, and she'd had it once and it used to take her a quarter of an hour to turn over in bed by the clock. Said goodbye to L and A. They're leaving tonight for Bath. Everyone's leaving London now – Redcliffe Road is like a street of the dead. Soon only Rupert and I will be left.

The all-clear finally went, so I dashed out, heading for the bathroom, and met Rupert carrying a struggling Henry in his arms. The poor cat keeps running back to the ruins looking for Prudey. Where on earth can she be? We know she spent Tuesday night at the Players but she hasn't been seen since.

Rupert and I had custard tarts for tea while we listened to the radio. The news was very cheering, with some MPs saying how extraordinarily brave we Londoners are all being – this made us feel very heroic.

Later while we were sorting out our salvaged loot I heard a cackle.

'Guess what I saved from the wreck with much danger to my life!' Rupert crowed, and out of his pocket produced those damned French letters in a very dusty envelope. 'Where on earth shall I put them? I know, I'll stick them inside your book on Gaudier-Brzeska.' Most unfortunate, as it's the first book people always look at when they come to see me!

The afternoon wore on and just as I was thinking I'd burst if I couldn't put my arms around Rupert soon he pulled me down on to the couch and kissed my wrist and lay with his head on my breast.

I held him and kissed him as if the devil were due to come and carry him away, thinking about how narrowly he'd escaped being killed. It really took that bomb on number 34 to make me realise how much I love him, and to think that he also wants to make love to me, and go around with me, and eat in my place, just passes my comprehension! It's the only really exciting thing that has ever happened to me and this is the happiest time of my life.

Friday, 13th

Another night of bombs. My mother's nerve has gone, and she says she simply must have a good night's sleep, so we took the train down to Eastcote and slept at the convent with the Ladies of the Grail. Then straight back to London in the morning to work at the first-aid post – St Mark's in the King's Road.

Went off duty at four, and had high tea with Rupert at Dossi's. Ate stale cakes covered in white coconut worms, paper roses on the table. Another siren as we finished tea.

'What with bombs and things,' R said as we paid the bill, 'we haven't got much further with your sexual decontamination, have we? Not that I care, life is so thrilling these days it's almost as good as an orgasm.'

When we got back to Redcliffe Road there was a palisade up across it and a notice – 'DANGER UNEXPLODED BOMB'. We were thrilled to think of it being there – why go to the pictures, as Rupert would say? In fact he has a singularly relaxed attitude to the whole business of explosives, as witness his adventure this morning. Apparently he was bicycling along in a trance, on his way to the Labour Exchange, thinking he was in the country, when he saw a wooden barrier, lifted the bar and rode through, replacing it to keep the cows in, saw a huge pile of sandbags, rode steadily up one side and down the other, oblivious of hoarse cries of 'get orf that bloody bomb!' etc. 'Oh dear,' R says, 'members of the lower classes, can't be in the country after all! What did you say I'd just ridden over? – unexploded bomb? Ah, thank you my good man,' lifted the barrier on the other side and pedalled on with dignity!

Most of Redcliffe Road has now been evacuated. At least a quarter of the houses are in ruins. This blitz has changed everybody's lives. Just think of the living organism that was number 34, each landing having its own atmosphere. Leonard painting upstairs, Prudey typing under him, Rupert playing his guitar, Leonard poking Agnes, the Baron poking Prudey, the whole house just bursting with life and intrigue, everybody lusting after everybody else and bumming meals off each other, just one happy family! In the good old days R says there was so much love-making going on that the whole of Redcliffe Road used to shake steadily from nine in the evening till nine the next morning.

In fact it's not surprising number 34 was hit; if any three things called for a bomb on them they were Leonard's painting, Prudey's novel and Rupert's poems! This is a fair specimen of his work:

> The sun has broken loose from its moorings
> And its face is splashed with oil from the spouting well
> The halting footsteps of blind spiders feeling their way
> Along a fractured thighbone –
> A pile of discarded genitals rusting in an old iron basket –
> Come to my party!

Another one begins: 'Sweet steaming cesspools disturbed fitfully by bursting balls of stinking gas'. Oh, dear.

Saturday, 14th

Slept with the nuns last night. Woke at half past six and heard my mother and Sid quarrelling in the next room. I could hear my name mentioned, and Sid saying something about 'a life of sin' and my mother was crying and saying, 'Please stop, you know I can't do without my sleep.'

Really, I thought, this is too sordid, so I got up, dressed, and came up to London by myself. The morning smelt of verbena and was cool and rainy.

The sirens went off as I was passing South Ken tube station, and I was held up there for half an hour, packed crowds fighting to get out, others, trying to get in. A lot of people are using the tubes as shelters.

Found Rupert in Jo's basement looking Goyaesque and pallid.

'What a night!' he said, as I turned on the light. He was sleeping under the table with the windows barricaded, the door wedged with a chair and a huge axe beside him to hack his way out with in case the roof fell in. He also had a candle stuck in a pudding basin and *The Red Fairy Book*.

Hardly had we got out of the house, when there was a violent explosion and a black pall of smoke rose over Earl's Court. It must have been a timebomb. The one behind Redcliffe Road hasn't gone off yet – if it sounds like that at Earl's Court, what the hell will it sound like here, I thought in panic – and ours is a thousand-pounder!

Even Rupert's famous nerve deserted him and we spent most of the afternoon sitting in the Redcliffe Road shelter. He tells me he is going to the country next week for a few days' peace and quiet at his ma's place but will be back on Tuesday. I said that if the invasion came on Monday, like they say it will, he might not be able to get back.

'Not get back?' Rupert cried, clutching his brow dramatically. 'Surely you know me better than that? Only to feast my eyes once more on your immortal beauty I would brave the fires of Dante's *Inferno*! Yes by Hecate!' – he seized both my hands – 'What are a few thousand Germans to keep me from your side?' Then he rubbed his cheek against my hand and said, 'I'm hungry.'

Everybody was in the shelter by now, and one by one we began talking about food until we had worked ourselves up into a kind of gastric frenzy. We each made up our ideal menu, and recited it amid groans of thwarted appetite and sighs of appreciation. 'Entrecote minute!', 'Irish stew!', 'Cheese omelette!' echoed among the steel girders that held up the roof. Soon we had all sunk into a state of exhausted lethargy, long silences broken only by an occasional mutter of 'roast beef and Yorkshire pudding' or 'treacle sponge and custard'. Some late arrivals aroused us to a new peak by bringing their lunch in from De Cock's, and eating it with champings and loud swallowing noises. I would have been happy to sit there all day with Rupert.

'I can't stand this,' he said finally. 'I'm going to make a dash for De Cock's and get some liver sausage sandwiches, then you can come and talk to me while I finish packing.'

So now Rupert's going. I'm glad I found out I love him.

Monday, 16th

This morning Sid and I nearly got bombed in the bus on our way to the first-aid post. Two dropped very close and we saw the smoke. Dovehouse Street first-aid post was short of clerks so we stayed till the all-clear at eleven. Lots of casualties streaming blood, very messy. There was a nice little doctor in gum boots who looked like Nero.

Came back to the studio to find Prudey in Madame A's room. *So* happy to see her again! She has been staying with the Baron in Oxford. We all drank tea and told our various experiences. Then Prudey and I went off to try and salvage some more of her stuff. I went too, hoping to find my *Apes of God*, which Leonard had borrowed.

When we got there it looked very dangerous, and Prudey said, 'Don't go in, you can't die a virgin!'

'But I'm *not* a virgin,' I announced proudly. Prudey did a double take.

'Oh really? Well that's fine, I expect you feel much better for it, don't you?'

'Well yes, I suppose I do.'

'I'm so pleased – did you use Volpar Gels?'

'No, but I'm going to.'

'You were lucky to have Rupert, of course. He's very sweet isn't he? It's terribly important to be poked by someone nice the first time. Most girls get awful men, and it puts them off poking for good.'

We climbed up into the ruins; my share of the pickings were a vacuum cleaner, an abstract picture by Gerhardt, a bottle of mayonnaise, two pairs of camiknickers and a roll of Jeyes paper. Prudey saved all her clothes and crockery, also her rubber douche and her copy of *Black Spring*, which is the most indecent book ever written, but she feels sentimental about it because of having slept with Henry Miller. We also found Prudey's will. She leaves £500 to Rupert, her carving tools to Gerhardt and her green silk Chinese dressing-gown to a tart in Bramerton Street.

Back in the studio we emptied the stones out of Rupert's gramophone and wound it up and it worked. We were playing 'I've got my love to keep me warm' when Madame A came up to lend Pru her novel, *The Hieroglyph*. It starts, ' "Are you a sadist or a masochist?" asked Iris Langford, idly burning the wrists of her companion with her cigarette end.' Great stuff!

Just then there was a rumbling noise like a landslide and we rushed to the window. Some of the ruins at number 34 had collapsed and white smoke hung over the street. Prudey and I ran downstairs squeaking with excitement.

The warden was standing in the street, looking distraught. 'There are two women under there,' he cried, dramatically. 'Oh no, they're not,' we said, 'we're here!' What a narrow escape!

Then the warden started shouting, 'Get back everyone! This may set the time bomb off!' So we thought we'd had enough and turned and ran back through the rubble into the studio. Prudey looked through her clothes, but couldn't find anything clean to change into. It was terribly hot and close.

'Have to eat dinner with the Princess Lowenstein tonight in these filthy trousers,' she said gloomily, dabbing 'Amour Amour' under her armpits. 'Hell, I've sweated into my best jersey!'

Tuesday, 17th

Lunch with Prudey at the Continental, and she poured out her soul to me, saying I am the only intelligent girl she knows in Chelsea because I can talk of something else besides cocks and poking.

'Now you're a *sensible* girl,' says Prudey. 'You're the only girl I've met in Chelsea whom I really like!' I returned the compliment and we settled down to talk poking ourselves.

Prudey thinks Rupert and I ought to get married – she says we'd make a lovely couple. She had seen us going out to buy our supper the other night.

'You both looked so nice and happy, you both wore trousers and had long legs and walked in a loose floppy way. You reminded me of two fauns trotting off into the woods to play.'

'That was the day I got poked.'

'Well no wonder you looked so nice!'

I said, 'But what about Squirrel?'

'Oh Rupert's very bored with her, she's gone on too long. But she's very good in bed because she's half-coloured.'

Prudey likes Squirrel because she is so beautiful, and Prudey is an imitation lesbian. She likes women to look at and men for their conversation, rather than the size of their cocks, that's why she likes the Baron, because he's so intense.

'Compared with Rupert,' she says, 'the Baron is like going up to the drawing-room after nursery tea. If you ask him an intelligent question you get an adult comeback, but if you ask Rupert he just looks at you gloomily and says "hornswaggle" or something equally unhelpful.'

After lunch, Prudey left in a taxi to go back to Oxford, with Henry Miller in a cat-box.

Half an hour later, return of Prudey and cat-box, Marylebone having been razed to the ground.

Thursday, 19th

Terrible news today.

The morning started quite cheerfully, with Leonard and Agnes arriving and saying, 'Can we eat lunch here, we've nowhere to go?'

Leonard very manly and responsible, Agnes somewhat *distraite* and tense in trousers, which did not suit her figure. Leonard said I looked charming, like a Brockhurst model, so I gladly shared my pilchards with him on the strength of it. Leonard, now in a position to show his *savoir-faire* in a crisis and dominate Agnes, is making the most of it. 'Do you follow me Agnes? Are you attending, Agnes?' Agnes, who seems in a daze, says 'Yes darling' to everything.

Suddenly, enter Rupert, back from the country, looking bright and cheery. He's obviously got something up his sleeve. 'According to Alan Stein at the American Embassy,' he announces, 'Herr Gerhardt Feldmann was drowned on the *Arandora Star.*' He gave me a piercing look to see what my reaction was but I didn't move a muscle and went on eating pilchards. 'Apparently it was heading for Canada, the bilges absolutely crammed with enemy aliens. Cheers me up no end to think of old Gerhardt, who was always so jittery, facing the last great dramatic moment!'

Leonard looked rather shocked. 'You sound very callous,' he said.

'Oh, I was just testing Joan's mettle, she being a bit gone on poor Gerhardt, you know. Can you see her wiping away any surreptitious tears, Leonard?' Still I didn't rise. Leonard, embarrassed, made some excuse about finding a place to live, and took his leave, Agnes trailing disconsolately behind.

There was a tense silence, broken by Rupert's cackle. 'That's shook you up, hasn't it? You look quite pale and intense. Don't you like to think of poor old Gerhardt being drowned, floating around all puffed up and bloated with crabs eating him – after a while you swell up and go pop you know.'

'Shut up, shut up!' I screamed, finally losing control. 'Anyway I don't believe it's true!'

Rupert exploded with laughter. 'That's what the girls on the cinema say.' He put on a high falsetto voice ' "I can't believe it, I *won't* believe it!" Now calm yourself like a good little girl. Yours was a great love that will go down in the annals of history, and no doubt you and dear Gerhardt will be happy ever after in heaven.'

I picked up the nearest thing to hand, which was a knife, and hurled it at him, but missed him by inches. He threw me heavily to the ground and held me there, and I bit his wrist, sobbing with fury.

'There there, Joanie,' he said finally, sitting astride my prostrate body. 'Have a cigarette to calm your nerves. Maybe it isn't true after all.' Of all the callous bums I've ever known, Rupert really takes the cake.

I went and lay down in silent gloom while he wrote some letters. 'Play me Stravinsky,' he said at last. 'A lousy composer but he passes the time pleasantly.'

I played him the whole of *Le Sacre du Printemps* while the rain dripped through the roof. I was numb with shock and the true sadness of it didn't hit me till I got home, and saw the dark skylight at the end of the garden.

More bombs at two a.m. Churchill has broadcast that nearly two thousand people have been killed in London this September. Poor old Squire has fallen down in the blackout and broken his ribs.

Rupert has gone to the country again for a few days' quiet with his ma. It will probably do me good not to see him for a bit, heartless bastard that he is.

Monday, 23rd

Lunch with Rowena at the studio. She is now so sexy that she astonishes her men and leaves them standing. She says she intends to be a grand courtesan and have thousands of lovers. Apparently her technique is simply terrific – I wish she'd give me a few tips!

'Think of all the time we've wasted, Joan!' she keeps saying. Can't say I agree with her.

After lunch she escorted me to a chemist to buy some Volpar Gels, but lost her nerve in three of them, dashing out after asking for toothpaste. She couldn't afford to buy toothpaste indefinitely, so finally forced herself to ask a fatherly gentleman in a dark shop near South Ken.

Wednesday, 25th

By this morning I had worked myself up into such a state of passion over the absent Rupert – I hadn't seen him for a week – that I didn't know what to do with myself. All morning at the post I was thinking about him and wondering how much longer I could bear life without him.

On the way home I saw seventeen German planes in arrow formation cutting through the blue sky, with hundreds of shells bursting around them. The guns were so loud I took shelter in the door of the Servite church. As I was cowering there I heard a yell – 'Woo hoo! Joanie!' – and there was old R lurching down the street with a cheery smile on his face, completely ignoring the guns.

'Lunch?' he said happily, pushing me ahead of him just as if nothing was happening. He was all brown and glowing, his thin cheeks flushed like pomegranates, talking about *Heloise and Abelard*, which he had been reading at his ma's – that is, he read all the sexy bits and skipped the rest. We brewed coffee on the oil stove, while I sat on the edge of his chair with my arms round his neck. He looked around the studio appreciatively. 'Gosh, you have cleaned the place up – you know this studio's quite classy now. It used to be a howling wilderness where Jo and his cronies painted – now he'd damn well have to take his boots off before coming in! Would you say your artistic career has come to a grinding halt? I don't seem to see the usual dreadful paintings around.'

I explained that what with the bombs and working at the first-aid post I really didn't have time for art any more.

'All the more time for looking after Rooples,' he chortled with satisfaction. I choked down my happiness and got lunch ready. Rupert had bought minute steak – it took the whole of his meat ration. I hadn't had any for weeks. He set about frying the onions and I sat watching him, marvelling more and more at his extraordinary physical charm. Why the handsomest man in Chelsea and Fulham should want to sit around my dump frying onions is more than I can fathom.

Old Madame Arcana has got her eye on him too; every time I go to the lavatory she comes up in her yellow-striped Arabian coat with the dove on her shoulder, and makes passes at him until I pull the chain – then she shoots into the centre of the room and pretends she came up to borrow a smoke.

Boy, what a steak! And what onions!

After we had eaten he wanted to lie down with me but I resisted, and we crashed down together on to the sofa, most undignified.

'Now this here Heloise,' Rupert said reprovingly, sitting on my stomach, 'she used to *glide* down to Abelard's couch – in fact she spent most of her time doing it, clad only in a loose-bodied gown and carrying a lamp. Now let's see *you* glide down to me, Joanie, ten stone or no ten stone.' Looking v. intense, I glided. 'You know I think I almost missed you,' R said.

After that we quit being funny and made love very seriously, and I was filled with peace and delight. You can't write about sensuality mingled with tenderness and pity, it just becomes maudlin or goes bad on you in some way – so call it love and leave it at that, one of the few transcendent and satisfying things left in this bloody awful life.

Friday, 27th

Got a bad cold, so Rupert had to keep his distance. He bought Benzedrine, Vapex and heaven knows what else – anyone would think he'd got the cold. We sat at opposite ends of the table and spent an enjoyable afternoon talking about sex and scandal. He told me all about the Chelsea set that used to be, before the war that is – about 120 people who'd all been to bed with each other once and were wondering what to do next.

'How many of them did *you* have?' I asked suspiciously.

'Not many, I'm a bit fussy – but of course I could have had them all! Take Peggy Guggenheim, for instance, I went round to see her at the Gallery to try and get Gerhardt a show, and there was this funny little woman with enormous gold ear-rings and a long sharp nose, bright red, glaring at me through the gloom with small, beady sex-mad eyes. "You're Guggenheim I guess," I said as she rushed at me. "You're sure right baby!" she replied, breathing heavily in my face. "Come to the country with me!" she howled. "Back in an hour!" I cried, eluding her, and dashed straight home to Gerhardt in a taxi, gave him a stiff drink, bundled him in and turned the taxi around. Two weeks later Gerhardt was driving Peggy's yellow Packard and his exhibition was on at the Guggenheim.'

After tea we lay on the floor and listened to 'Children's Hour' – Rupert is crazy about it, he loves hearing fairy stories. He was still too scared of catching my cold to make love to me, but held my hand to show he still likes me.

Sunday, 29th

Thetis and I took Rupert to the Ballet Club for *Dark Elegies*. I found myself faintly out of sympathy with the spotty young men in green corduroys, and their uncouth females glaring with alert intelligence from under monstrous fringes. I don't really think young men should draw attention to themselves by dressing conspicuously, unless they're at least as handsome as Rupert. All the arty girls stared at him as if they'd like to eat him.

'That boy with the long Celtic head isn't bad,' R said. 'And so's that snakey Jewess.' I suppose he meant Frank and Celia. He doesn't think much of ballet on the whole.

Tuesday, 1st October

Double bill at the Forum with Rupert. *Elizabeth and Essex*, and a gangster film where somebody actually *did* say 'Stool on me would ya, ya doity rat!'

R and I walk quite differently every time we come out of the cinema. Today he strode along the Fulham Road as if he had fifty pikemen trailing at his heels. We both love playacting – I suppose it's one of the biggest things we have in common. Even going downstairs from the studio becomes a drama. Sometimes he's carrying me on his back out of a burning house, sometimes we're a doddering old Napoleonic general and his wife descending to the ballroom. 'Come m'dear,' croaks Rupert, 'the Emperor awaits us! You've got a huge bosom remember, mind you carry it properly!' And together we creak downstairs, the violins playing a Strauss waltz.

But today there was a piece of real-life drama awaiting us at the bottom of the stairs, a letter addressed to R. C. A. Darrow, Esq., On His Majesty's Service.

'Oh my God!' Rupert said, holding the letter up to his eyes in the dark hall. 'My calling-up!' I felt sick and shut my eyes. 'Oh no it isn't,' he went on cheerfully, 'it's only my ration book.'

'You'd better not cry wolf too often,' I said, 'or you'll spoil the effect of your *real* calling-up. I'm saving a first-class swoon for that dramatic occasion!' Rupert looked pale and said nothing.

Friday, 11th

My eighteenth birthday. Can't say I feel as old as that, with Rupert persistently treating me like a naughty child.

After lunch we went to buy his present to me and found two lovely green budgerigars, in a shop off Sloane Square, that he bought with 10/-

he'd borrowed off Jo. Then we found a big wicker cage in a second-hand shop for five bob and bought that as well. We washed it in the bath and put the birds in it and in two minutes they were making love like nobody's business.

Saturday, 12th

Decided I'd better go to Confession – after all Rupert hadn't poked me for nearly two weeks, and I thought maybe he never would again, which is as near as I'll ever get to a firm purpose of amendment, so I'd better go while the going's good.

I was petrified and started straight off with the bit about making love to get it over with – my first mortal sin! I could almost hear Father Corato's hair rising on his scalp. He could hardly wait for me to finish before launching his attack.

'And er – how many times have you – ah – have you –'

I thought, oh God the record's stuck, but just then he got a brainwave, and called it 'committed this sin'.

'Oh,' I said cheerfully, 'only twice, and we used birth control once, and he's *not* married!'

After that I was given a long talk on preserving my chastity in future, to which I replied rather unconvincingly that I'd do my best. I have an awful feeling he *can* recognise my voice! He jolly well should do, he's been to supper enough times. Finally I got *fifty* (!) Hail Marys right off, and staggered out feeling distinctly chastened.

Sunday, 13th

Cold, with a damp white mist and the sun like a great orange ball. It's nearly winter. Now that the leaves are fallen I can see Gerhardt's skylight again. I still have the feeling he's alive and imagine I can hear him hammering away on the other side of the wall.

Winter always reminds me of Gerhardt. Even now when there's frost in the air I find myself feeling sick with remembered fear and loneliness at the corners of stairs or coming out of the bathroom. I don't think I could have been quite normal when I loved him. Well, I couldn't have anything much more normal than Rupert, could I? He'll do a lot towards making me get over it. I'm very lucky really.

Monday, 14th

Unexpected visitation to the studio by Mummy, who found a very domestic scene. Me one side of the fire darning Rupert's socks, he opposite practising his guitar, the birds singing and the dinner bubbling on the oil stove, just as if we were married. I really don't know what she imagines our relationship is! I don't think that she believes I'm his mistress, but Sid does. She's fanatical. She didn't speak to me for days when she first began to suspect it. She went all pale and sour and awful for weeks, as if she was ill, and wouldn't come near me or touch me. She told Mummy I was leading a filthy life and she was just blinding herself to it.

R acted very sweetly with Mama and I think she likes him and feels a bit motherly towards him. He could make anyone like him.

After she went I told Rupert about my going to Confession, and he was furious. 'Chastity!' he bellowed. 'What do you mean, preserve your chastity? You've lost it haven't you? Damn it all girl, you can't pull a fast one on God like that!'

I tried explaining about absolution and penances. 'Christ,' Rupert said, 'that stuff's only for half-wits! What happens if you sleep with me again, and again after that? Do you get excommunicated or something? Anyway what's the problem, are you afraid to die unshriven?'

'I'm afraid to die in mortal sin. I'm afraid of going to hell.'

At this Rupert could no longer restrain himself – his amazed laughter nearly choked him. 'Hell? This is fantastic! Oh you funny little girl, you really *are* a funny little girl – why, you're a museum piece!'

I slapped his face hard.

He didn't say a word but just lay there, breathing as if he were asleep, his back turned to me. It was as if all contact, mental and physical, were cut off between us. I went cold with misery, I felt so helpless and so frightened by this frigid immobility. It lasted for hours or seemed to, and then suddenly he turned towards me, and took me in his arms. He pulled the rug up over our shoulders, and we went to sleep together in mutual warmth and amity.

When we woke it was late afternoon. We leant out of the window and saw it had turned to a lovely evening with an enormous double rainbow over Redcliffe Road. We could see three bombed houses to the left and two to the right, plus a church with the steeple blown off, four air-raid shelters, several piles of broken glass and wreckage, barrage balloons over-head and this amazingly lovely rainbow stretching from one end of the street to the other with a fainter repetition above it.

As we were admiring it we heard the sound of marching soldiers in the distance. Redcliffe Road heard it, and pricked up its ears. The soldiers swung out of Cathcart Road with pipes and drums in front, and it was the first time I'd seen soldiers marching since the war began. It seemed to make it all more real. Old grannies were coming out of their cellars, weeping and wringing their hands for joy in the streets.

Tuesday night, 15th

This is certainly hell and no mistake. Hardly a minute's pause between each load of bombs and each one sounding as if it's going to hit our house. Gosh, it's awful; this is the heaviest bombing we've had since the war began, the absolute poetry of destruction. I sit in the shelter in my new navy-blue siren suit, reciting Rupert Brooke – 'If I should die think only this of me/That there's some corner of the Fulham Road –'.

Wednesday, 16th

When we emerged into the Fulham Road this morning there didn't seem to be much of it left – they'd certainly buggered it up! The whole place was a shambles like the last days of Pompeii, with shop windows shattered and their goods destroyed, the road thick with glass and the air with dust. Tulley's has been burnt out and there are two houses down in Limerston Street. People still digging for the bodies. Huge crater outside the tobac-conist with a burst water main spouting in it. Poor old Redcliffe Road has lost another two houses, three bodies in the wreckage and my skylight broken.

As I approached number 48 there was a huge explosion and the time bomb finally went off behind 37; black smoke hung in the air and everyone ran as big bits of masonry hurtled towards us. The studio looked very dirty with bits of glass everywhere.

Went off to see if Rupert had been hurt but met him half way – all that was wrong with him was a chill in his stomach, which he'd caught last week from leaping naked out of bed and putting out a firebomb in his mother's garden by peeing on it. He was wearing his famous black overcoat that he used to impress clients with when he was in advertising. It hangs down to the pavement like a box all round him and has such huge padded shoulders that old ladies in buses turn pale when they lean up against him and half of him collapses.

While he was rather unwillingly patching up my skylight, Madame Arcana came up, pale and ghastly after the night's terrors, and said she hadn't been able to sleep because she had gone to bed in her stays, and when she had finally dozed off she dreamt that Aleister Crowley was trying to rape her, and woke up in a cold sweat just as the time bomb went off.

Friday, 18th

Rupert back to his ma's again.

St Mark's for night duty. Was given truckle bed beside the phone, the mattress liberally sprinkled with what looked like blood. Mongrel dog, bombed out of his home, slept on my stomach.

Saturday, 19th

Staggered back to the studio this morning, exhausted and dishevelled and longing for sleep, to find Prudey, of all people, ready for a nice gossip.

'I am so glad to have caught you,' she says. 'Now we can have some coffee and a good long talk.' I groaned inwardly. 'Now how's Rupert, he *is* sweet isn't he? Are you still feeding him? And who's his chief girlfriend, you or Squirrel? How often does he poke her? How often does he poke you? Are you happy? And do you still do charming ridiculous things like going to Confession after he's poked you? I've always thought I should like to be a Catholic, it must be such fun to tell a priest you've fornicated.'

'I don't put it quite so bluntly,' I said. 'I just call it "living with a man".'

'Oh my dear, that's much too sophisticated! I believe in the good old-fashioned words, don't you? Though of course,' she added ruefully, 'I've never really been *able* to fornicate, you see, it's always been adultery with me as far as the Catholic church is concerned – even my husband was married before!'

'What a shame,' I said.

'Well, I'm so glad you're happy, darling. Actually I'm quite happy too, living in Oxford with the Baron. It's been so lovely seeing you again, and after all, what does the war matter when you've got a nice boyfriend?' She paused at the door. 'Where is he by the way?'

'Oh,' I said, 'he's gone to the country to recuperate. He caught a bit of a chill.' Then I told her about Gerhardt drowning.

'I always had a queer feeling about him,' she said. 'He was the sort of person one expected to find hanged.'

After she had gone, I went to the Forum to see *The Mortal Storm*. Sat in the usual one-shilling seats and began thinking of dear Rupert in the country with his ma and what a pity he was missing this smashing film and so on. Happened to turn my head down the row just as someone lit a cigarette which illuminated his face. It was Rupert. He was with Squirrel, who was powdering her nose from a gold compact. The match lit up her slim brown hand and long red nails, and her brown wrists clinking with barbaric silver bracelets. The fleeting impression I had of her was completely native. My blood boiled! Rupert had deceived me, telling me he was going to the country, and here he was with Squirrel!

He was only sitting two seats away from me so I fixed him with a glittering eye. The mortal storm that raged on the screen was nothing to the one going on inside my breast as I gave myself up to planning our next meeting. Perhaps I should have a special hair-do before Monday, something hard and sophisticated – and if my new coat arrives from Harrods . . .! Damn Rupert and his mistress! I couldn't wait till then, I'd have to accost him in the cinema, give him a fright, and that would enable me to be quite blunt and frank on our next meeting.

I spent the rest of the film thinking up opening gambits, most of which started with 'Well, you low double-crossing snake in the grass . . .!' The moment came when Squirrel and Rupert rose to go. I stood up to let them pass, and when his head was level with mine I hissed 'Hello' down the back of his neck in a menacing sort of way.

He didn't even have the good breeding to start. 'Oh hello Joanie – how are you?' he said. 'Dreadful film, isn't it?'

'I'm enjoying it very much,' I replied icily.

'Hello Joan,' said Squirrel.

'Hello,' I said.

I breathed fire and slaughter for the rest of the evening, and looked forward to a good row.

Sunday, 20th

Arrived home from night duty to find Milborne Grove wrecked. Eight bombs had fallen within the Boltons alone; one, three doors away from our house. Our windows and shutters had been blown in, the doors jammed, and half the tree on the front lawn had fallen through the drawing-room window. While we were working on the house, collecting up broken glass etc., who should ride up to the wreckage on his bicycle but Rupert.

'Hello,' he yelled up at the window. 'Are you all right? I expected to find corpses!'

I ran out completely forgetting about my rage, and began talking cheerfully about the bomb. Then I suddenly remembered and snapped out, 'I thought you'd gone to the country!'

Alas for my suspicions! His ma had put him off till Monday, so there was no row after all – v. disappointing.

My new plum corduroy coat has arrived from Harrods, very smart! Luckily my bedroom hasn't been destroyed by the bomb so I could try it on.

We went for some beer to a little pub near Dovehouse Street, very warm and cheery, then wandered round the Fulham Road looking for a cake shop but couldn't find a single one; they'd all been blown up!

'No more custard tarts,' I told Rupert. He came and sat on my lap and put his head on my shoulder and said, 'You rock me to sleep like my old nanny used to do, very comforting.' I bounced him gently up and down and sang him 'Rock a Bye Baby'.

Friday, 25th

Workmen still clearing the rubble out of our house in Milborne Grove. Had a lovely day at the studio; made colossal stew while R practised his guitar and played me his new farruca. Suddenly he hit a discord, clutched his stomach and said, 'Oh, I've got an awful pain just here – do you think the meat was off?'

'You've probably got wind,' I said.

'No, it's not that, I've been feeling a bit peculiar lately. Not quite myself you know. Do you believe in premonitions? I feel the way I did just before the house was blown up.'

Saturday, 26th

Thetis came to lunch. She's hoping to go to Bermuda with the Censorship, lucky bastard. The room was looking very nice and lived-in, stew on the fire, guitar music lying around, Rupert's boots on the floor, and beside the typewriter a poem by Rupert that starts, 'O cock! Thou gilded barnacle!', with a note from the cleaning lady scribbled on the back – 'Mr Darrow, you owe me three shillings, could you let me have it before this evening as I am relying on it'!

Everything seemed so normal, and I felt at peace with the world. 'Come on Teta,' I said, 'let's go and try to find a cake shop that's open.' As we went downstairs I saw there was a big yellowish envelope in the letter-box. I pulled it out and saw 'R. C. A. Darrow, On His Majesty's Service'.

'Oh Teta! Do you think he's been called up?' I tore it open and the nightmare sprang. 'Report for Military Service – Royal Navy – and from thence to His Majesty's training ship *Raleigh* – 7th November.'

'Oh no!' I cried, 'I can't bear it.' And I sat down on the linoleum because my knees had given way.

Thetis looked surprised. 'I didn't know you cared for him so much,' she said.

I kept thinking, 'I must get away from here and join the WAAFs or the WRAFs or something, or go to Bermuda with Thetis, anything to get away from London.' I looked at myself in the hall mirror. I was wearing a pale blue hat with a pink feather and my plum corduroy coat and I thought, 'What a mockery, I ought to be wearing sackcloth.'

About six o'clock, after Thetis had gone and it was getting dark, there was the familiar sound of someone tearing up the stairs. I jumped to my feet and Rupert came in wrapped in his huge black overcoat, glowing with the cold. I put out both my hands and said, 'I've got bad news for you. You've been called up!'

'*Called up?* Where? When? How soon? What for?' He seized the paper from my hands, glaring in horror at the four shilling postal order for his train to Plymouth. I could almost see how sick he was feeling. He dropped the forms on the floor and looked at me despairingly. 'You see what this means, don't you? I'm done for, finished, it's all over! I'm trapped – *worse than school!* – and for the next two or three years probably! And you *never* get leave – oh Joanie!'

'Oh Rupert!' He sat on my lap and we rocked together in misery.

'Do you think I'll get killed?' he asked. 'Do you think they'll let me practise my guitar?'

I tried to reassure him on both points. Horrible pictures were now racing through Rupert's mind of himself wielding a marline-spike or clambering aloft to the crow's nest. 'It's getting late,' I said, at last. 'We'd better go.'

We stood up feeling awkward, and Rupert's fear filled the room. He put his head clumsily against mine and our lips met. He had never kissed me standing up before. It is the only one of his kisses I shall ever remember properly.

'Do you really think it will be all right?' he asked, like an apprehensive child.

'Of course it will,' I said. 'Come on, I've got to go.'

There was no moon. The road was swept by a cold wind and cats prowled like coyotes around glistening piles of wreckage.

'Do you remember how cheery this road used to be?' Rupert asked. 'Pianos tinkling day and night, guitars on hot roofs, people on balconies taking tea under striped awnings, hundreds of typewriters tapping, thousands of paintbrushes squeaking – why, it must have been one of the jolliest streets in London! It'll never be like that again.'

Two lighted shops at the end of the street reminded me of Christmas. 'Oh God,' I thought. 'Christmas alone.' Christmas is always the worst time at home, with pictures in the magazines of parties that I never get asked to.

'Maybe I'll be drowned,' said Rupert as we walked slowly down the street. 'And I'll meet Gerhardt floating around in mid-Atlantic, and me and Gerhardt and the fishes will all have a lovely Christmas together. Darling Joanie – will you come and rescue me when I'm in wicked old hell? Will you save me from the devil?'

'Of course I will.'

'And we'll get on a bwoomstick and wide and wide through the twees, wicked old devil hot in pursuit?'

Hutchinson's was warm and bright, so we went in to buy cigarettes and while we were there the siren went for the evening blitz. The guns began in the distance.

'Oh dear,' Rupert said, 'what are we going to do? There's nothing we *can* do. Only ten days! It's like the last week of the hols.'

'Never mind,' I said, 'remember you're serving your country.'

'Yes, like *Elizabeth and Essex*.'

He left me and I ran back through nightmare streets, cold and dark and the guns going, past a time bomb barrier, running into ropes that held me back like spiders' webs, and treading on broken glass that cracked horribly underfoot and made my heart jump.

Monday, 28th

Arrival of Rupert at the studio, walking as if he had a wooden leg, one eye screwed up under an imaginary patch, wheezing, lurching and belaying, and doing the sailor's hornpipe all over the studio.

'Man the poop stick!' he yelled. 'You just wait till I get my first leave, my girl, I won't have seen a woman for twelve years!'

'Nonsense,' I said, 'you'll frequent bordellos, sailors always do. Or you'll fall in love with some nice little midshipman.'

Rupert, ignoring these insults, began cooking steak and put a tinned fruit pudding on the boil. After lunch he told me awful stories of naval disasters like the *Camperdown* and the execution of Admiral Hawke. 'Think on Cadiz, my Lord of Essex, think on Cadiz,' he muttered as he slumped in his armchair. 'Are you lugubrious? As lugubrious as sixpence?'

'Why, do you want me to be?' I asked.

'Of course – for men must work and women must weep, that's what I keep telling myself. Come and lie down, it's the universal cure for all misfortunes.'

So we lay down under the grey sheepskin rug and kissed and felt warm and sleepy and even happy, with the waltz from *Un Carnet de Bal* on the wireless. After that they played Handel's *Acis and Galatea* – 'The happiness of the lovers is threatened by the giant who comes on with ample strides,' announced the BBC suavely. 'Somebody always comes buggering in,' Rupert muttered.

Just then the music faded, which usually means a raid is on the way, and Madame Arcana came up to lend me a book on black magic.

'You'll be lonely without the boy, won't you?' she said, looking coyly at Rupert. 'Poor child, they tell me it's hard in the Navy!'

Tuesday, 29th

We have nine days. Everything is heightened and speeded up. Took Rupert to the dentist, as he's heard the Navy pulls all your teeth out as they haven't got time to stop them. No holes luckily, as R invariably knocks dentists out if they hurt him. Felt like a mum getting her son ready for school. Afterwards we went to Schott's to look for guitar music, and the sirens went off on top of Liberty's. We could see it up on the roof yelling its head off so we yelled back our defiance into its teeth.

'Gosh,' R said, 'look at all the people running! They're not as tough as we are in the Fulham Road.' It was really quite exhilarating shouting back at that siren, and it made us feel hungry too, so we went to the Tottenham Court Road Corner House.

'I adore this place,' I said. 'It's a mixture between a public lavatory and the Taj Mahal.' I think I'd read that somewhere, but Rupert thought it very original and funny. We ran up the marble stairs and found a very classy café called the Mountview, with a band in red coats playing 'Ciri

Ciri bin', and a conductor who waved his violin and executed curious Latin dances. We clapped every number and laughed and ate enormously – rum babas and fruit slices and cherry flan, with hot chocolate to drink. The huge mosaic pillars glittered under the lights and I was so happy I felt almost drunk. I don't think I've ever enjoyed a tea so much.

We were played out to the 'Nightingale in Berkeley Square', and wandered our way back through the wreckage of Shaftesbury Avenue to find no buses running from Soho, so walked all the way home singing *The Beggar's Opera*.

Wednesday, 30th

Rupert tries to keep up his spirits and be cheery, but his nerves are very bad. Today he actually hit me, quite hard. We were walking down the Vale towards King's Road, having a slight theological discussion, when R said something about the Pope which annoyed me rather more than usual. I struck him, quite lightly, but he replied with a stinging blow. In rage I hit him harder, making his nose bleed. He responded with a back-hander across my face of such colossal force that it shattered my glasses. I felt the concussion, saw flying glass all around me and thought I'd been hit by a bomb. Then I saw Rupert's bleeding knuckles and realised what had happened.

I was so stunned I couldn't move for a few minutes but stood with my hand over my face. Rupert, thoroughly unrepentant, began dragging me along by the wrist, blood pouring from his nose, to the goggle-eyed delight of two butcher's boys.

The extraordinary thing is, I bore him no malice although I pretended to. My nose still felt pretty sore and I couldn't see anything without my glasses. To get me home through the blackout, I had to hold on to his sleeve like a blind man.

Thursday, 31st

Mummy is suspicious, because I haven't had the curse for two months.

'You're either anaemic or pregnant,' she said, 'and I mean to find out which.' So she's taking me to a doctor. She keeps on asking me if I'm still a virgin or whether there's any cause to believe I'm going to have a baby. She's really put the fear of God into me – it's not so much the thought of having a baby, it's the ghastly maternal fuss that would attend such an occurrence.

Friday, 1st November

Alfred came to tea, and we picked texts from the Bible as it was All Hallows Eve. Next week Alfred's off to Dorset, where his mother lives, to join the Home Guard. Played mah-jong with Mummy, and sang to our ukeleles.

Saturday, 2nd

While I am still lying in bed, Mummy comes in and says in would-be normal tones, 'The doctor will see you on Tuesday. It's over two months now, isn't it? I do hope you're not pregnant – how terrible it must be for a girl who *has* slipped up when she misses her curse for two months! Just think of the agony she must go through!' She can be a very cruel woman sometimes. I wondered if she was deliberately torturing me.

Couldn't eat breakfast. Was Sid looking at me strangely? Funnily enough I hadn't given much thought to this pregnancy thing till now, but all at once I began to feel more and more certain that I was in for it, that it was true, that nothing could stop it. I was buggered and bitched.

I broke out in a cold sweat and tore back to the studio. There I found a bottle of quinine pills left behind by Prudey, and I remembered how she told me the girls in Redcliffe Road used to take them when their curse was late. It said 'Take one or more as directed'. So I took six, swallowing them with water.

Sitting now at the switchboard I feel queer, giddy and remote. If I hold out my hand it shakes and I can't feel my fingers much, they're all cotton-woolly. Oh dear God, get me out of this, never no more, I promise! It's not the baby, it's the home fuss that worries me. Sid *must know* by now – I couldn't face her, that would be too much. Wish my fingers didn't miss the holes when I dial. Wonder how soon it will show. I tried looking it up in books where girls have babies, but they never give accurate dates. Why did this have to happen to me?

Sunday, 3rd

When I went over in the morning Rupert was sitting at the table writing to his ma and listening to Beethoven on the wireless. 'God,' he said as I came in, 'what a bad writer Beethoven was!' He seemed very cheery. 'The great problem facing me now,' he went on, 'is how to become an officer, preferably an admiral, as soon as possible. I'm concentrating all my guile and cunning to that end.'

I was just wondering how to break the bad news when Prudey called in, full of bounce and go. She has acquired a new image, her hair combed straight down like an intellectual, calling everybody darling this and darling that, much to R's disgust. He thinks she has gone off terribly since she began living with the Baron.

'And how are you, darling?' she asked, turning to me. 'You look a bit pale and tired.'

I took a deep breath and pulled my shabby old coat around me. 'Yes I suppose I do – Mummy thinks I'm pregnant.'

I watched Rupert's face change from cheerful cynical amazement to blank horror.

'What?' he shouted, as the realisation hit him.

'Yes,' I said calmly. 'I haven't had the curse for two months.'

'Haven't had the curse for two months! Then you *are* pregnant! Oh my God, I feel sick and ill!'

Prudey prowled around shaking with laughter. 'Oh, how exciting, I *am* glad I called on you this morning! Have a cigarette, darling. Now do be careful, won't you, and don't let Rupert throw you down the stairs.'

'I can't stand this, one staggering shock after another. The whole world seems to have turned upside down since Saturday. I'm in a cold sweat,' he went on, wiping his brow with the back of his hand. 'Prudey for God's sake leave us alone.'

After she'd gone I waited for Rupert to say something.

'Thank God I'm going to the Navy on Wednesday,' he said finally. 'How long have you thought this might be happening?'

'Oh, on and off for a month.'

'Why the hell didn't you tell me before?'

'I thought it might have made you lugubrious.'

'Yes but then I could have taken you to a doctor straight away and it could all have been settled by now. Christ almighty, I shall be in the Navy and I won't be able to manage things. You *must* have an abortion, and pretty damned quick too.'

'But I don't want an abortion,' I said.

'What do you mean you don't want one? What *do* you want?'

'Well, if all else fails, I'll have the child.'

'You're crazy, you don't know what you're saying! Do you realise what an illegitimate child means? No man will marry you, they hate illegitimate children, and the child will always feel ashamed and inferior.'

'Never mind. I told you I've always wanted a child. If it feels inferior then it's a fool. I won't have an abortion. The Catholic Church forbids them.'

'*Oh – God-damn!*' Rupert said slowly. 'I always knew the fucking Catholic Church would get me in the end. Now listen Joanie, I know it's all very strong-minded of you, but just be practical for a minute – nice girls like you don't have bastards and *I* certainly can't stand the idea of marriage. The responsibility would give me the most awful claustrophobia. On the other hand, I'm a kindly chap, not cut out to be a betrayer of young maidens and all that, not my *métier* at all.

'Oh God I'm going to kill myself, I can't cope, my brain's buzzing! I don't think I've ever felt so lugubrious before in all my life. Has your curse ever stopped before?'

'Never for so long. Perhaps you'd better throw me downstairs after all.'

I didn't mention the quinine I'd taken in a moment of panic although I was feeling dreadfully ill. 'Please,' I said, 'this is like a scene in a play, I keep on wanting to laugh – let's go and have some lunch.'

It was pouring with rain and I couldn't eat. The rissoles tasted like putty, and I shovelled my beans on to Rupert's plate. 'You're not attacking your food in your usual fierce way,' he commented.

After lunch we were back in the studio talking about abortion when Squirrel rang the bell. 'What a cheery party,' Rupert said with a grim laugh as he threw the key out of the window to her. 'Three mistresses in one morning.'

She came upstairs. She was wearing a very expensive fur coat, sleek and soft as a second skin, and tight leather gloves on her tiny hands. Her fragility infuriates me, it makes me feel six foot tall with enormous feet like Little Titch, all Kirbies and cardigan and size 7 sandals.

The atmosphere in the studio was icy, our nerves strained to breaking-point. I hardly spoke, and Squirrel showed her uneasiness by trying to make conversation. Rupert, under an indolent exterior, was thinking hard and littering the grate with his cigarette ends. After a while he made some excuse to leave with her. I could imagine him confiding in her and saying, 'Ought I to marry the girl?' and Squirrel saying, 'Of course not, you just ring up Billy Bolitho.' Billy Bolitho is a fashionable abortionist who always fixes up Squirrel's curettings for her.

I went on sitting there with my coat wrapped round me, staring into space, cold and frozen with fear. Then I went home and played Bach. Mummy and Sid were going to Confession, so I went with them, back to the stale incense smell and the virgin with the seven swords sticking into her heart, who never had to bother with problems like mine. There was a Catholic Truth Society box in the dripping porch and I managed to extract some leaflets that gave the Church's views on birth control and abortion, without my mother noticing. One thing's certain, I thought, no God-damn abortion if I can help it. Back home with Mummy, Sid and Alfred. Felt like an outcast among strangers. Never, never felt so sick. This is the first time I've felt that I was inside a nightmare, knowing that it was real. My legs ached and my body shivered.

Went to bed and lay curled up as if I was back in the womb. About midnight I felt a terrible pain in my stomach. Went to sleep and dreamt I was brought to bed of a fine boy, dark and perfect and the image of Rupert.

Monday morning, 4th

Still a terrible pain in my stomach. Could the quinine be working? It feels like – yes it must be!

Later

I could feel the blood coming out. I dashed into the bathroom, fell on my knees, thanking God again and again. I nearly wrecked the bathroom in my jubilant frenzy. The nightmare veil lifted and I suddenly saw the room with sane eyes again.

After Mass I ran to the telephone and phoned Rupert. 'Darling,' I said, 'I've got the curse!'

Rupert's voice was completely unemotional. 'Oh have you? Well that's a relief. You working this morning? OK I'll be round in half an hour.'

I suppose my nature must be very uncontrolled, for I would like to have fallen on his neck and cried with relief, but with Rupert it's not possible. He sheaths himself in icy calm after coming through any stress. In fact he came in without saying anything about it. The most he would offer after ten minutes of triviality was, 'What a bloody awful hour to ring me up – I was asleep! As a matter of fact,' he went on, 'I made a few plans last night. If all else failed I was going to have you kidnapped and forcibly aborted. I actually rang up Billy Bolitho and he said it was quite easy. He'd give me something that would bring your curse back in two days and cost me exactly five bob. I told him you wouldn't take it so he promised to give it to me in powder form so I could mix it surreptitiously into your food.'

I didn't tell him about the quinine because I felt rather guilty about it already. Had I been pregnant? Had the quinine worked, and if so, is it as big a sin as an abortion? I suppose I will never know. In any case both Rupert and I dropped the subject and he'll probably never mention it again.

Tuesday, 5th

Only two days left! I have a plan to get a night with Rupert before he goes, a whole blessed twelve hours of darkness. I was dreaming and yearning about this night so much in the summer that I was quite ill for wanting it. Supposing I say I'm staying with Thetis, who is alone in her flat – I can easily spend the last night with Rupert and he could join his ship the next morning. I don't want him to poke me or anything, I just want to go to sleep and wake up beside him.

Of course it did occur to me that after that pregnancy scare he might never want to sleep with me again, so I was doubly relieved when he said today what I'd been hoping he'd say, i.e. 'Do you think we ought to go to bed together again before I go away?'

I said, 'Yes, if you like', and told him about the Thetis plan.

'Good,' he said, 'but it won't be much fun in this ice-box. Try and get hold of some decent blankets and I'll fiddle around with the gas and see if I can make it work.'

I kissed him and was filled with peace and delight, but when I told Mummy she looked a bit strange. I could see she didn't believe me and later she just said, in an offhand manner, 'Oh by the way I don't think you ought to go and stay with Thetis tomorrow – they've been having a lot of bombs round there lately.' She must have seen my fury for she went on, 'After the war when you're living alone you can do as you please, but right now you'll do what *I* say!'

When I told Rupert he looked really huffy. 'That's a bit gloomy, isn't it?' he said crossly. 'I was really banking on having dinner with you on Wednesday and I've turned down another invitation for tomorrow night because I thought I'd be having dinner with you.' I really felt like crying. Rupert didn't seem to care, at least not in the way I did. Being done out of my night with him was hurting me like an aching wound and all he could think of was his dinner.

Wednesday, 6th

Rupert had lunch with his brother Robin. I don't know where he is tonight – with Squirrel probably.

This evening at home has been hell, lying in my bath, getting into bed, and every minute of it thinking – now we should be talking in the lamplight, now warming water on the stove to wash in, now a last cup of coffee before going to bed, and Rupert laughing at my cotton nightdress for not being glamorous enough. Then the lamp turned out, and the guns shaking the sky, and his warm body in my arms; peace and contentment so deep that nothing could break it. Oh how I hate mothers! Never mind, I can wait.

'After the war,' says my mother, 'you can do what you like . . .' After the war . . .

Thursday, 7th

Rupert's last day.

My mother attacked at breakfast, just as I was bolting down my last piece of toast, ready to dash over to the studio and find him.

'I'm worried about you and Rupert.'

'Oh, why?'

'I'm not as blind as you think Joan, I'm afraid he'll ask you to sleep with him because it's his last day and you'll be swept off your feet and agree.'

'But I'm not like that,' I lied glibly. 'I think things out for months ahead.'

'Yes, but you're emotional, and impressionable, and all your artist friends think nothing of immorality. Of course if you *did* become pregnant, I'd put your father on to him right away and he'd have to marry you!'

'Oh no he wouldn't, and anyway I wouldn't let him. Besides if I had his child I'd still get half his pay as his unmarried wife.'

'Good heavens, you seem to have thought it all out – I believe you *have* been sleeping together!'

'No,' I said shaking my head firmly – I had to get that look of horror off my mother's face. 'You see, Rupert is not a very highly sexed young man, and we're very happy being just friends.'

Just then the front door bell rang, and it was Dr Brownlow, come to examine me for anaemia – what a farce! He made me strip, looked me over, said I seemed a perfectly normal young woman and gave me some pills to encourage my ovaries. He must have realised at once I wasn't a virgin so I can only hope he doesn't tell Mummy – perhaps there's some kind of professional secrecy, like with the confessional.

Finally escaped to find Rupert in my studio cooking cauliflower and reading John Donne. After lunch we lay down.

'The last snooze,' Rupert said lugubriously. 'Where are those dreadful things?'

'They're in the *Life of Gaudier-Brzeska* – and I've got some Volpar Gels.'

A look of settled gloom had come over his face at the thought of the aforesaid 'things'.

'Do you think if we were to take all our clothes off old Madame A would come up?'

'I'll lock the door – it'll be a bit cold so I'll get some extra blankets.'

He took all his clothes off and looked fine, striding around the studio with an erection, brown all over from the Serpentine, except for his behind which was white as a shelled nut. I sat up in bed smoking a cigarette, and watched him with quiet amusement. Finally he jumped into bed, very cheerful, but as soon as he thought of those wretched French letters his cock fell down! Poor Rupert, it's a real fixation with him. I suppose the trouble with people like us is that we think too much – even in the middle of making love, both of us bathed in sweat and shuddering in each other's arms, Rupert's green eye will meet my grey one, the cold eye of intelligence bridging the blind gulf of passion, and we'll know that the boring old thought barrage is hard at work – think, think, think – and if I'm not thinking about Rupert poking me I'm thinking about something irrelevant like getting leaf-mould for my gum tree, or whether I've remembered to feed the birds.

Still he managed to make love for a bit, and it was gorgeous. I quite began to see what all the fuss was about.

Then, just as I was beginning to lose my sense of identity, I was dragged back to reality by Rupert giving a howl of anguish and collapsing on the bed beside me.

'Oh damn, damn, damn,' he was saying in a small strained voice. 'I've had it outside you!'

'Well never mind, does it matter? Don't be so gloomy!'

'I am gloomy. Every time I get going I seem to see a vast French letter floating in front of my eyes and everything goes flat.'

'What a shame. I am so sorry. Maybe we should use the Volpar Gels on their own.'

'No, it's not safe, the best thing is for *you to go to some clinic and get properly rodded up, ready for my next leave!*'

It was almost time for me to go. I could kill my mother for not letting me spend the last night with Rupert. I can't help feeling there's a lot to be said for the good old-fashioned double bed, where people sleep together all their lives. Prudey says one of the things that makes Rupert nicer than other men is that he looks so sweet when he wakes up in the morning. It's sad to think that she's seen him and I haven't.

There was so much for him to do, laundry to be fetched, trunks to be packed, so we got up and went out. Rupert was flushed and his hair seemed to have gone out of curl from fear. There seemed to be very little in his suitcase, just shirts and towels and a tin of cold cure tablets.

'You'll write to me won't you? Don't forget our code. Anything that has "quite" before it means the opposite, i.e. "our officer is quite a nice chap" means "fucking awful bastard".'

'I'll remember.'

'And send my pipe on to me.'

'Uh huh.'

'Hold my hand.' I held it and we walked to the bus stop and stood there quite unemotionally until the bus came.

After he had gone I walked back feeling very much alone and curiously self-reliant. Being alone doesn't seem to bother me now I've got something to wait for.

Friday, 8th

It seemed funny to have the studio to myself at last, for the first time since I'd rented it. On the divan the cushions were still dented from our last embrace, and smelt of his hair.

I realised almost with surprise that if I wanted to paint a picture today I could, so I put on Rupert's dressing-gown, very old and smelly, and set up a still-life – a copper jug and some apples.

Just as I was getting started Prudey turned up saying, meaningly, 'Well darling – how *are* you?'

I told her it had all been a false alarm, but worth it just to shake Rupert out of his damn complacency.

'And so beautifully timed, darling, the disclosure I mean, just when I was there to enjoy it!' Prudey is moving back from the country into a new flat in Covent Garden. 'Incidentally darling,' she said, 'you might let me have back that indecent novel of Henry Miller's – Zwemmer's have offered me ten bob for it which will just pay the removal men.'

I told her I'd lent it to Madame A, so we went downstairs to retrieve it, and found the old besom dancing around in her nightgown to the 'Merry Merry Pipes of Pan'.

'I had the most extraordinary dream last night,' she said, as the record ground to a halt. 'A bull came into my bedroom with its horns pointing straight towards me, the tips sheathed in rubber.' The poor old girl didn't seem to see the significance of this at all.

Prudey has asked me to tea as soon as she has settled in.

BOOK V

Letter from Rupert:

Joanie dear, this place is hell – am pretty sick and downhearted. I'm in a huge camp with 5,000 other men, *all* lower class!!! I'm in an awful gloom. It rained all yesterday and today. I've got a sore throat and we had to get up three times in the night so I am tired too. You know how depressing rain is in town, well here it's ten times worse, cooped up with a lot of babbling half-wits and nothing to do. My head feels as if it will burst. When I think the war may last for years, I think I shall go mad. It's like being in prison, cut off from everything that gives me pleasure in life, from the people I know and the things I like doing. Tell me – what does it feel like to be free and only to see and talk to people you like – I've forgotten. I curse myself for not having got a government job before it was too late.

If all goes well I shall see you again in three months – but not for long, not long of what I want and ages and ages of what I don't want.

I haven't spoken my special language since I've been here . . . I do miss it. The other men hate me 'cos I'm not lower class, so I've hired a hooge Cornish boxer called Joshua Pengelley to be my protector. I pay him 5/- a week and he stops them beating me up.

Perhaps this war will make a man of me – do you think so? People say I'm not grown-up. Is that true? Is it a good thing to be grown-up? I suppose it is sometimes. I sometimes think I'm lacking in strength somewhere but I don't quite know where. Please give me your opinion.

It would be wonderful to hear from a sane and interesting person again.

Well after all that, how are you Joanie dear? How are the birds, the oil stove, the gramophone and the leaky roof? Do you still wear Kirbigrips and glasses, now that I'm not there to tick you off? Do you still eat in the studio? Unless you've got a new boyfriend you must be very lonely. It must be very boring and gloomy for you. If Squirrel comes round for my clothes, be nice to her.

Please write to me soon. Lots and lots of love from Rupert.

PS. Can you rescue my bed from the ruins and get it over to Prudey's friend, Annie Rietti? She lives at 41a Rosetti Studios and she's going to look after it for me till I come back.

PPS. I think they're putting bromide in our tea! This will undoubtedly destroy the last tottering remnants of my manhood.

After I'd read this I burst into tears, though I was laughing at the same time. When I'd washed my eyes with cold water I went round to the post and tackled Rupert's friend Ralph, who is a stretcher-bearer, about moving R's bed. He says that once I have got it down on to the pavement he will hire a handcart and help me push it.

Saturday, 16th

Ralph is lean, dark and wolf-like with filthy clothes, untidy hair and a gap in his teeth. He paints when he is not being a stretcher-bearer.

The soldiers got the huge bed down from the ruins, supervised by a very gallant officer with a cane. On it were the same sheets I was seduced in. We loaded it on to the cart and began the long trek towards the Embankment, both pushing from behind, pretending we were a poor young couple who'd been bombed out with nothing saved except our double bed. It only needed a howling infant perched on top of the mattress, waving a Union Jack, to complete the picture.

Ralph is full of grim anecdotes about his work with the stretcher party. He finds he is beginning to look at everyone from the point of view of whether they'll make a good corpse or not!

Our conversation went something like this:

ME: 'I think our best bet is to go down Beaufort Street.'

R: 'My God, I could tell you some stories about that Beaufort Street shelter that would make your hair curl!'

ME: 'Or cut down Bramerton Street?'

R: 'If you'd only seen what I saw in Bramerton Street the night of the land-mine!'

ME: 'Or maybe Lawrence Street?'

'Christ!' howls Ralph, practically upsetting the bed. 'The bodies I saw in the Holy Redeemer Crypt in Lawrence Street!'

We finally reached Rosetti Studios and deposited the bed with the care-taker, then went back to have lunch at the Fulham Road Communal Feeding Centre. Burnt rabbit stew which was mainly potatoes and swedes, but it only cost 9d. Ralph leaned back with half-closed eyes and asked me if I was a good girl – he then suggested that he should teach me to play chess but I declined politely. I am v. suspicious of men who want to teach me chess – or anything else for that matter.

After he'd gone I went back to the studio. It poured with rain and the skylight dripped. Then the gas came on, so sat by the fire and made toast for tea. The birds are quite tame now and sit on my head. Missed Rupert terribly, it was the kind of afternoon you felt like sharing with some-body.

Monday, 18th

Answered Rupert's letter. I wrote:

My darling Rupert,

It was lovely to get your letter, but when I finally finished it the gloom was so awful I burst into tears. I'm praying you get your com-mission even if you are a villainous old heretic!

I'm not too lonely on the whole. I think most people are awfully boring unless you like them terribly and I've always been an unsociable person. Sometimes I feel almost happy when the studio's nice and warm and smelling of paraffin, and coffee's boiling on the stove, and rain dripping into six saucepans and a guitar record on the gramophone that sets the birds talking.

I should say the war will last about two years – and after that we can become normal and forget this 'damned interference' and go to Spain, and you can sleep all day if you like.

I hope the war doesn't *completely* make a man of you! There's a good deal of femininity in your nature which is very attractive, at any rate to me, who doesn't really like virile men. Of course if it cures you of hypochondria and laziness, then well and good.

No, I agree with you, you're definitely not grown-up, and thank God for it! I mean unless you want to be Prime Minister or something what's the point? It doesn't really get you anywhere, either in this world or the Kingdom of Heaven.

I wear your dressing-gown to paint in – my God, it's old and smelly! I'll try and be nice to Squirrel if she comes round for your things but she really scares the pants off me, being so small and glamorous. She makes me feel ten foot high and sticking out in all the wrong places.

Did you get the pipe safely?

Going to see Prudey now in her new flat. Lots of love, Joan.

PS. Took your bed over to Annie's.

PPS. Don't take any bromide for at *least* a week before you get leave.

Monday, 25th

Prudey's new flat is over the Covent Garden market. You fight your way through baskets of fruit and vegetables to a small opening in the wall of a warehouse, squeeze through and find yourself at the bottom of dark stone stairs leading to the studio. She spends the day there and sleeps on the floor at the Players Theatre during air-raids. The studio is entirely brown. Brown corduroy chairs, a big modelling stand, a model's throne used as a table with a big bowl of oranges on it. Also scattered around are abstracts by the Baron, very phallic, but Prudey is having special shelves built in the lavatory to accommodate them.

She was looking great in scarlet dungarees, with her hair done up in a handkerchief. We sat in her blue and red bedroom with a big window overlooking the market and drank coffee round the stove.

She has a new lower-class lover who is decorating the flat for her while the Baron is away. She also goes around with a 'set', the one that sleeps at the Players every night. I wish I had a set.

While we were drinking our coffee (which I put sugar into, although Prudey said I shouldn't), I showed her Rupert's letter and pumped her about his sex life with S.

'Well,' Prudey said, 'I don't want to depress you darling, but Rupert used to sleep with Squirrel a hell of a lot! You see, whatever else one can say against her she had one great thing, she was simply wonderful in bed. Rupert says it's because she's from Fiji. He was always telling me about how she used to put salt on his cock and how thrilling it was, and so on. And just because she's terrific in bed he'll probably never give her up.'

'But she's terrible,' I said. 'She's so Knightsbridge, and she has no intellect.'

'Oh I know, but Rupert always has to have two girlfriends, one for sex and the other to talk to. I suppose that one was you,' she added rather tactlessly. She squinted sideways at me. 'Aren't you terribly lonely without him?'

'Yes, I nearly went crazy at first. You get used to having them around don't you – and of course with Gerhardt dying too –'

Prudey looked at me in blank amazement. 'You weren't *fond* of Gerhardt, were you?'

'Very fond of him,' I said, rather taken aback by her tone.

She looked at me as if she had never seen me before. 'But you couldn't have been – it's *impossible!*'

I didn't say anything more because I didn't want to put myself beyond the pale in Prudey's eyes.

It was so cosy there sitting round the glowing stove that I didn't want to leave, but Prudey had to get dressed to go to the Players before the air-raid started. While she was darkening her lashes she told me about the last man she had slept with which was on Saturday. 'I feel awful about being so promiscuous,' she went on, putting Apple Blossom fragrance behind her ears. 'One of these days I'll really reform and live alone with a cat and play chess with myself all day.'

Today a surprise visit from Jo, just as foul-mouthed, just as coarse, and just as anxious to pinch my book on Picasso. His calling-up for the RAF has finally come through.

'Jesus wept!' he said, getting off his bicycle. 'This road's a real bugger isn't it?'

I asked him up to the studio and told him about the pregnancy scare which caused him much amusement. 'So Pussy had the pip eh? Why don't you use a—?' (Using some word I didn't understand.)

'A *what*?'

'You know, a bowler hat! Mean to say you've never heard of them? You go to a birth control clinic and get yourself fitted up for free.'

His next question was more to the point. 'Do you like fornicating?'

'Quite,' I said doubtfully, not wanting to discuss it with him. He looked at me scornfully.

'I guess you don't wiggle enough.'

I cooked him lunch and when he had polished off the last slice of apple tart he leant back in his chair, gave a lewd chuckle and said, 'Oh by the way, you have a new admirer.'

'Really, who?'

'A chap called Yurka Darkovitch who used to haunt my caff. I guess he must have seen you there. He's been boring me shitless all morning, talking about how wonderful you are.'

'Oh really? Where does he live?'

'Just across the road, number 21. That ground floor room with the dirty curtains. I told him to drop round and see you.'

'You did *what*?'

'Sure, you're lonely without Rupert, aren't you? He's a nice chap, even if he is a bit serious.'

So there you are, I now have Yurka Darkovitch haunting my doorstep. He is a fiery Slav with fine dark eyes and long lashes, brown skin with high cheekbones, a prominent nose and nice hair that flops over his forehead. Jo's right, he's a very serious type, mad keen on politics and, I think, very lonely. He's asked me to his room next Sunday for lunch.

Sunday, 1st December

Today I had a typical Redcliffe Road meal. My host met me on my way in the street and said, 'I have no knives or forks, please bring some.' When I returned laden with cutlery I was greeted by a fearsome smell of burning.

'It is Armenian pilaff!' says the harassed Yurka as we fight our way into the smoke-filled kitchen. 'But somehow the rice is all black!'

'So I see,' I replied without much enthusiasm.

Nothing dismayed, he decides to wash it, but then finds there is no collander so we empty the tea-leaves out of the filthy strainer in the sink and wash the rice in that, then dry it in a dirty tea towel. Even then it's a bit grey and damp, so back it goes into the frying-pan and burns again.

Hardly have we snatched it from the fire when the soup boils up all over the stove, and the blackout collapses, plunging the kitchen into total darkness. I was laughing so much that I couldn't speak.

Yurka wrestled with the blackout, muttering fierce Armenian curses, while I cleaned up the stove and put some chops on to grill.

After that we had black coffee in his living-room, which is also his bedroom. A single bed with a rug thrown over it and a couple of sagging armchairs. Bare walls, except for the spectral shapes, outlined in dirt, of mirrors, wardrobes and pictures belonging to the previous owner, grubby net curtains and a map of the Balkans over the mantelpiece. I have an awful feeling he is going to fall in love with me.

Wednesday, 4th

Rowena rings to say, in a dead sort of voice, 'The worst has happened, Billy Bolitho says I'm definitely pregnant. Can you lend me fifteen quid till Saturday?' I said I could give her six, which was all I had, because I know just how she feels, and if she doesn't have the abortion before Saturday it will be too late. I met her in Dean Street and we wandered down to Durand's in the icy cold for a *delicious* lunch. Christ, their pastries are good! Poor Rowena couldn't eat anything.

She says that her only other chance is to put lots of ether soap up her bottom for ten days. Billy Bolitho says it's tough going but infallible, but

R says, 'How will I keep it from my Mum if I go around smelling like an operating theatre?'

Sunday, 8th

Yurka is definitely improving. Today he took me to Mass at the Russian church in Moscow Road and then to Josef's in Greek Street for lunch, where he gave me stuffed vine leaves, apple strudel and Tokay. The bill came to 16/11! And he paid! Amazed at such extravagance, I asked him what his present job was and he said he did translations, and wrote occasional vignettes in the style of Chekov – doesn't sound too lucrative to me!

After lunch we wandered round a bit, then went to thé dansant at the Café de Paris with Ken 'Snakehips' Johnson and his band of grey-suited Negroes. I hadn't danced for a year. Gosh it was fun! I got transported into a kind of ecstasy. So did the band, thudding away at an ever-increasing speed, so did slim grey beautiful Snakehips with his refined nigger face, swaying lightly on the balls of his feet, while the band played 'I can't dance – I got ants in my pants'.

I apologised for not knowing how to dance properly, but Yurka said, 'What do you mean, you're a positive choreographic nymphomaniac!'

When we were too tired to dance any more we sat on the balcony. Down below were all the smart Jewesses and the tarts, and the barmaid from the Redcliffe Arms and Benny the Fulham Road tailor, all jigging away together on the packed floor like amoebas seen under a microscope. Yurka by now was showing alarming signs of infatuation. He heaved meaningful sighs, gave vent to the occasional groan, and uttered half-finished sentences, like 'well, well' and 'so here we are'.

I told him all about Rupert, which sent him into a frenzy of jealousy. 'What chance do I stand against the guitar and the Navy!' he shouted.

He calls me his 'black angel' and says I have 'it', whatever that may be. The trouble is I'm just not cut out to be a *femme fatale*.

Thursday, 12th

Yurka's gastronomic excesses continue. He called for me today all spruced up for the West End, hair cut and a piece of cotton-wool sticking to his chin. He has to shave several times a day because his beard is so strong. It's a pity about the hair-cut; it makes his ears stick out.

He was all set for what he calls a 'hot night out' so we had chicken paprika at the Leicester Square Bierkeller and danced to a nice continental band.

Unfortunately Y has been chucked out of his translating job and is not eligible for the dole because he is a foreigner, so I don't see my way to many more chicken paprikas.

After dinner he took me to St Mark's for night duty in a taxi and when we said goodbye he clicked his heels and kissed my hand. His manners are quite amazing, he won't sit down unless I do and when I get up he leaps to his feet in a most unnerving fashion – how different from you know who!

Friday, 13th

Tea at Quality Inn with Rowena, who is still haemorrhaging pretty badly after her operation. Welsh rarebit and chips. R felt sick but ate it just the same. After tea we saw *Waterloo Bridge*, all about a girl who becomes a tart and then won't marry Robert Taylor because of dishonouring his regiment. What silly things girls do on the flicks!

Coming out into Leicester Square a huge bit of shrapnel whizzed on to the road in front of me and I was running to pick it up when another bit cracked down just where we'd been standing! All the people sheltering in the cinema made a rush to grab, but we got there first. It was still hot when we picked it up.

Felt very sexy going home in the bus. I get like that some days, especially on buses.

Sunday, 15th

Scratch anyone in Redcliffe Road and you find a painter. Y has now asked if he may 'have the honour of doing my portrait in sepia'. Went to his squalid room where he plied me with cheap port, then arranged me in a chair by the fire.

All the time he was drawing me he kept up a running commentary. 'You have an inquisitive nose and a lustful underlip. You are capricious in the extreme, irascible, cunning and sarcastic, you are one of those women who can be utterly wicked and utterly candid at the same time. I know the type, it is very dangerous. Forgive me if I ask you a personal question. Are you in love with Rupert?'

I said 'Yes', and went on to explain how things stood between us. That I loved him but he didn't love me because he kept another mistress.

'Oh, so you mean you don't give yourself to him?' Yurka asked hopefully.

'Oh yes,' I said, looking into the fire, 'I do.' To my horror I began to cry, only by now it was getting too dark to show.

'My God, these Englishmen,' Yurka burst out, 'how I hate their attitude to women, how I loathe it! Why don't you put him to the test, tell him it's either you or her. Have the courage to find out if he really loves you. If he doesn't then you're well rid of him.'

I said I hadn't got that kind of courage.

'I knew a girl in your position once,' said Y. 'He left her, as was inevitable, as Rupert will leave you. And afterwards you will be pursued by a great many men, and you will succumb – oh yes you will, because you will be so bored and disillusioned. Then they in turn will bore you, but you won't have the guts to break free and so it will go on – *un cercle vicieux*.'

He kept giving me more and more port, so I had to throw it on the fire while he was out of the room. It flared up nicely. Nevertheless I was drunk enough to tell him everything. All about Gerhardt and Jo, and Rupert and I socking each other in the street, and how I sat for Leonard in the nude. This seemed to make him very angry. He said I must have no sense of honour or aesthetics – a woman who stoops to a thing like that will stop at nothing.

'But it was only a business deal,' I protested.

'If I were to become a gigolo that would also be a business deal!' he snarled, and went on to tell me that I had been debased and degraded, that bad company – Jo and co. – had resulted in a kind of fragmentation of my personality – in French, *avilissement* – causing me to see everything of spiritual importance as just a huge joke. I was, in fact, incapable of real love. I was enraged by this and acted like dames do on the flicks when they're seething underneath, chain-smoking and drinking strong tea without milk and giving him dagger-like glances. How dare he say I don't love anyone!

Yurka just looked out of the window and chewed his nether lip.

I suppose the trouble with Yurka is I have no feeling of kinship with him.

Wednesday, 18th

Yurka continues to call and I continue to treat him cruelly. I suppose it's just because I used to suffer the same myself. It sort of gets it out of my system to vent it on him.

He sits and watches me, sucking his long cigarette holder and drinking more black tea than I should have thought any human being could hold, while he talks about the Balkans. He seems obsessed by the wretched things. Today I got so fed up I found some old cheese that stank appallingly and gave him my mousetraps to fix, hoping it would keep him quiet for a bit, but just as he was fixing the last trap something must have slipped, for there was a fearful yell, and Yurka was hopping madly round the studio, the mousetrap hanging from his fingers like a Laurel and Hardy film.

I laughed so much I cried, while Yurka stood staring at me huffily and sucking his fingers. Then, thank goodness, his mouth began to twitch too.

'You devil in skirts,' he gasped, 'what are you trying to do to me? If I were to fall seriously in love with you I should be finished!'

It was a bit of a test really. If he hadn't thought it funny I would never have seen him again.

I write Rupert a running commentary on Yurka. I hope it's keeping him amused.

Thursday, 19th

Squirrel called to see about storing Rupert's things.

'Why do you want those awful prints?' she asked, pointing to *The Birth of Bacchus* and *Minerva visiting the Muses*. I couldn't tell her that when

I was being seduced by R and opened my eyes in pain and bewilderment they were the only things I could see, grey in the brown gloom.

So we packed everything else into a kit bag and bribed a soldier to carry it to the number 14 bus stop. Everyone whistles after Squirrel. Some girls manage to look cute no matter what they're doing, others look ugly when they're not looking beautiful. I belong to the second category, Squirrel, I'm sorry to say, belongs to the first.

She and her sister Bosie live in a typical glamour-girls apartment, with stockings and suspender-belts drying everywhere and the radio playing jazz. When we arrived Bosie was sitting at her dressing-table putting oil on her eyelids. She is v. glamorous and native, and was wearing plaid trousers and a transparent white shirt through which her breasts stuck like spears.

The phone kept ringing, and it was always men asking them out to dinner. Rupert says it's not because they're tarts, they just have to do it to balance their budgets. I suspect Squirrel must love Rupert – she kept playing a record called 'Oh, there's a lull in my life'!

Monday, 23rd

Lunch with Y, who now wears a clean white shirt every time he goes out with me, and an amazing brown sports outfit with a silver-buckled belt. He has also taken to smoking a long pipe like a German student, shaves within an inch of his life and baths so often he has burst the geyser.

Over lunch he showed me photographs of himself taken on the Riviera – glad to see he hasn't got hair on his chest, as I'd feared.

I wish I was dead, I want Rupert so much, so why do I care whether Yurka has hair on his chest or not? Life is very puzzling. I suppose the fact is I like to pose and dramatise myself with Yurka. I thoroughly enjoy playing the roles that he offers me, and that's all there is to it.

After lunch we went to a News Cinema. Italy is about to crack, it seems. A crowd of Greeks was shouting 'Zitos y Hellas!' as Himarra was taken.

After some bad coffee we walked back across the Park. Talk, talk, talk, I just don't listen any more – whenever the Balkans are mentioned I turn pale. Talking and smoking, walking through Green Park from Piccadilly to Chelsea, nothing but talk, talk, talk, and when there are no more cigarettes he sucks at his long holder between sentences.

And I am so responsive, so sympathetic, I make all the right noises in the right places, my face composed in a mask of tolerant gentle understanding, and not a word do I hear.

An amazingly rude, bad-tempered letter arrives from Rupert, saying I am behaving childishly over Yurka, and ticking me off like a Father Confessor. He says that what I am doing is the thing that men hate most about a girl, and I'd better cut it out immediately or at any rate not tell him about it, as it makes him very cross. This put me in a bad mood for the rest of the day.

Tuesday 24th, Christmas Eve

Snow. The whole of Redcliffe Road is smooth and white. Yurka uttered cries of joy and danced a gopak down the street, leaving fantastic tracks behind him. Whenever he sees snow his mind rushes to Cossacks charging over the moonlit ice, himself at their head, all in black with a single diamond at his throat. His favourite fantasy is to be a young Russian cavalry officer, one of those who make it a point of honour to light a cigarette while they're charging. They fight with light fencing swords and never kill their opponent if they can only wound him – then, when he kills them, they die looking surprised.

I sometimes wonder if Rupert has made me so cynical that he has spoilt me for other men.

Christmas Day

Woke to carols on the wireless, and an orgy of present-opening. I got Damon Runyan, Wodehouse and Thurber, a book on Surrealism, a record by Scarlatti, some new green trousers, milk chocolates and cigarettes, a book on chess problems, cold cream and stockings.

Mummy had to go on duty, so Yurka took me to the Brasserie for lunch. We had turkey and plum pudding, and I wore my new pink shirt and grey beret and was looking particularly glamorous and old. He wore a brown double-breasted overcoat with a velvet collar and dark-grey knitted gloves. His nose is always pink in cold weather.

Over lunch he trotted out some real old chestnuts to go with the turkey, like 'You are the sort of girl who should be met at dawn by fifty outriders with drawn sabres glittering', which added to my enormous appetite. I drank quite a lot of beer too, although I can't stand it, in the hope that it might make me tight. It didn't.

Walking back to the post for night duty the pubs were all full of happy, drunken people singing 'Tipperary' and the latest Army song which goes 'Cheer up my lads, fuck 'em all'. I spent a dreary night in an unheated room, sleeping in my clothes on a hard bed. Talk about Christmas night in the workhouse!

Sunday, 29th

Lots of excitement. The post had issued me with a tin hat so I could go out in the shrapnel, which is just as well as things turned out.

I'd been having lunch in Yurka's room when the first guns began. He said I must wait till there was a lull – only there wasn't one, for, as the papers said next day, 'At half past six the full blast of the Nazi fury hit the capital.' I'll say it did! This was the night they set the city on fire, including six churches. St Bride's and St Laurence's were gutted, the Guildhall burnt out, and St Paul's only just escaped. The aeroplanes never stopped and the sound of their engines dive-bombing was deafening.

We stood on the steps of number 21 watching. The sky was already red as blood – it looked as if half London was on fire. Flares lit up the street like daylight and the stars were all put out.

Yurka stood behind me and pulling back my head he kissed me till I thought my lips would break. A bomb began coming down making a noise like an express train.

'For God's sake, get in!' he said, pushing me into his room, and shutting the door. 'You can't go home in this.'

He pressed me up against the bedroom wall, and began making love to me while I stood rigid, staring straight ahead. The room was dark except for the fire. I'm sorry to say I was a bit nervous, thinking that each bomb was for us, but Yurka didn't seem to notice. He was in ecstasy. I thought, at all costs I must keep quite still or he'd see how nervous I was, and tried to control the trembling muscles in my leg.

'Now do you believe I'm serious?' he asked, his eyes boring into mine. Too true I did, as something that sounded like a land-mine exploded right outside our front door. As he pushed me down on to the bed I could hear the glass falling out into the street from the windows in Redcliffe Road, but he was oblivious, whispering about my Giaconda smile – a grimace of sheer terror, probably – and framing my face with his hands.

Then he kissed me for a bit, and I was actually beginning to enjoy it when he had to ruin everything by asking, 'What are you thinking about?' – the most maddening question in the world. I didn't want to hurt his feelings by telling him.

By now he had slipped off my blouse and was kissing my shoulders, and I found myself automatically stroking his forehead and caressing his hair, just as if it was Rupert. My God, the old familiar gestures and positions – how I hated myself. But Yurka was like someone possessed – he kept saying 'don't speak', and pressing his fingers over my lips like a man in a dream.

I didn't let him actually seduce me – my trousers were well fastened up with safety-pins, as luck would have it – but I felt sorry afterwards for leading him on. 'You are pitiless, my dark angel,' he sighed wearily as he went off to make some strong tea. The raid seemed to be quietening.

As we sat by the fire with our mugs he looked at me with a funny sort of smile and said, 'You really don't know what you're missing. If you were to let me love you it could be something that you would neither forget nor regret for the rest of your life.'

Round about seven there was a lull in the firing, so I put on my tin hat and Yurka borrowed an old French sentry's helmet from O'Connor, the warden, and we went round to Milborne Grove where we were welcomed with cries of relief. Everyone fell on our necks and we were plied with sherry. I could see Mummy and Sid were enormously impressed by Yurka's beautiful manners – Sid particularly took a shine to him and in no time at all they were locked in a furious debate on – you've guessed it – the Balkans!

Friday, 10th January 1941

Letter from Rupert at last, saying he was only teasing and not to be huffy. He says he hopes he doesn't meet Yurka, 'cos he's sure he'll giggle. He gets leave as soon as he has done four weeks at Chatham. 'No doubt,' he writes, 'your grandma's historic couch will be glad to bear the weight of a fighting man again.'

Saturday, 1st February

Poor Yurka bores me more and more. The fact is, I prefer men to be slightly caddish and knock me around, and not to love me too much. I like men who think they are God.

Rupert, of course, has all the self-assurance in the world – never looks foolish or put out, is completely at ease with the universe and thinks himself a lord of it. He belongs to that class of person that is adored by shopkeepers and servants – 'Dear master Rupert, such a fine lad he's grown into!' – and Rupert smiles his gentle smile that means nothing, and strides on in glorious self-absorption, six foot of indolent golden manhood in a spotlessly white unbuttoned shirt, his trousers just a little too big for him. There is a kind of aura about him that suggests green cricket fields and white flannels, though God knows he detests all sport and exercise. He has that irresistible lazy charm that often goes with decadence and overbreeding – just like my father.

How different from the dark heat and turmoil of Yurka! For the last few weeks I have been avoiding him as much as possible, so as not to rouse false hopes.

It's now February 1941 and we are expecting the invasion by the spring. The night bombing is not quite so bad, and Mussolini has been defeated in Greece and Africa.

Mummy has suggested I should join one of the Women's Services. Naturally I'd prefer the Wrens, but she doesn't like the idea of my being at a seaside town when the invasion comes. The main thing of course, to my mind, would be to get away from Mummy and Sid and lead my own life.

I was cleaning out the birds' cage when the bell rang. Half-way down the stairs my knees gave way and I knew it was Rupert. I had to lean against the wall to open the door.

At first I thought it was a stranger standing there, thin, brown and clean-shaven, with shadows under his eyes, wearing a filthy old mackintosh, all brown and worn like a sandstone statue against the white driving snow.

'Hello!' He smiled.

'I knew it was you,' I said.

'I'm very ill,' Rupert said. 'I've been through a great deal. Is there any tea?' And so he came back.

He looks much younger with no beard and with his cheeks all hollow and sunken.

'How did you get leave so soon?' I asked.

'Oh that's easy,' said Rupert. 'I bribed the Master at Arms ten shillings.'

He looked very ill. Old Madame A came up, wearing a black satin Moorish cloak which she called a Hidalgo, and welcomed him back like an only son, giving him cigarettes and half her butter ration. Then I went out and bought doughnuts, meringues, custard tarts and coffee for tea. How lovely it is to have him home. After tea we lay under a rug on the sofa, and I fell into such a state of peace and joy as I'd forgotten it was possible to experience. What a relief to be able to return love a hundred-fold after that queer abortive affair with Yurka where I never permitted myself a single responsive movement. Our mental contact is still as complete as before. We still have the same values and laugh at the same things.

While we were still snoozing the doorbell rang. It was Yurka, and I threw the key down to him. He must have thought that Rupert was still in Chatham. Half-way up the stairs he heard the give-away cackle, but by then it was too late to retreat.

The room was in disorder, the bed crumpled, and Rupert's and my shoes were neatly disposed by the side of it. Yurka's eyes darted to and fro like rapiers. I made some tea to relieve the tension and Yurka and Rupert sat on either side of the fire discussing Greece and the Balkans.

From there Yurka progressed to God, absolute truth, patriotism and so on, sitting on the edge of his chair, all burning and intense, swinging his latch-key like a flail.

Rupert, reclining like a grandee, said he didn't believe in absolute anything and all he really wanted was a villa in a hot country and plenty of down-trodden peons to beat, and exercise his *droit de seigneur* on.

Yurka's eyes flashed scorn, and he said that personally, he was going to join the Greek Volunteers to see a bit of action. R merely looked incredulous and then with great deliberation began putting on his shoes. 'One two buckle my shoe,' sang Rupert cheerily as Yurka watched in cold fury.

I went down to borrow some cigarettes from Madame Arcana, and when I came back he had gone off without saying goodbye. Then Rupert went off to see Squirrel.

Wednesday, 5th

Rupert's younger brother, Robin, turned up today demanding lunch. He is a born sponger like Rupert. He is about nineteen with floppy blond hair, receding chin and pointed ears, rather like a goat.

'I thought I'd better warn you about Ma,' he told Rupert, 'just in case you were thinking of visiting her. She thinks Doctor X is after her again, and the whole house is crawling with workmen setting up booby traps – you can't walk upstairs without setting alarm bells ringing.'

'Christ,' Rupert said, 'thanks for warning me. I'm going down there on Thursday.'

'Oh, and the mice are back.'

'What?'

'The mice in her wooden leg. She says she can hear them squeaking.'

Later on when Rupert went off to see Squirrel again, Robin and I had a little talk. He told me that their mama is not really looney, just eccentric, and thinks Queen Alexandra is still on the throne.

'Rupert, of course, is another matter,' he went on, fixing me with his prominent blue eyes. 'You realise, of course, that he is a conscientious hedonist with schizophrenia?'

'What on earth's that?'

'Oh,' says Robin, who has been reading Freud, 'it's a sort of madness where you can't feel any emotions at all. It's a very dangerous condition and unless something comes along to snap him out of it, he may never find himself at all.' He looked at me sideways. 'What he really needs, of course, is to find himself a soul-mate.'

'Oh,' I said, 'has he got a soul?'

Robin didn't reply and soon after he went off to firewatch on top of a shop in Bond Street, leaving me alone and strangely depressed.

Wednesday night

Thick soft heavy snow. I was on night duty. The thought of Rupert sleeping with Squirrel never left me, and I couldn't sleep for jealousy plus indigestion. I had the most awful stomach ache after the canteen dinner and kept seeing vivid photographic images of R's head lying on Squirrel's brown bare arm. I once saw a picture of her in the nude in Lilliput, so I knew what she looked like, sleek and brown as a native, with round shining breasts, laying aside her Knightsbridge veneer with her clothes.

Monday, 10th

Sunny day like spring, blue sky, wonderful feeling of exhilaration. The snow has almost melted and Rupert is back from his ma's. We met at Hyde Park Corner, where the crocuses were just beginning to show in the wet grass. That afternoon was one of the happiest we'd ever spent together. We were two minds with a single thought, or rather lack of thought.

Rupert's latest ploy is to challenge Yurka to a duel, and when he fires his pistol, one of those things you get in crackers that make a rude noise will shoot out and hit Yurka on the nose. He wouldn't think that funny. Rupert's idea of fighting a duel is to wait until his opponent is busy saluting him, then pick up his sword with both hands and cut him in half.

After lunch at Bertorelli's we went to a peculiar French pub in Dean Street, called Berlemont's, full of French tarts and Air Force pansies, and sailors trying to look like Jean Gabin and smoking in a very French way. Monsieur le patron has wonderful moustaches, and a nice-looking daughter behind the bar. It seems rather an arty place with photos of prize fighters and vaudeville stars stuck on the walls. When I told R I had never had absinthe he insisted on my trying a Pernod. It's a pale yellowy-green colour and you drip water through a lump of sugar into it through two pipes and it tastes like aniseed cough mixture. About half-way through the glass a delicious melancholy pervades your soul, and you begin to know how all those French poets wrote their stuff.

We were turfed out at closing time and wandered round the Charing Cross Road in a blissful Pernod haze, wishing we were in France where we could have sat in cafés getting drunk the whole afternoon. The pavement sang beneath my feet as we weaved our way down Covent Garden and called in at Prudey's studio. A dreadful arty girl called Fifi was alone there.

'Prudey is at La Coqu*ille* with Ber*tee*!' she drawled affectedly. 'And after lunch Ber*tee* is painting '*er* and after that 'e is coming 'ere to sculpt *me*!'

'Oh my God, goodnight!' said R, backing away in alarm. We fled. Prudey's new set is really too much.

Tuesday, 11th

Robin brought over his psychiatrist, Dr Evans, for lunch. Rupert and I were crawling round the floor playing bears when they arrived. Dr Evans simply can't get over his good luck at stumbling on such a rich vein of looniness as the Darrow family. We drank lots of sherry and then Rupert, who hates psychiatrists, lapsed into his usual infantilism and played 'puff-puffs' on the hearthrug while Dr E asked us searching questions. It seems that Robin is a masturbator and Rupert has dementia *praecox*, while I am a masochist with repressions!

After they'd gone R and I went back to Covent Garden in search of Prudey, and found her sitting on a couch beside the emaciated but glamorous Fifi, who appears to be having an affair with her. She was idly modelling a clay face on a small board and eyeing Rupert with naked antipathy.

Prudey seemed embarrassed by our presence and hardly spoke. Rupert, a little put out, talked his most potent brand of nonsense. The lesbian asked with cold disdain, 'Do you always talk like that?'

'Ah – yes actually,' says R. 'It took me years to learn it.'

'Why do you bother?' snaps the lesbian, but gets no change from R, who goes off into high-pitched cackling laughter and sings nursery rhymes to Henry Miller. When the strained silence continued he turned his attention to the *objets d'art* on the wall.

'What's that?' he asked, pointing to a piece of twisted aluminium adorning the mantelpiece.

'That,' says the lesbian, after a few impressively consumptive coughs, 'is the Baron's "Wunschtraum". It's what everyone subconsciously wishes for without knowing it.'

'Can't say *I'd* fancy it,' says R.

A deeper chill fell on the assembly. Rupert went on eating huge slices of cake spread with strawberry jam. I could see that Prudey was torn between her old tenderness for Rupert and the high intellectual standards demanded by her new smart set. She must have known quite well what Rupert was thinking under his maddening mask of nonsense, so in desperation she began boasting, trying to prove to us how thrilling her new life was – the parties she'd been to, the people she knew and the painters she'd sat for. Rupert said nothing, and soon her narrative fizzled out. When we got up to go she hardly said goodbye.

Rupert and I, on top of a homebound bus, laughed helplessly, tearing Prudey to pieces and tacking her together again, discussing her with feverish interest like two gossiping old women. We are a secret cabal against the world and against all stupidity other than our own. Sooner or later I must force Rupert to marry me, whether he likes it or not.

Friday, 14th

St Valentine's Day. So much for my romantic dreams. Instead of a Valentine from Rupert, he announced that as he was seeing me at lunchtime, it was only fair that he spent *all* his evenings with Squirrel! I was so cross that I kicked him, and he put me under his arm and spanked me, saying, 'You forget I'm immensely strong after the galleys, like Ben Hur.' Nevertheless he must have realised he had behaved like a cad, because he agreed to take me out to dinner, just this once.

Went to the Majorca, a basement Spanish restaurant all green and watery, with dark ferocious waiters. Rather rashly I ordered shellfish and rice and spent a frenzied fifteen minutes battling with things in armour with long whiskers that sent the rice hurtling over the tablecloth. Rupert watched with malicious enjoyment. We drank a whole bottle of excellent red wine, called, I think, Olivias, smoked a Ramon Allones cigar, very classy, black tobacco with a white ash. Getting a little tight by now but terribly happy. Rupert has such nice ears. In profile he looks rather like Toby Tortoise, now he has no beard. The bill was 39/10!

Back in the studio we put up the blackout, and lay down on the bed with the rug over us.

'Take your clothes off.'

I slipped the top of my dress down, and Rupert ripped everything else off with one pull and chucked it on the floor, then in two seconds was naked himself. 'Much better without clothes,' he said, and lay down beside me. I was feeling sexier than I'd ever felt in my life before, when to my amazement he said, 'Mustn't seduce you though – mustn't seduce young girls when they're drunk!'

'But why on earth not?'

'*Enfants terribles,*' he muttered, 'lots of little Joanies toddling around calling me Poppa – goodnight! No bloody precautions – *enfants terribles!*'

'But why can't you use something; there's still a couple of packets left inside *Gaudier-Brzeska!*'

He looked at me quite crossly. 'You know I can't stand those awful things – why haven't you got yourself fixed up? Why are you so selfish? I never have this sort of trouble with Squirrel.'

After that it was all ruined as far as I was concerned. We made love for a bit but he pulled out before the orgasm.

'My God, I hate coming like that,' he whimpered. 'It's no pleasure at all. Christ, when I think of the dangers of being nude with you! You know I haven't got over that fright you gave me a few months ago. Never again, I told myself, and here we are! What on earth came over me, I must have been crazy!'

I got up and slowly started to dress – my clothes were all in one piece, the stockings dangling from the suspender belt. It looked squalid and I felt awful. I really must get myself fitted up, I thought.

Wednesday, 19th

Rupert in a bad mood. He can be very strange sometimes. He bought us two eggs for lunch, and when he couldn't find a clean saucepan he just took them and smashed them on the floor, then sat without saying a word looking furious, miserable and hungry. I went out and bought two more, and fried them. Gradually the smell roused him. 'Those for Rooples?' he asked, looking like a naughty child.

'Yes,' I said, 'and you ought to be ashamed of yourself with the price they are now.'

'I get rushes of adrenalin,' he said, 'but I'm better than I used to be. Anyway I'm fed up 'cos I can't seduce you properly.'

Fearful raid on, so I left early to go on duty. Flares silhouetted Lots Road power station and there were bombs across the river – Battersea as usual 'getting it'. Lots of casualties at the post. Bombs at Beaufort Street, Limerston Street and St Stephen's Hospital (22 killed), also Paulton's Square. Our air-raid shelter has a big new sign on it in black and white saying 'POISON GAS'.

Friday, 21st

Yesterday had lunch with Rupert's artist friend Ralph, the one who helped push the bed. He is currently considered a pariah because he is prostituting his art by making huge plaster casts of teeth, modelled from dreadful yellowing specimens, and selling them to a dentist. He has even bought a shiny blue suit on the proceeds, and looks like a dentist himself.

We talked about ways of making money and Rupert thought I should write awful articles for women's magazines, things like 'Why are your elbows like nutmeg graters?'

Ralph's mistress cooked a ghastly meal, fish-head soup with ground maize in it, and we ladled it out with a tin mug and ate it on the scrubbed kitchen table. Ralph is a Marxist, and is very shocked by my Catholicism. He says Christ was a bad yogi, and why don't I read something called *The Coming Struggle for Power*.

Afterwards we strolled back to my place, and lay down on the bed and made love. For the first time it seemed to me that Rupert realised I was actually *there*, that he was aware of me as a person and was making love to me knowingly, with his mind as well as his body. We're all right now, I thought, we've made contact, we're safe. We've bridged the gulf and fixed the cable.

He was looking down at me broodingly, as if he really saw me, and there was tenderness in his hands tracing the lines of my face and in his eyes that looked into mine quietly, not laughing any more. I thought that perhaps after all he really loved me in spite of pretending to have no heart. The minutes slipped by into darkness and we are still unable to leave each other. Thank God, I thought, now at last I know he finds some real satisfaction in me. He was lying with his arms behind his head, arms that are smoother to kiss than any woman's, when he said, 'I feel huffy!'

'Oh, why?' I asked in dismay.

'Because I'm tired of pretending to seduce you through about six layers of the most incredible underclothes and I can't seduce you properly because you won't take precautions – although you *know* how much I hate having to do it myself. Anyone would think you wanted to be pregnant, the way you carry on – you're like those dreadful lower-class mothers who write to the *Daily Mirror* –' he put on a high-pitched cockney voice – ' "Even though we did 'ave a bomb on our 'ouse, not to mention a bomb on me stummick when I was expectin', they can't stop me doin' my bit and now I'm the mother of a luverly boy. Of course he 'asn't got any 'air or fingernails and one of 'is feet's missing, just the same I 'ope to have six or seven more before this war's over!" ' He fixed me with a steely gaze. 'Well you're not going to have them with me. It's not so much that I can't stand children – which I can't – but you've got to have money, then you can get someone else to look after them and ignore them yourself.' He got to his feet purposefully. 'Now Joanie, you get yourself properly rodded up! You've got lots of sexy girlfriends who simply bristle with contraceptives so why don't you ask them about it? If I wasn't such a vague chap I'd have made you do it months ago. I don't know how I've stood for this nonsense so long!' He faced me across the table. 'But honestly, don't you think it's about time I went to bed with you properly again?'

'Yes – I guess so.' Then, in a small voice, 'I suppose you couldn't wait until after the war?'

'No, I certainly could not!'

'OK,' I said, 'I'll do it right away. I'll ring Rowena tomorrow.' He smiled and patted my cheek. 'Good,' he said, 'I'll come round early tomorrow with my guitar.'

But later Rupert rang me to say he'd been called back to Chatham at once. 'Return forthwith,' the telegram read. 'Signed Commodore'. 'I'm doomed,' Rupert said. 'That means my ship's come. Get my guitar from Jo's and look after it for me. I think some money fell out of my trouser pocket tonight. You'd better keep it. Oh dear! Aren't you gloomy? I am! Do you think I'll ever come back? I'm leaving at five tomorrow morning.'

I felt stunned for the rest of the evening but it wasn't until this morning when I woke up and thought of how Rupert had said he would be round early with his guitar, that I had to go into the bathroom and cry and came into breakfast with swollen eyes.

Now I'm the last survivor of the old set in Redcliffe Road and soon I'll be gone too, as I've definitely decided to join the WAAF.

Tuesday, 25th

My mother says she is giving notice to Wheeler and Atkins that I leave the studio at the end of next month. Yurka is leaving London too. I saw the van taking away his furniture. He turned up at Milborne Grove this afternoon, saying he couldn't possibly leave without seeing me.

Meeting him again made me very nervous and irritable. Something is wrong with the shape of his head. It's straight at the back instead of round like Rupert's and he's got hair growing out of his nose. And his being foreign and laughing at the wrong sort of jokes – all these things irritated me to the last degree! If his sleeve as much as brushed my arm, I shuddered and moved away.

'Goodbye *ma belle amie*,' he said as he kissed my hand, gallant to the last. 'I am not eighteen so I shall not die for you!'

I never want to see him again. Why did I ever let him touch me? I'd like to cut off my lips and flay off my skin – Jo and Leonard too! I feel sick when I think of it.

Saturday, 1st March

Laura Cavendish came round, just out of the sanatorium and looking lovelier than ever. She has to go to bed after tea on account of her TB. I told her all about Rupert, Prudey, Jo, Yurka, and the rest. She seemed amazed and said, 'Well my innocent little friend, you've certainly got yourself in with a queer lot.' But she seemed glad to hear I'd got seduced. She's been living a very dreary existence herself, shut up in a sanatorium. I love Laura, she is really a terribly attractive girl.

One of my birds has died. I buried it in the window-box among the dead geraniums. Old Madame A says she saw the bird's ghost the night it died, coal-black and huge as an ostrich.

Sunday, 9th

Last night the raid was bad – it was the night they hit the Café de Paris, where Yurka and I danced.

I felt dreadful about it; the bomb fell on the band killing them all except the drummer – gentle, magnetic Snakehips Johnson with his thin elegant face and his joyous rhythm – the best swing band in London gone.

They were dancing to 'Oh Johnny' when the bomb fell. The couples on the floor, killed by the blast, stood for some seconds as if they were still dancing, just leaning a little – then fell, heaped on top of one another.

Today I masturbated for the first time. It came about almost involuntarily. I was thinking about Rupert and when it became unbearable my thoughts started to turn themselves into acts and soon I found a way to bring it about. I was crying out loud with short, hoarse gasps.

God, I thought, coming to myself again and lying back exhausted, what a dreadful business, what am I coming to? I really mustn't let it happen again.

Monday, 10th

Made an appointment with Billy Bolitho for my cap – dreadfully exciting! I felt glad Rowena was coming with me. It's an embarrassing thing to have to go through with, but I've promised Rupert.

We waited a few minutes in a pokey little waiting-room. Rowena took out her knitting and said, 'My new boyfriend's a Brahmin, he's going to take me to India – did you know that yoga's terribly good for sex?' Then Billy Bolitho came in and I eyed him with fascinated horror. This beautifully turned-out man with a terrible face has perfected his technique – he is the perfect woman's doctor, kind and suave, who makes you feel completely at ease. At the same time he made me shudder with repulsion. Impossible to think of him as a man apart from his job.

'She doesn't want a . . .' Rowena put in quickly. 'I mean she isn't going to have a –'

'No, thank God,' I said. 'I just want to have a cap fitted.'

'A cap. Now tell me, have you ever used any type of cap before?'

'No, none.'

'So what have you been using then? Volpar Gels?'

'We – I – well we used French letters,' I said rather apologetically.

'I see. Well, of course they're safe, but they're not very nice things, are they? Incidentally, how much does your friend pay for his French letters, do you know?'

'I don't really remember – about 10d each I think.'

'Ah, well, that's all right then. Some people pay three or four shillings for them, which of course is utterly scandalous! Now tell me my dear, have you ever been pregnant?'

'No,' I said firmly.

'Good – now let's see what we can do for you. If you don't mind taking off your things behind that screen?' The things one can come to! I took off my clothes and lay down on the couch with my head on a small pillow, and he came over and said, 'Would you mind lying over on your left side? A little bit more please. And the leg up. Like this.' He wears an immaculate grey suit, and his eyes are too close together. I think he's kind and probably sincere – he believes that to forbid abortion is a crime – but he is horrible, quite, quite horrible.

He bent over me and inserted his finger. 'Unfortunately, you have an exceptionally long vagina, and an exceptionally narrow one too. It's going to be rather difficult I'm afraid. Still, we can try.' He fiddled around for a bit, very uncomfortably. 'Now I think this one will be a little bit too small for you – tell me if I hurt you, won't you – now let's see if you can get it out for yourself. You'll find it rather difficult without practice I expect.'

I certainly did! No matter what contortions I went into it was no good. I did everything except stand on my head, and still the beastly thing eluded me. When he had got it out for me, he told me he hadn't got quite the right size so he'd have to write off for it.

We emerged feeling stifled, and took deep breaths of fresh air as we ran across Green Park. 'Well, my dear,' I cried, in my 'Bolitho' voice, 'apparently I've got a terribly long vagina!'

'I know, so have I darling – isn't it hell?'

We ran laughing across the park, and had a good blow-out at the Old Vienna Café, with Rowena telling me all about the lesbians in Paris and how the courtesans have boudoirs fashioned like dungeons, with iron manacles and whips.

Monday, 24th

Letter from the WAAFs at last. They order me to report immediately to Victory House for my medical and end, 'Yours sincerely, Commandant in charge of WAAF recruiting. PS. Do not come when your period is in progress.'

Went to Knightsbridge and saw old Bolitho, but the cap hadn't come yet.

Tuesday, 25th

Ten a.m. Victory House.

Was interviewed by glamorous officer called Pearson, the first WAAF to be decorated for gallantry. She was charming to me, asked how long I'd been an art student and whether I'd enjoyed it and so on. Then she put me down for special duties which are very hush-hush – map-plotting and so on – and sent me in for my medical to see whether my eyes were good enough.

After sitting in a vast room full of girls all shaking with nerves, one or two with suitcases and in tears, I was sent by a corporal into an inner room and made to sign a paper saying I had never suffered from fits, bed-wetting, suppurations of the ears, St Vitus's dance, or venereal disease. I wrote 'no, no, no' till my hand was exhausted but noticed my neighbour, earnest and sweating, giving each item her full consideration, with pen poised doubtfully over sleeping sickness.

I finished the list and was pushed into another room, weighed, measured

– ' 'at orf, coat orf, be'ind that screen' – and wrapped in a dirty towel while my hair was searched for nits.

The next stop was a canvas booth with partitions, where a bored and weary woman murmured without opening her eyes, 'Please pass water for me, dearie,' and handed me a bottle. I managed to oblige her after a strenuous effort, poured the result into a UD milk bottle and marched back through the crowded room carrying it in front of me with some embarrassment. Horrified mutterings from the girls who were waiting. 'Cor! Look wot they make you do!'

'Looks orlright to me!' said the lady who'd first seen me, holding it up to the light, then, turning on me again, 'Dress orf, undies orf, be'ind *that* screen!' There I was confronted by a lesbian-looking doctor, completely hung around with stethoscopes. 'Undress!' she said in a deep bass voice.

'Completely?' I asked nervously.

'Completely!'

She then punched and pummelled me, listened to my heart, hit my reflexes with so much force that my foot shot up and nearly knocked her out and finally said, 'Well, you seem pretty fit,' and then with biting scorn, 'And what brought you in then? Mr Bevin?'

'Not at all,' I said huffily, 'I just got sick of my job. I was at the first-aid post and there didn't seem enough to do.'

Finally, after someone had stuck tubes down my ears and blown down them, I had the dreaded eye test. Of course I couldn't see a thing on the chart without my glasses, but I fooled them because I had learnt lots of it off by heart while waiting my turn.

So I was passed, registered as fit for special duties, and told to be ready for call-up in five to six weeks' time.

Bought some Maltesers and went to the Forum to see Peter Lorre in *Island of Doomed Men*. Wish I could write about important things instead of the nonsense that I do. Sometimes I feel the significance of what is going on in the world, but even then I can't put it into words. This war is probably the biggest thing that's happened in history, one half of the world trying to destroy the other. Nothing will ever be the same again – we are gradually reaching starvation point as rationing becomes stricter. Civilians, for the first time, are living under fire. We are expecting the invasion in the spring, poor Rupert's going to sea and may be killed, bombs fall every night and so on, but I don't feel any different to what I did in peacetime, except that I'm a bit happier.

In Zwemmer's window today I saw a huge print of Picasso's *Guernica*. It made me feel something of the awful chaos in which we live. I was considerably moved, but normally I just don't think about it.

Thursday, 27th

Great day. Had my cap fitted and found I could get it out quite easily this time. It's a sort of a twist and a wriggle; you soon get the knack of it, like getting winkles out with a pin. In fact I got it out right first try, much to Bolitho's admiration.

He was very sweet and kind and said it should be almost impossible for me to get pregnant wearing that cap, but I should use a Volpar Gel as well. Also to be careful in the WAAF and hide it when they have kit inspection – if necessary put it where it's meant to go until the danger's past!

Then he told me it would be a guinea, wished me the best of luck and off I went with it in a little box.

Sunday, 30th

Cleared out the studio ready for the removal men, a very gloomy business. Said goodbye to old Madame A and the empty room. Dreadful feeling of finality and of the old life being over.

As I left, the night was illuminated by a flare which lit the whole of London, dropping very slowly down and occasionally letting fall showers of burning sparks. Four others also dropped slowly in a parallel line to the east, turning red as they came lower.

Monday, 31st

Called up for WAAF – I go in a week, 7th April. All of a sudden I feel dreadfully depressed. Rowena and I went to the Galeries Lafayette and bought tarty underwear.

Tuesday, 1st April

Sid and Mummy stayed over at the Grail House last night, so was alone in London for the first time since the blitz started. Went up to Sid's bedroom and read all her juicy books about psychopaths and sexual abnormalities and the symbolism of dreams. There was one by Kraft Ebbing that got me so excited that I remembered something Leonard had told me and took a candle from the little altar. Now I suppose I'm completely beyond the pale as far as the Church is concerned.

Wednesday, 2nd

Went to say goodbye to Laura, and sat beside her while she had dinner in bed, and shared her fish. She says she is desperately lonely and has lost touch with everyone. She doesn't think she'll ever get back into the swim again or meet people, because this damned TB makes it impossible for her to go out in the evenings. She sees no one but old women.

I showed her Rupert's photo and told her all about him, and described our affair and how it came about. Laura is several years older than me. It seems unfair that she should be lying in bed like a pink and gold angel while I tell her the facts of life.

Thursday, 3rd

Letter from Rupert. Amazed and impressed to hear that I am now a member of the Armed Forces – and of my own free will! He says he's going to be posted to Canada but he's waiting for his ship.

Last week he went on manoeuvres and spent most of his time in the crow's nest, covered in icicles with only his nose sticking out of his balaclava. He says for the most part the sea always looks the same – no trees and no cake shops. Poor Rooples.

Sunday, 6th

My last day before joining the WAAFs.

I wanted to spend it with someone I loved, and who had also loved Rupert, so I called on Prudey after lunch. She was still in her blue corduroy dressing-gown that she sculpts in, so I played the Mozart C minor quartet, while she bathed and dressed. Her toilet is simple in the extreme – she wears no underclothes, summer or winter, except for a thin pair of flowery cotton pants. Over that go her violet jersey and scarlet dungarees, red socks with black shoes, and a blue sheepskin coat with a scarlet lining. All the reds are just slightly out of tune with each other.

Today her hair was brushed straight across and fastened by a slide. Although she brushes it for hours every day and slaps brilliantine on it it still sticks up like the hair of a young schoolgirl. She covered her raddled boy's face with Ardena powder, painted her lips scarlet, and said, 'I wish I knew how to make up!' Prudey is thirty but you'd never think it. I don't know why I love her so much.

'What did you think of Fifi?' she asked. 'Didn't you think she was turribly, turribly pretty?' She has a new voice now that she's going out with smart people. 'Guess I'm gonna get TB,' she went on. 'Guess I should have a blood test or something. Everyone who sleeps with Fifi gets TB.'

I suppose this was meant to shock me, but it didn't. 'What's happened to the Baron?' I asked.

'Oh we had a terrible row when he came back to find I'd put his sculptures in the lavatory. How about you, are you still faithful to Rupert?' When I said 'yes' she seemed amazed.

'What a good little girl you are. I was never faithful to the Baron for a minute. No, I tell a lie, I did manage it for a fortnight once, but the reaction was so dreadful that I slept with the entire Players Club in rotation for a month afterwards. My dear it was *dreadful* – such guilt! – but the fact is, I just adore love-making. You see, since I've had my neck stretched I've actually started having orgasms, not every time of course, but when you think how frigid I used to be . . .!'

'But darling, how wonderful!' I exclaimed, falling into her jargon. 'But what's your neck got to do with it?'

'God knows, angel, something to do with the nerves in the spinal column, but pretty good going for me don't you think? Of course it's very embarrassing now at the Players not remembering whether I have or haven't been to bed with someone, because if I *have* it's all right for him to give me lobster thermidor at the Lansdowne, but if I *haven't* and he *does*, then of course I feel I *have* to! Oh dear, I do hate these moral obligations, don't you?'

We got to the Players Club about seven and I met Prudey's 'set'. Very smart and chi-chi and talking bitcheries, most of them drunk or on Benzedrine. I felt nervous, then I drank huge whiskies and felt better. The toast was 'The WAAFs, God bless 'em'.

Prudey got squiffy on gin and vermouth, and kept squinting at me through the smoke-haze with her Chinese eyes, as if she was sizing me up. I lay back against the black velvet seat and smiled at her almost reassuringly, as if she was lost or something. Prudey puzzles me, she is so nice really, but I hate her set. I suppose I'm afraid of them.

After a while the show started and we had Peter Ustinov doing Lisalotte Beethoven-Fink – a masterpiece – and then Alec Clune's recital of 'The Bachelor and the Doll'. He was wearing a dead-white make-up, red wig, and a stove-pipe hat with a black overcoat, too short in the sleeves. His style was sinister and brilliant.

Afterwards they cleared the stage and I danced the polka with a bearded Polish dwarf who came up to my waist. As we one-two-three-hopped round and round I lost my shoe and he talked about art.

'You know who did the wall decorations? It was Felix Topolski, a very clever man and a very brilliant artist – but of course a Pole, and all Poles are brilliant.'

The lights were lowered and we waltzed to 'L'ombre s'enfuit, adieu mon rêve'. Prudey had given up hope of a lobster thermidor, so we had egg and chips at a small, dirty French café in Soho.

Home alone with a full moon shining on wet streets. Sad music from behind shuttered windows. Number 34 now demolished to the first floor, the bedroom and studio open to the moon. I went up the few remaining steps and stood in the corridor in the dark.

Saw a series of ghostly pictures, Gerhardt lying on the couch at Prudey's party when I was young and green, me climbing the stairs to sit for Leonard, sweating with nerves, Rupert running down in his clean white shirt with his bathing things under his arm. Oh that house, I certainly love it!

Goodbye to London. Goodbye Fulham Road and Redcliffe Road, De Cock's, Deschuyter's and Hutchinson's. Goodbye to the Forum Cinema and Cavaye Studios.

Nothing will ever be quite the same again.

BOOK VI

Monday, 7th April

GLOUCESTER

This afternoon reported to Victory House, along with forty other miserable recruits, all clutching our suitcases. We were conveyed to Paddington in camouflaged cattle-trucks, hurtling from one wall to another as we went round corners, and arrived in Gloucester at six p.m.

The depot is like a huge town of green huts and straight white roads on which WAAFs and Airmen wander in the failing light. It has its own cinema, churches and shops, and in the centre a huge parade-ground with a flag-post.

For what seems like hours we were marched and counter-marched up and down the camp for no apparent reason with a corporal shouting 'left right left right', carrying our tin mugs, cutlery and heavy suitcases.

Then to the FFI hut (Free From Infection) to have our heads searched for nits. Sprightly conversation of the girls as they run their fine-toothed steel combs through our hair – 'How about you, Cecily? Get any? I got two!', 'Oh good show Marjorie' and so on.

Next stop the NAAFI canteen for supper – great chunks of meat with tomato sauce and slabs of cake, all on the same plate. It seems a cheery enough place, with a broken-down piano. For the first time since we arrived we began to thaw out and feel more cheerful. I sat next to a rather nice girl called Samantha, who looked even more lost and desperate than me.

'This is just like hell isn't it?' she said. 'You know, like that line in Milton, "smells and sounds and sights unholy".'

We sleep twenty-eight in a Nissen hut with no heating, and our pillows are canvas nosebags stuffed with hay. At the end of the hut is a small curtained cubicle where our sergeant lurks and entertains her friends late into the night, with much coarse laughter and clinking of glasses. She is an Irish lesbian with her head shaved at the back, v. hearty and full of *bonhomie* towards her girls. She slouches up and down between the beds, her hands behind her back, each step seeming like an arrested fall.

Her goodnight speech to us on the 'Spirit of the Hut' ended with the immortal words 'And if I finds any of yez leaving STs where you didn't ought to leave them, there won't half be a steam, be Jasus!' By then poor Samantha, who has the bed next to me, was in a state of semi-hysteria.

I slept with two thick jerseys over my nightie. Samantha slept with her pearls on, because they're real and she says that if she takes them off they will die. We slept very badly. It was bitter cold and the hay pricked our ears.

Wednesday, 9th

Up at six thirty – hot water for washing in the Ablutions hut over the way. Then huge breakfast of cereal, treacle, bacon, beans and enough butter for a week's ration, washed down with lots of sweet strong tea. Thus fortified, we troop into the gym for physical training. Modesty is thrown to the winds as we are drilled by male PTOs in our 'black-outs' – i.e. long, black service knickers, and no stockings. All of us – long thin housemaids, huge fat cooks and outraged debutantes – hop up and down in our underwear. We are a macabre sight, everything that can shake or wobble does, and everything that can come loose, comes loose. It's very embarrassing.

Next we are issued with our uniforms – extremely unflattering, particularly the cap, and brassieres made to fit *expanded chests* – no casualties on the parade-ground that way! Then straight out on to the square for drill. Most of the afternoon is spent marching to the commands of a bellowing sergeant, thousands of WAAFs, their buttons glinting in the sun, like some huge Nazi youth rally.

In the evening our first lecture on constipation, nits, STs and scabies – this is called 'Hygiene'. Then a very smart officer comes on and talks about discipline. It seems we are now under military law and can be shot! Quite a few of our batch have decamped already. They took one look at the barrack square and legged it through the gates, heading for home.

Officers keep begging us not to pack up and leave in despair, they say we mustn't judge the WAAFs by this dump, and things will be quite different once we're posted. It's a *marvellous* life, and so on! Personally, I rather like this dreadful hysterical schoolgirl existence. The girls in our hut are great fun, particularly the ones from London – Lyon's nippies and Marks and Spencer's shop girls. We southerners live in terror of a tough gang from up north, run by a large fierce woman known as Ma Kitchen, and inevitably there are scapegoats. A lot of time is spent 'avoiding Gladys', a poor Welsh girl who had nits in her hair at the last inspection, and who tags around after us, looking miserable.

The corporals are a lax and jolly lot, the officers pleasant and very upper class, but the sergeants are low and bloody-minded.

As for me, I'm beginning to feel rather like a piece of meat going through a sausage-machine, from which I'll eventually emerge about five foot tall, plump, pink and well-groomed, and leaning forward permanently at an angle of 45 degrees, with one hand at the salute.

Thursday, 10th

Last night we had an audition for the camp concert in the NAAFI. After five WAAFs had sung 'Trees' and seven had sung 'Only Forever', a great fat sergeant got up on to the stage and recited 'There are fairies at the bottom of my garden', jumping up and down and flapping her arms. I've never seen anything so incredible in my whole life – but anything can happen in this amazing place.

Friday, 11th

My first pay parade. Got ten bob and tried to look suitably grateful. Still very cold, but apple blossom is flowering between the huts.

We're getting to be seasoned warriors now, our discipline is terrific. You should have seen the suicidal precision with which we marched, three abreast, straight into a stone wall the other day because we hadn't heard the 'left wheel'!

It's been pouring with rain and the parade-ground is covered with deep pools, which we try to skirt when on the march. 'Go through it, you slackahs!' yells our sergeant. 'A little watah won't hurt you!'

The food gets better and better. This morning for breakfast we had stewed figs and baked beans on toast with *real* coffee!

In the afternoon we had some free time, so Samantha washed out her knickers and put them on the line outside the hut. When she came back after tea there was a note pinned in their place saying, 'These drawers are now the property of Aircraftman Jenkins. If you wish to reclaim them please report to hut nine at eight o'clock.' Poor Samantha is very upset as they were her best knickers.

After tea, a lecture called 'Current Events'. A blank map, and an officer with red chalk. With a short bitter commentary she filled in the last few years with red for Germany. Soon the map was nearly all red. We cried, till our faces were stiff with tears.

Tinned pilchards on fried bread for supper. Someone played the NAAFI piano, and lots of WAAFs jitterbugged with each other. Then at eight o'clock, our big treat of the week, the camp cinema showing *Tarzan of the Apes*. The cinema is very small. You can't see and you can't hear, and sometimes you have to share a stool, but, as the airmen only go there to pinch WAAFs' bottoms, it doesn't really matter. All of our hut sit crowded together at the back, because, as Ma Kitchen so rightly says, no bugger's feeling us for thruppence.

After the film Samantha and I ate kidney pies and drank bottled beer in bed – a strategic blunder as I afterwards discovered. Two pails are placed at each end of the hut, so, sweating and shivering alternately, I got up to be sick, finally fainting across Ma Kitchen's bed.

In a week's time we go before the Special Duties Board to see if we are temperamentally suited, or something. We are all very apprehensive about it; they probably let off a pistol behind your back to see if you jump.

Saturday, 19th

After hours of sitting on wooden benches with our feet up on the pipes, alternately freezing and sweating (and how some of us sweat!), the Board finally materialised.

Instead of ten commodores sitting round a table letting off pistols as we'd expected, there was just one colossal woman, very formidable, but nice and friendly. I've got through as a plotter and so has Samantha and several of my friends. Apparently we all sit round a huge table with a map of England and the French coast, pushing little aeroplanes around with sticks to show the advance of German bombers, and our fighters going up to meet them – just like in the war films! It sounds v. exciting.

We plotters have been moved to a new hut, run by Corporal Levi, a fourteen stone Jewess with a big nose and an Eton crop. Every morning she gives us our routine orders for the day, sitting on her bed in black satin pants, cutting the dead skin off her heels with a pair of nail scissors.

While waiting to go to our new hush-hush camp for training, we work as Runners, which means we are general dogsbodies, cleaning the officers' quarters, lighting their fires and polishing their shoes.

Night duty is hell – you have to go round the entire camp inspecting the blackouts, and the ground between the huts is like the floor of a crater. What you don't trip over you fall into, and when you return, a semi-cripple and nervous wreck, you are sent stumbling over miles of ploughed field to get some damned officer her hot water bottle!

When we were finally settled cosily round our stove in the dark, listening to the bombs on a nearby aerodrome, who should come charging in but Corporal Levi, lit up like a church at Easter, the hut positively reeking with her gin-sodden breath. She was in full cry after some wretched girl who'd left an ST in the Ablutions, and had lost her after chasing her round the huts in the dark.

'My God!' she screamed. 'The way you bloody women let down the services, leaving your filthy STs in the Ablutions hut, it's a pretty shaky do, my God it is!' She went on like this for hours, like a record that's stuck, her language getting worse and worse. We were all terribly tired and didn't know how to stop her – this sanitary towel business seems to be a phobia with corporals. Anyway, the upshot of it is that we're all confined to camp until whoever left the wretched thing there owns up. At least it was found behind the bath – one turned up in the washing-up machine last week!

Saturday, 26th

The station dance. Great excitement, everyone hoping to get off with a pilot. Wings, of course, are the thing; if you don't have wings you don't stand a chance, but the men turned out to be dreadful, all mechanics and technical chaps. The hut was small and crowded, boiling hot and smelling of Brylcreem and sweat.

We had a bet in our hut to see who could get the most – I got five, each one worse than the last, and a date for tea at the Regal, which I ought to keep but can't, because our hut is being kept in over the ST scandal.

Samantha is laid up with a sprained ankle. She fell over a slag-heap running away from a mechanic after the dance last night.

Tuesday, 29th

Great joy – our papers have come through, and we're off to Leighton Buzzard in two weeks' time, for training.

Just before we go we are going to get a long weekend's leave, so I have written to Rupert to see if he can join me in London. The only problem is that Mummy and Sid have fled to the country and are staying with the Grail Ladies at Eastcote almost permanently. It seems that the last big raid on the 19th was too much for their nerves. Anyway, Milborne Grove has been shut up as one of the walls is still unsafe after the last bomb.

I went to see the Welfare Officer and she gave me the address of a place called the Catholic Women's League for Service Girls – sounds pretty ghastly but any port in a storm!

The days drag on. Every morning now, at eight a.m., an army lorry comes to take us to a hush-hush camp where we learn about plotting.

Wednesday, 30th

Inoculated today. Lots of WAAFs fainted on parade. Rupert writes that he is still in Portsmouth waiting for his ship but he can come to London more or less when he likes while he's waiting, although he could be recalled at any time. So he thinks he'll definitely be able to make it! That would be just too wonderful for words.

Thursday, 8th May

Our last day! After a nervous address from the Padre, we went through the gas van. My mask was too loose, and made rude noises through the rubber bits behind the ears, like a horse farting.

In the afternoon we had the grand passing-out parade, marching past at the salute in an icy wind, after which the CO, who is quite ga-ga and has no back teeth, gave us a singularly uninspiring address.

Big emotional goodbyes in the NAAFI, then a lecture on syphilis and gonorrhoea, and what happens when a WAAF gets in the family way.

This was followed by the grand finale, a talk called 'Esprit de Corps'. We rather liked this one. The main theme seemed to be keeping the pilots happy and off the booze, giving them a home atmosphere and so on. We all felt we could do this rather well.

Friday, 9th

CATHOLIC SERVICE WOMEN'S HOSTEL, LONDON

Came up to London feeling strange, excited and alone. All the time I had been marching around on that awful parade-ground I had been thinking about Rupert and making love to him in my head.

Arrived at the hostel just as it got dark, to find a telegram waiting for me, saying to contact him at Rosetti Studios. The name sounded familiar – wasn't it where Ralph and I took his bed?

Nearly choking with excitement I ran all the way, not even bothering to change out of my uniform. As soon as I saw Rupert wearing his mother's fur coat and jumping up and down with excitement at the sight of me I felt all right, and all the old feelings of tenderness and intimacy came back to me. He danced around me, pulling my hair and calling me 'WAAFI'. In the kitchen beyond I could see a huge woman making stew, wearing patched corduroys, a Breton smock, and a Tibetan cap perched on top of masses of dark hair.

When this monumental statuesque creature turned towards us, a frying-pan full of black sausage still in her hand, I saw that as well as being fat, or at any rate in spite of it, she was also colossally sexy and attractive. So this was the Annie that had Rupert's bed.

'Hello,' she said, 'you must be the famous Joan we've all been hearing so much about.'

As she was talking I slowly realised that Rupert must have been on leave for quite a few days already. I had a quick look around but I couldn't see any other room – so where was he sleeping? I was still pondering this when there was a tremendous rushing noise like Niagara Falls.

'Oh don't worry about that,' Annie said cheerfully, 'that's Robert Savage from upstairs – every time he washes his teeth, or has a pee, the entire liquid contents hurtle through my room in a pipe.' She thumped the frying-pan of sausages on to a wooden table, and began cutting up a large loaf of home-made bread.

'Who's Robert Savage?' I asked.

'Oh,' she said, 'he's a randy sculptor. He'll probably fall madly in love with you, you're just his type.'

During dinner, Rupert told me lots of funny stories about the Navy. He's an officer now, and has actually shot down a Dornier! He says to the ratings 'Scrub those floors scum!' and they reply 'Fuckin' RN, fuckin' RN!'. He is still trying hard to pretend he is barmy so that he can get invalided out as a schizophrenic.

Went for a booze-up at the Lord Nelson in the King's Road. It was great seeing peculiar people again after the Services. Rupert played with his new toy, an Ashanti war-drum, which has only two notes and you play it with your hands. He says he walks around with it in the blackout, frightening people. He taught us to drink something called a Matelot's Embrace, which is beer with a tot of rum in it – v. intoxicating. When the pub closed he walked me back to the hostel, still playing his war-drum. Outside the door we kissed and clung together.

'Do you remember,' Rupert said, 'this is like the lovers under the trees at the end of Redcliffe Road – I used to shine my torch on them. It's really not my thing at all you know, kissing girls outside front doors at midnight.'

I said there was something I'd read about in Harris's *Life and Loves* that people could do standing up and Rupert said, 'Mmm – I'm very keen on that – but I'd never dare do it with you!'

'Why not?'

'You terrify me – you're so virginal.'

'All right then,' I said, 'go on home to Annie.'

Nevertheless it was nice to see how keen he was to spend the night with me. I kissed and hugged him and his ears were very cold. Then I went in to my Catholic Service Women's bedroom which was even colder, and smelt of Jeyes Fluid.

Over my bed is a picture of *The Sacred Heart*, all wreathed in thorns and dripping with blood. Warder-like women patrol the corridors. How am I going to work it so that we can sleep together?

Saturday, 10th

Lunch with Rupert at Annie's studio. Met R. Savage the randy sculptor who shot one look at me and said, 'God you're beautiful!' He had wild frizzy hair covered in stone dust which stood up almost like a mane all round his head. He has been given a commission to sculpt a bee bath for Bim Bravington. What on earth is a bee bath? I can't imagine. Anyway he seemed very chuffed about it.

Annie, meanwhile, is painting something on commission – a very fierce-looking French freedom fighter brandishing a gun, with a dead German lying at his feet. Also cooking meat balls and potatoes for lunch.

During lunch Rupert and I had one of our religious arguments, just like old times. 'Everyone knows,' he declared, 'that when Christ wasn't making up to John he was whopping it into Mary Magdalene!' So of course we fought and had great fun and I threw my baked potato at him, but he went on saying the most terrible blasphemous things about Holy Communion and transubstantiation. I couldn't possibly write them down. I laughed in spite of, or perhaps because I was so shocked.

Then we all had a little snooze together on the same bed, because Savage has promised to take us to a real Chelsea party tonight and we wanted to be in good form.

It was supposed to be fancy dress, but as it turned out no one took this very seriously. Robert put a wastepaper basket on his head and stuck some flowers through it, and I put on a black artist's beret with a floppy tie. The only person who really went to town was Rupert, who wore a huge picture hat with flowers on it, and we made him up with lipsticks and mascara. He primped around holding a feather fan, looking absolutely ravishing, just like Lily Langtry. Annie wore a long black evening dress, with her hair piled on top of her head and a black mantilla.

Then we bought some bottles of wine from the Black Cat Café and set off for 410 Fulham Road, which is like a little Italian village composed entirely of studios. The party was being given by a white-robed Indian poet in a vast studio, with a grand piano and a radiogram that never stopped playing all night. Off the studio was the bedroom, shrouded in darkness, with necking couples piled two deep on the bed, and off that the bathroom where people went to be sick.

Everyone was very, very drunk except for us, and for the first quarter of an hour we felt as if we had suddenly strayed into a lunatic asylum, with everything distorted and out of focus.

When a man came up and asked me to dance I said, 'No, wait a minute until I get drunk.' Then I had a tumbler full of Marsala, some gin and lime, another glass of some sweetly-scented Cypriot wine, and a glass of beer, and then I was drunker than I'd ever been in my life before. The people round us came gradually back into focus and seemed to be behaving in the only right and natural way possible, and the evening began.

We four were the lions of the evening because we were new blood, and everyone was talking about us. Annie seemed to have annexed Rupert, so I went off with Robert, who said I was a swell girl. I put my arms around his waist and we began to dance. 'Rupert,' he cried in his funny rather high-pitched voice, 'Rupert old chap, she's going to love me! God what have I done to deserve this?' I was laughing and laughing, I felt so happy. My arms and legs floated out at beautiful inconsequential angles from my body. Just then the air-raid siren went.

Over Robert's shoulder I could see Annie, very drunk, her Queen Mary figure, like some vast and awe-inspiring statue, rocking to and fro on its plinth. Then I saw Rupert pick her up and whirl her round his head, her feet narrowly missing the chandelier each time she whizzed round. Her hair had come down and hung in a heavy curtain over her eyes, her evening dress had split from top to bottom and all we could see were her white lace drawers.

Two lesbians were doing a scarf dance, and some smart women in evening dress were dancing in trilby hats and yashmaks. We could hear loud thumps in the distance, but no one took any notice.

I was still dancing with my arms around Robert's waist when I heard stifled chuckles behind us and suddenly, amid cheers and encouraging cries, we were propelled into the dark bedroom. Rupert banged the door after us.

The room was filled with faint murmuring sounds coming from supine bodies. Sitting up I said in faint bewilderment, 'What a funny place! Why are we here?' Someone on the bed laughed in a kindly, rather pitying way.

Robert started to kiss me and undo my buttons. Then suddenly he stopped and seemed to come to a decision. 'Come on,' he said, 'let's get out of here.' He pulled me up and dragged me back into the lighted room where Rupert and Annie were sitting with their arms around each other on the sofa beside the piano. We lay on the floor underneath it and Robert began kissing my neck and making love to me. All I could see beyond the piano were a pair of large bare feet belonging to Annie, and Rupert's black Navy shoes beside them. Suddenly there was the most tremendous whining noise followed by a loud 'crump' and the piano above my head shook and vibrated with a noise like a harp.

The buzz of the party died down for a moment and then swelled up anew, and from where I was lying I could see people's feet begin to twitch and stamp again. It was round about then that I began to feel very ill indeed. The room started to spin round and I realised I had to be sick.

The next thing I knew was that Robert and Rupert were carrying me across the room and through the bedroom into the bathroom, where I sunk to the floor and let my head droop over the lavatory pan. From far away I could hear Robert saying, 'She's not human, she even looks good when she's puking.' I remember feeling vaguely gratified and very much better for having got it over with. I'd never been sick from drink before.

Rupert held my head and saw that my hair didn't dabble in the water, while Robert wiped my face and held a cold sponge to my forehead. I was amazed and touched by their lack of disgust at my condition. I kept apologising and saying how awful it was but they seemed to take it as part of the day's work. Then I returned refreshed to the party and we all did the conga. Soon I was feeling happier than I had ever been before, not because of Robert or Rupert – just beautiful impersonal happiness like a dream that nothing could penetrate. Every time I asked someone what the time was they said 'quarter to nine', but I knew it wasn't true.

Just to prove I was still in control of my legs I did thirty-two *fouettés* till I could hardly stand up, my pink snood flew off and my red skirt spun right out.

Then I was sick again and this time it was Rupert who held my head and

Robert who sponged my face, while the Indian poet, who was very nice and kind, made me drink hot water to bring it up. By now the guns were going like mad and the bombs seemed to be coming closer.

The last part of the evening was spent with Robert and I underneath the sofa necking, Rupert and Annie necking above us, just like a four-decker sandwich.

Rupert kissed Annie and let his hands slide caressingly over her swelling black velvet bosom. As I watched his lips kissing Annie's – familiar lips and familiar kisses – I felt the first and only prick of sad reality penetrate my happy golden haze that night.

I think Robert must have thought he was going to sleep with me because I heard him hiss into Rupert's ear 'I say old boy, how are you off for FLs?', which made Rupert hoot with laughter. Meanwhile Annie was stuffing Rupert's pockets with hundreds of our host's cigarettes. It was now about two o'clock and people were beginning to go. Robert was kissing my hand and saying he'd give anything to be as young as Rupert again. Annie, with childlike and elephantine deliberation, turned two somersaults and then remarked that someone had been sick on her cloak. The party was over.

Outside all hell seemed to be let loose. I'd never actually been out in the streets in such a raid before, but we were all too drunk to care.

Robert supported me while Rupert staggered along under Annie's weight, her voice echoing down the Fulham Road. She was bellowing out a little song which went 'Ermintrude, Let some sperm intrude', and under every lamp-post she stopped and kissed Rupert.

Robert seemed a bit put out when I told him I had to get back to the home for Catholic Servicewomen, but he behaved like a perfect gentleman and saw me back here, in spite of the bombs which sounded terrifyingly close just over by the river. Rupert and Annie had disappeared without saying goodbye.

Sunday, 11th

Rang up Rupert. 'Well Joanie,' he said, 'what an exhibition! Never have I seen anyone as drunk as you were! What I could see of you, that is, when you weren't necking with Robert under the piano!'

'Oh my God,' I groaned, clutching my aching head, 'what a terrible night!'

'Mmm, it was a bit rough,' R said. 'They blew up the Houses of Parliament and Westminster Abbey, not that you were in any fit state to notice of course.'

'To hell with Westminster Abbey,' I cried, 'what about you kissing Annie!' *He* claimed it was just my drunken fantasy and denied it. I knew better, and felt a bit doubtful about going round to Annie's for lunch, despite Rupert's insistence.

Annie was wearing a magnificent pair of red corduroys with a hole in the seat. Robert was in rather well-cut tweeds with a flamboyant tie. It was really quite a shock seeing him now that I was sober, he looked so old. In the light of day everything was quite different and there was a great deal of restraint between us.

Perhaps because of my hangover, or because of lack of sleep, my perceptions were heightened and I kept noticing little things between Rupert and Annie that hadn't seemed significant before. I kept noticing how he said and did things that were the same as when he first became interested in me. All the little signs I knew so well, the intensely personal familiar things that at the time one thinks are for oneself only.

At one point he let slip a mention of something that happened three weeks ago – some party they'd been to – and I realised he must have been up on leave before without telling me.

Annie is Rupert's mistress. I can't think why I didn't realise it before. What can I say about it? There's nothing to say.

I am sure he isn't in love with her, nor she with him, but she has his bed which is big and comfortable – the bed that I lugged half across London – and Squirrel's away and so am I, and as he has nowhere else to stay he sleeps with her. That's the way Rupert lives, taking whatever comes along provided it suits him.

Just to watch them together was agony, so I pretended I needed some fresh air and took a walk in Ranelagh Gardens. I walked around as long as I could, looking at the trees in blossom and feeling sick with rage and misery. When I got back it took Annie rather a long time to answer the bell, then she opened the door and I saw her rumpled hair and the state of the bed. Annie saw my look.

'Rupert's little snoozes,' she said, 'you know.'

'Yes,' I said, 'I know all about Rupert's little snoozes.'

I stood half in and half out of the doorway, not knowing whether to come in or to go. I could see Rupert sitting on the bed, looking at me like a stranger. In the end I stayed out of sheer embarrassment, not wanting to make a scene.

Annie did the washing-up, and I played *The Beggar's Opera* on the piano while Rupert lay on the bed. I could feel he was very angry about something. After a bit he called out roughly, 'For Christ's sake stop that ghastly row, it's getting on my nerves!'

Something seemed to snap inside me. I went over to him, gripped him by the hair and slapped his face. He made a rasping noise like an animal, raised his head and hit me with his open hand, knocking my glasses on to the floor. I caught his wrist as he tried to hit me again and we rolled over on to the floor together, kicking and biting. Then he suddenly put his head on my breast and sighed once or twice, laughing because the buttons hurt his cheek, and said, 'Oh dear, what a military bosom!' Then I think he slept for a bit.

He can't help getting moods like this. They soon pass. I sat beside him for a while while he slept. Annie very tactfully disappeared in the direction of Robert's studio.

After a while Rupert opened his eyes and said, 'I've got a little speech to make to you –'

'Oh yes,' I said, knowing what it was going to be.

'I think you're pursuing me too much. I mean I don't mind us being friends and seeing each other now and again, that's all right, but I'm afraid you're becoming enamoured of me and I just can't stand it. Hopping into bed by mutual consent is all very well, but this business of being in love is just too much for me, it always has been – I can't take it, it makes me feel guilty. Soon you're going to expect me to spend all my leaves with you and then I shall feel tied down and get claustrophobia.'

I tried to protest, but he wouldn't listen. 'I was watching you and Annie today,' he went on, 'I saw you looking at her the way you used to look when Squirrel was around. And it makes me feel guilty because I'm a kind-hearted chap really. It's not that I don't want to see you – I do, I like seeing you very much, in fact if I'd arranged to spend my whole leave with you I would have done, but as I didn't, and I'm staying with Annie and we like each other – well it's just not on.

'I simply can't stand it when girls get possessive – you know I'm not seeing Squirrel any more? That was the trouble with her you see, I kept telling her, *get another boyfriend*, but she wouldn't and she began to make scenes if I went with anybody else, so Squirrel and I had to say bye-bye. You know I'm a peculiar chap, I'm never fonder of a girl than when she's madly infatuated with somebody else. I sometimes think there's something not quite right with me.'

'If you ask me, you're plumb crazy,' I cried, 'and as for being infatuated with you, I may have been once but I'm not any more and your colossal conceit staggers me! If you really want to know there's nothing I'd *rather* do than get a new boyfriend, if I could only find one!'

'Well,' Rupert said, '*I* think you're pretty enamoured of me, because I've got eyes in my head. So either we break off altogether or we continue as friends because frankly I can't stand being tied.'

'Suits me,' I said trying to sound cool and off-hand. 'Actually, I'm glad we've had this little talk because I always like to know where I am.' I felt nothing for him at all at that moment, except perhaps contempt and a kind of wondering pity.

After that we went out to the Nelson, like the best of friends, and Rupert ordered a Matelot's Embrace and we drank to the friendship that is not lit with passion.

'You see,' he explained, 'I'm not really very sexy, that's why I need someone like Squirrel to get me all worked up. Squirrel and I were really quite good together. The thing with you is I get embarrassed when I'm in bed with you, because you obviously have no interest in it at all.'

'But I loved it,' I said, 'I loved being in bed with you!'

'Of course you did, you're romantic. You thought I was going to carry you off on my white horse and love you forever amen – only it just doesn't work out that way.'

'Hadn't you better get back to Annie?' I said, unable to keep the misery out of my voice.

'Poor Joanie,' he said and I could see he was smiling in the darkness outside the pub. 'If it isn't Squirrel it's Annie. Are you terribly, terribly jealous?' I was too upset to answer, so he kissed me goodnight.

I suppose I should hate Rupert, but I can't. When I'm with him I can only think that he's right, and all the other people who say he should be faithful to me are wrong and stupid.

The last day of my leave. Rupert couldn't see me till the evening, so I killed time, looking at bookshops in Charing Cross Road and eating in a milk bar.

When I rang him up he said, 'Where's my guitar? You know I left it with you to look after.'

I told him it was stored at Milborne Grove, along with all the other stuff from the studio, but the house was locked up and my mother was away.

'OK, let's bust in! I'll really need my guitar if I'm going to be called up for Canada – jolly sea-shanties in the mess-room and all that!'

The idea of breaking in seemed rather exciting. I said OK, I'd get some food and we'd cook a meal there, just like old times.

'Isn't this fun?' Rupert said happily as we raided the larder for my mother's tomato chutney and lit a fire in the dining-room. It had been amazingly easy to force the lock on the downstairs window with Rupert's penknife. We put some soup on to heat. All the old studio crockery had been put away in the gas room downstairs, along with the old furniture and pictures etc. – v. nostalgic. Even the empty bird-cage was there.

'Oh look, the famous couch,' Rupert laughed, 'and there's my guitar.' The last shreds of our estrangement disappeared and it was just like being back in Redcliffe Road. I changed into my green trousers and found him some flamenco music I'd copied out so that he could see if his guitar was still OK. We ate our supper by the fire. It was the friendliest evening we'd had for ages, sitting on the floor with our heads together looking at an old Spanish atlas that I'd found in the ruins, poring over the map and planning the towns we'd like to visit, singing their names like a song, Malaga, Barcelona, Seville, Valencia.

'After the war,' Rupert said, 'I'd like to live in Spain and spend my whole life in one colossal orgy compared to which that party the other night would be a vicar's tea-party, boozing and boozing until I fall unconscious and grape-vines grow out of my ears!' He played his guitar, the farruca and the soleáres, and we talked about sex and how it wasn't the most important thing, and I told him about my recent experiments with the candle and he seemed very amused.

We were in the happiest possible mood for making love, it would have been perfect. All evening I had been terribly aware of how great his physical attraction was for me, even if his hand touched mine I felt like crying out. Everything was right, the room, the warm firelight, and he and I sitting side by side with our heads leaning together in perfect contentment.

'You know our couch downstairs?' Rupert said. 'Why don't we spend the night on it?'

'What about Annie?' I gasped, unable to believe my luck.

'Oh she won't mind. She's like me – doesn't want to be tied.'

'But that would be wonderful,' I said. 'Do you realise we've never spent the whole night together? And now I've got my new cap you don't have to bother about those awful things any more.'

The upstairs rooms were locked, but we managed to find some blankets and I made up the bed while R opened another bottle of Spanish wine. I felt all warm and glowing with happiness. At last, I thought, I'm going to wake up beside him instead of running home through the blackout to my mother.

We half sat, half lay on the bed, drinking red wine out of tooth mugs and kissing each other while the empty gas-masks grinned down from the mantelpiece.

'If your ma could see us now!' Rupert chuckled. He was just starting to unbutton my dress when the telephone rang, sharp and menacing, tearing the silence. Who could be ringing at this hour in a house we no longer use?

'Don't answer it,' R said.

For a moment I hesitated then, like a fool I ran upstairs, groping my way in the dark, and picked up the receiver.

'Hello?'

'Hello, is that Joan? This is Annie. Is Rupert with you?'

'Yes.'

'Well, can I speak to him?'

I went and called downstairs, 'Rupert it's Annie.'

'Oh my *God*,' said Rupert, 'you should *never* have answered it.'

'Why,' I said, 'I thought you said she didn't mind?'

But then, as I stood on the stairs and listened, my heart turned cold and sick inside me.

'Oh God!' I heard. 'Oh Annie – yes – yes – all right, I'll be right over. Yes – I'll get going straight away.'

I just couldn't bear it, the disappointment was too much for me, the misery too acute.

Rupert came down and put his arms round me. He said, 'My calling-up telegram's just arrived. It was delayed. I should have been back at Portsmouth last night. I'll have to rush back and start packing right away – catch the first train in the morning.'

I said nothing, just stood numb with unhappiness by the mantelpiece. Rupert came over to me and took me in his arms and we kissed and I clung to him. I loved him then to distraction, his ugly hands, the back of his head and his kind eyes.

'Write me some lovely letters,' he said, his cheek against mine.

I walked with him as far as Annie's house and we kissed again at the bottom of the steps. I stood in the street after the door had banged shut for about ten minutes, then I walked slowly back to the hostel.

Tuesday, 13th

I'm in the train going to Leighton Buzzard, with my belt and buttons newly shined, ready to start training for Special Duties. At least it will keep my mind occupied.

I suppose I could meet someone new, a pilot or something, who won't be queer or paranoid or schizophrenic, who won't be self-centred and cynical or have had VD, or take drugs or play the guitar, and who certainly won't be a painter! And what's more he won't be a hypochondriac or a hedonist, or hate children or laugh at religion or think the lower classes ought to be shot at sight; he'll have a heart and a soul, and all the right feelings at the right time.

And he won't beat women up and have rushes of adrenalin and smash things or keep two mistresses at the same time, he'll do the washing-up and buy me flowers and take me dancing, he'll see me home in air-raids, think I'm beautiful and write me love-letters and ask me to marry him!

But I'm sure I'll never like him half as much as Rupert.